Feast *of* Laughter

An Appreciation of R. A. Lafferty

Volume 3 - November 7, 2015

Ktistec Press

Feast of Laughter
An Appreciation of R. A. Lafferty

Volume 3, November 7, 2015
Published by The Ktistec Press

Front cover: "The North Shore" © 2015, Lissanne Lake
Front cover layout: Anthony Ryan Rhodes

ISBN-13: 978-0692586518
ISBN-10: 0692586512

Editor's Note

Often on long road trips with my family, I tell shaggy dog stories. My favorite is the story of John the test pilot, Nate the 4672-year-old talking snake, and the lever that holds the world together. If I'm feeling inspired, and we have enough open road, I can spin the story out to 45 minutes or an hour, building larger and better plot elements and twists before arriving at the inevitable punch line, "Better Nate than lever."

This volume of *Feast of Laughter* was intended for publication on November 7, 2015 in honor of R. A. Lafferty's 101st birthday. It is far larger than any of our previous issues, and has even better essays, stories, and interviews. It also was a lot of work for our dedicated core of Ktistec Press volunteers, all of whom have families and day jobs and other such distractions. So here it is December 26, and this has taken far longer than we expected. I hope you will accept my apologies and agree with me, better late than never.

Table of Contents

Dedication

This issue is dedicated to the memory of Cuyler Warnell "Ned" Brooks, Jr. (1938-2015) of Lilburn, GA, USA. Ned was a science-fiction fanzine publisher and archivist of more than 12,000 fanzines and 300 typewriters. He collected R.A. Lafferty's works and met Ray several times at southern conventions. Ned generously provided *Feast of Laughter* with access to R.A. Lafferty fanzines such as Dan Knight's *Boomer Flats Gazette* and Guy H. Lillian III's *Challenger,* helping us to preserve priceless Lafferty history.

This work © 2015 Anthony Ryan Rhodes

Introduction

Once was a phenomenon, twice was amazing, three times—we may just be onto something.

This is the third issue of *Feast of Laughter* in celebration of R. A. Lafferty's 101st birthday on November 7. When we started this a little over a year ago, we had no idea how well it would turn out, how huge each issue would become, and just how much effort would go into it from a small army of artists, editors and publishers. Our originally conceived fanzine has grown into a "bookzine" (a neologism from Michael Swanwick, for which we are thankful). This is truly a collaborative effort, and tremendous thanks must be given to the members of the editing team, neglecting family and day jobs to bring this labor of love to fruition. See the list of contributors at the back of the book.

We have something else to be thankful for in this issue. The rights to Lafferty's literary estate are now owned by the Locus Foundation, and represented by the JABberwocky Literary Agency. They are among the good guys. They are working to promote the literary recognition and success of writers of real impact and merit. We owe a tremendous debt of gratitude to the fine folks at Locus and Eddie Schneider at JABberwocky for arranging permission for us to reprint "Tell it Funny, Og" and "Configuration of the North Shore."

And while I am thanking people, we need to acknowledge The University of Tulsa McFarlin Library. They are the only reason we have access to some of the manuscripts for which Locus and others have granted permission, from R. A. Lafferty, Alan Dean Foster and Dan Knight.

And add another note of thanks to Warren Brown for the photograph of Lafferty's office door that graces our back cover. Lafferty covered the door of his office with pictures he clipped from books, magazines, and posters turning it into a work of art in itself. The door was exhibited in Tulsa recently when Neil Gaiman came to give a public reading and honor

Lafferty's memory. Warren and several others are working on an analysis of the imagery on the door. I hope we will be able to publish the resulting article in a future issue of *Feast of Laughter*. Look at the images on the door and see if you can connect any of them to Lafferty's stories.

Mark your calendars and plan to be in New Jersey this summer for the first LaffCon in Lawrenceville, NJ on Saturday, June 4. You can meet some of the Ktistec Press and many fans and writers, small and great, inspired by Lafferty. You can share in the celebration of what most of us have discovered on our own. See the last page of this volume for details.

This is what we are on to: Lafferty's writing is inspiring. Many of the greats in literature, from Michel Houellebecq, the enfant terrible of contemporary French letters, to Harlan Ellison, the former enfant terrible of science fiction (former enfant, still Great and Terrible) have heaped praise on Lafferty and his influence. Many of us among the less great are inspired to create by Lafferty, be it literary or theological exploration, personal essays, or art and fiction. You can decide who in this volume is numbered among the greats. Your answer may be different from mine. Every contribution in this volume is inspired by Lafferty. Every piece is different, because every individual experience reading Lafferty is uniquely his or her own.

Join in the fun. Read the essays, stories, and other contributions here, be inspired, and write a piece of your own for the next *Feast of Laughter*. Then join us in giving thanks for the unique literary genius of R. A. Lafferty. For your thanksgiving, this Feast is served.

Tuck in to whichever dish you like in whichever order you prefer, but you may want to start with a second appetizer, the following essay by a pioneer who came before us. Dan Knight's introduction to his own Lafferty fanzine the *Boomer Flats Gazette*, from back in the 90s, will welcome you even further into this feast and this fellowship.

Kevin Cheek
November, 2015

Introduction to the Boomer Flats Gazette

by Dan Knight

"We few! We happy few!"
-Henry V
Shakespeare

It was never intended that our Fellowship, the Fellowship of the Argo, of Epikt and Roadstrum, of Dana and Okla, should be an exclusive thing. The table was prepared and the bar was stocked for as big a bash as ever was seen. There was something for everyone. A magical feast. Take as much as you want. Stuff your pockets and fill your purse. It would make no difference. There would be just as much when you were done as when you started. This is fish and loaves stuff. (Are not all good stories fish and loaves stuff by their very definition?)

Well, the feast was readied and the invitations were sent out and a most peculiar thing came about. All of the folks to whom they were sent found excuses not to come. The Host was a gracious man. "Perhaps I have not worded the thing properly," he said. So another round of invitations were prepared and dispatched. Years passed (feasts like this don't just happen overnight, you know). The Gracious Host is still waiting. The beer is still cold and the pheasant warm. The steaks are thick, the hot sauce is the hottest around, and the bread is fresh, fresh, fresh! But the hall is still empty and perhaps it will always remain so.

Or at least almost so. They would be easy to miss in such a vast place. But here and there, sometimes alone and sometimes in small groups, figures move through the magic place. Tasting. Drinking. Stopping here and there to sample that most prodigious board. And when they meet, at the intersection of the Great Tables, there is much back slapping and laughing and joy at what they have found. Family of the Empty Hall. You can hear them if you listen close by the doors.

But why wait at the door?

Did I not say that the beer was cold? That the whiskey was the whiskeyest and the wine-ah, the wine, there's been no cheap-jacking about the wine! So come. One day the Hall may indeed fill with guests. And they will require guides. The Invitation is yours. The Fellowship awaits.

There now, we've had the Invitation and the Invocation. What started as a suggestion by Steve Pasechnik of Edgewood Press fame (thank him for IRON TEARS, I do) has taken on flesh, as it were. Let the Sherlock fans have their funny hats and pipes. Let the Trekkers have their ears (by the way, if you look carefully at Clint Eastwood in The Unforgiven I believe you will see where the make-up guys got their ideas for Worf). We don't need any of that stuff. Nope. Not us. We're special. We're the guys with the pointy minds and odd reading habits. All together now "We got style! We got Verve! We don't find this stuff absurd!" Sing it to yourself. Everyday. It'll work wonders.

There is no way I can let this go without thanking Shinji Maki for assistance far above and beyond the call of duty. It was his mailing to me of the checklist you'll find inside that really started the ball rolling. I wish him and his family every joy and success. I also acknowledge a debt to Mr. Asakura for his contribution and to Gene Wolfe for allowing me to reprint his Lafferty poem. (Hiroshi Inoue, where have you gone?! I would have loved your translators insights.)

I am hoping that those of you who are talented with pen or brush will be kind enough to contribute to The Boomer. Short essays will be warmly embraced. Commentary and letters are encouraged. I would love to do future issues around Lafferty in Italy, in Britain, in France, Holland etc. If anyone out there can help, please, please do.

A regular feature of this irregular endeavor will be the free classified ad. Individuals looking for anything specific for their Lafferty collections (and we will keep this to Lafferty material) can send me their want lists in ad format. Also those interested in selling things. Feel free. We'll start this with issue two if there's any interest.

Enough of me for now. Welcome again to Boomer Flats, Home of the Hairy Earthman.

This work is © 1993, 2015 Dan Knight.

Dan Knight is the creator of United Mythologies Press and an important publisher of Lafferty's work. His Boomer Flats Gazette periodical was a seminal outlet for Lafferty scholarship and appreciation.

"They lay down in the red roaring river, and one of the giants set a heavy rock on the breast of every person of them to hold them down."
R. A. Lafferty, "Boomer Flats"

Illustration © 2015 Anthony Ryan Rhodes

Ray

by Rick Norwood

When Ray came to New Orleans, one of his favorite cities (as everyone who has read the Argo trilogy knows), the New Orleans Science Fiction Association adopted him. We all thought Raphael Aloysius Lafferty was an amazingly cool name, and that Ray Lafferty was an amazingly cool drunk. He seemed very mild. We loved the way he said, "Yes," drawing the word out as if it had three syllables. All the teenage girls liked to sit on his lap. He liked it, too.

But you couldn't talk him into anything. I remember once we tried to get him to come with us to a meeting of the Society For Creative Anachronism. Ray was not interested and he would not come with us. We were surprised – we took Ray for an amiable drunk, but when he said "No," drawing the word out the same way he drew out the word "Yes," he meant it, and we could not change his mind.

Another time Ray surprised us was at a science fiction convention when someone proposed a question about the resistance between two diagonal nodes in an infinite rectangular array of one-ohm resistors. Ray answered the question. We knew he was an electrical engineer, but that information had not really sunk in with us.

At a Nebula Award Banquet in New Orleans, one of Ray's stories was nominated for a Nebula. Ray and I were sitting at the same table. Joe Green read the five nominees from the fifth place up. After four stories had been announced, Ray's story still had not been mentioned. And then Joe said, "And the winner is – no award." Ray didn't show any emotion, but that had to have hurt.

Ray did win a Hugo Award for his short story "Eurema's Dam," tying with a story by Fred Pohl and C. M. Kornbluth. At the convention where the awards were handed out, the committee decided to give two Hugo spaceships to Pohl, one for himself and one for the deceased Kornbluth, and none to

Lafferty. When I found out about this from Ray, I pestered several later Worldcon committees to set this right. They never did.

Ray was always cheerful and yet always seemed a little sad. If I had known him better, I suspect I would have learned about greater disappointments in his life than the two I mentioned.

I got into publishing because I learned about books written by major authors that nobody wanted to publish, books by authors like Hal Clement, Alfred Bester, and Ray Lafferty. I published the Clement and Lafferty and was about to publish the Bester when another publisher snatched it up, changing the name from *Tender Loving Rape* (which is probably why nobody else would publish it) to *Tender Loving Rage*. But I had the pleasure and privilege of publishing Lafferty.

There are two editions of *Archipelago* from Manuscript Press, both very limited editions. The general edition of 500 copies has a red binding and a white dust jacket. The signed, numbered edition of 100 copies has a two-tone black and gray binding and a cream dust jacket. It also has an extra poem, "Fill every bucket, every pail".

Archipelago is, chronologically, the first book in a trilogy which I called *The Devil is Dead* trilogy. I didn't know any better, and the second book in the trilogy, the only one published at the time, the only one ever published by a major publisher, was titled *The Devil is Dead*. Ray never corrected me, but after the book was published I found out that he called it the *Argo Trilogy*. I wish I'd known.

By that time, I understood that friendly, tipsy, Ray Lafferty was a major writer. I took proofreading the book seriously. I corresponded with him in detail about the text of the manuscript, and he replied in kind. One of my happiest memories is sitting at an outdoor café on a lovely spring day and amending the typewritten manuscript based on Ray's answers to my numerous questions.

I was discovering the serious side of a man who was seldom serious and often funny. Ray was serious about religion and he was serious about writing, but when he was socializing he rarely talked about either.

Eventually, the final book in the trilogy, *More than Melchisedech*, was published by U. M. Press in three volumes, *Tales of Chicago*, *Tales of Midnight*, and *Argo*. The books were nicely printed and bound, but sadly riddled with typos.

There is a little bit of a Lafferty revival going on now, in 2015. Two collections of his short stories have appeared recently. Neil Gaiman often mentions Lafferty as a major writer. I hope someone, someday, will publish the *Argo Trilogy* in a uniform, carefully edited edition.

Rick Norwood edits books for both Manuscript Press and Fantagraphics Books. He is the editor and publisher of Comics Revue *magazine (www.comicsrevue.com) which reprints classic comic strips such as* Alley Oop, Rick O'Shay, *and* The Phantom. *His stories have appeared in* Analog, F&SF, *and other magazines and anthologies. He also spends way too much time editing Wikipedia.*

"Lafferty in the Green Room" © 2015 Anthony Ryan Rhodes

One Cannot Give Too Many Instances
by John Ellison

I.

Christopher Dawson in an essay titled "St Augustine and his Age" gives the following quote from Augustine:

> "Christ is the straight way by which the mind escapes the circular maze of pagan thought".[1]

In examining certain passages from R.A. Lafferty's writings in the course of this essay this quotation can serve as a useful reference point. In previous essays I have suggested a tension between the linear and the spherical that occurs at a thematic level in Lafferty's work.[2] On re-reading many of his stories it is surprising how explicitly, and how often, this point is made. The following passage is from the short story "Ishmael into the Barrens":

> ...She was tending the flowers as if they were in straight lines, as if they were in rows, going down one file of them and back another.

This "lineate" behavior is recognized by a sympathetic character who warns how subversive her actions would appear to the authorities.

By contrast, in the short story "Interurban Queen" we are shown a world where straight-lines are celebrated:

> By law there must be a trolley line every mile, but they

---

[1] Christopher Dawson, "St Augustine and his World," in *A Monument to St Augustine*, (London: Sheed and Ward, 1930), p.69

[2] See Feast of Laughter volumes 1 and 2. –Ed.

were oftener. By law no one trolley line might run for more than twenty-five miles. This was to give a sense of locality. But transfers between the lines were worked out perfectly. If one wished to cross the nation, one rode on some one hundred and twenty different lines. There were no more long-distance railroads. They also had their arrogance, and they also had to go.

I wish to suggest here that the sense of inter-connected and local lines of travel is itself analogous to Lafferty's methods of narrative technique. His cast of mind is similar, though not identical, to the political-ecological ideal of 'Small is Beautiful'. Rather than being just a bland assent to the concept of the local the Lafferty-vision is also a pursuit of densely packed detail and unexpected configurations of persons and events. We are shown in the next passage from "Interurban Queen" how the passengers in the trams have the time and capacity to take in the details of the landscape they pass through:

> The Saturday riders passed a roadway restaurant with its tables out under the leaves and under a little rock overhang. A one-meter-high waterfall gushed through the middle of the establishment, and a two-meter-long bridge of set shale stone led to the kitchen. Then they broke onto view after never-tiring view of the rich and varied quasiurbia. The roadway farms, the fringe farms, the berry patches!

After this passage there is a long list of different types of berries. Rather than being monotonous we can acknowledge how the use of lists in many of Lafferty's stories function as a kind of oral storytellers' technique; the lists do conjure up the visual and extended aspect of the world being described. A paradox of all this, which will be explored in other passages, is that an ordered and linear world can be productive of a textured sense of differentiation. By contrast the sphere has been chosen in this essay, not for any personal critique of it as a mathematical form but for its strong association with ideas of enclosure and totality. This may make more sense as we examine details from the short story "Thou Whited Wall". Here we are shown a world in which a large part of the population are "guided persons" who watch a global communicating medium known as the "prime wall". There are multi-layered aspects of metaphor and analogy at work in this story which presents a startling and bleak vision of humanity gone wrong. The people of this near-future society have some resemblance to the astrology-reading and horse-race-betting populations of the past. But in addition to the old narratives of fate, such as the horoscope and the "daily double," a new zodiac based around the visceral and sexual sensations has been constructed. As these daily prompts to sensation are followed in a slavish and addictive fashion we see a parody of traditional human relationships unfold:

> "Mother, father has opened his veins and bled all over everything," small son Hiero Gilligan was hollering. Hiero's early stridence always gave an unpleasant cast to a morning.
>
> "Yes, dear," his mother Evangeline told him, "but be tolerant. It is his personal privilege."
>
> "Personal privilege nothing!" Hiero exploded. "I never said that papa could use my vein opener. He should have asked me first. I wish people would leave my things alone."

Later in the story Evangeline struggles to bury her husband's body in someone's garden but is restricted by the received wisdom of the "guided persons" that the acidity of the body will be bad for the plants. Just as the new modes of behavior have reduced people to a narrow, and alien, set of actions so too the communicative force of language and consciousness is similarly distorted.

> ...The message of Joe Snow was still there on the prime wall. The background of it had darkened somewhat, but it was still too much white-on-white to be read. And Joe Snow himself was there...
>
> "Perhaps the message won't be readable today at

all," the thick-tongued Joe Snow mumbled. "Amateur artists are careless and they are writing over my message. I try to chase them away, but as the afternoon goes on I get sleepy and then there is no one to chase them off. But imprint my message on your mind and hold it there. The snow-colored message itself will not darken, but your mind will become grey and grimy by evening. The contrast will enable you to read it."

The combination of weariness and passivity in response to a violent and chaotic world is familiar. Augustine's description of the "circular maze of pagan thought" that Lafferty recognized as being re-established in the twentieth century is even more firmly in place today. The enclosing sphere of the "prime wall" may correspond quite closely to our own era's digital and behavioral networks on which "splatterings" are seen and copied every day.

Turning to similar themes in the short story "The World as Will and Wallpaper" we find a hero who is filled with wonder as he starts out on his journey to the *Wood Beyond the World*.

The cliffs and caves were fabricated and not natural cliff dwellings, but they looked very much as old cliff dwellings must have looked...It was pleasant there. Sometimes the people sang simulacrum Indian songs. There wore patterned blankets, brightly colored, and woven out of bindweed.

"All different, all different, every block different," William murmured in rapture.

The climax of the story, though, confirms the slowly-revealed secret that in this new world the wallpaper designs of the writer William Morris have been used as its formative template. Seemingly intricate and beautiful at first examination, it is, as William whimpers, "...the same thing over and over and over again."

There is a significant passage in the middle of the story which evokes the feeling of torpor and resignation in "Thou

Whited Wall":

> ...Something a little sad here, though; something of
> passion and pity that was too empty and too pat. It
> was as though this was the climax of it all, and one
> didn't want it to be the climax yet. It was as if the Top
> of the Town and Night-Life Knoll (and not the Wood
> beyond the World) were the central things of the
> World City.
>
> Perhaps William slept there awhile in the sadness
> that follows the surfeit of flesh and appetite.

As in "Thou Whited Wall" there is a kind of parodic
portrayal of familiar concepts such as will, work and appetite.
The direction in which these distortions lead us is towards
termination. A passage in the story describes the fate of
William and others like him:

> ...They are happy, they are entertained; and when they
> are convinced there is no more for them to see, they
> become the ancients and go willingly to the choppers.

The discourses of the Programmed Persons in the novel
Past Master echo similar themes concerning life and
consciousness. The following passage is Boggle talking to
Thomas:

> "...Who needs it? Who wants it? Who thought it up in
> the first place?...We have, and men have, an appetite
> for life. Men programmed it into us, but we are now
> programming it out of ourselves...We do not know
> how men came to have such a strange appetite. We do
> not know how men themselves, or anything
> whatsoever, came to be. But it was a bad idea from the
> beginning. As soon as we here present have lived our
> lives to some fullness and have satisfied our curiosities
> (curiosity is programmed into us, but it is not
> programmed into our final generation) then we will
> phase out these appetites in ourselves. We will phase
> out reproduction also; in fact, we have recently done

that for ourselves. We will terminate it all. We will close down the worlds and make an end to life."

In the same novel we have Evita talking to the Emperor Charles about the inhabitants of Astrobe:

"...Nine out of ten persons ask for termination long before their normal life term is run...The people are so weary of perfection they ask for termination at earlier and earlier ages..."

The significance of these passages is the way that the spirit of resignation is connected to the acceptance of the given contents of consciousness. For the Programmed Persons appetite is just an aspect of thought rather than something to be shaped and used for new modes of "narrative-shaped" consciousness. Analyses of the addictive personality have shown that the addict is bounded by the way things are in the present moment. There is no opening on to discourses that reveal how things may be in any way different. They lack the awareness that old narratives of life can be over-written and that a new linear path can break them out of the closed-circle of habitual behavior. I want to try and bring all of this together with some reflections on the role of the Christian mystical tradition in Lafferty's thought.

In a series of commentaries on early Christian thinkers Olivier Clement makes the following observation:

...The World for a Christian is a Trinitarian text, or better it is a woven cloth: the fixed threads of the warp symbolize the Logos, the moving threads of the woof the dynamism of the Pneuma.[3]

The significance of movement and spirit is suggestive within this quote. The deadening of the will portrayed in Lafferty's future dystopias is linked to lethargy and immobility. By contrast the structure of Trinitarian thought

---

[3] Olivier Clement, *The Roots of Christian Mysticism* (London: New City Press, 1993), p. 214.

in Augustine revolves around the fertile connections of memory, understanding and will. I wish to argue that the narrative- and world-making tendencies in Lafferty's work, noted by critics such as Andrew Ferguson, can be seen as grounded in Catholic and Augustinian spirituality. In these traditions there will only be a true unfolding of history when love and the creative use of the will are at the core of social being. Without these aspects the 'City of Man' stays locked in the circularity of secular politics and domination.

2.

The themes of the protean and the sense of the plenitude of being will be examined in the remaining excerpts from representative stories. In painting the descent into vice of Charles Chartel in the short story "The Man Underneath" there is a quite nuanced portrayal of why things have gone wrong.

We have the following exchange between the two "versions" of Charles:

> "I've shown you a hundred times, Charles...But why do you want money?"
>
> "It's just that I have a passion for collecting it, courlis."
>
> "Collecting we can understand, but the true collector will have no desire for duplicates...The avid people have spoiled it for us. But you have not the true collectors' spirit, Charles."

This interesting passage brings out the sense that a ravenous pursuit of money locks the pursuer into a closed-cycle of repetition. The true collector, though, has an affinity with the unique and the original.

In the story "little C" is described as "protean and...not at all plausible"; he is told "You change forever in appearance and name"; little C says "To be serious is the only capital crime"; the narrator says of Charles Chartel, "It is an awful and sickening thing to see a good man grow rich and respected"; little C says, "Good things can go on forever, except that—now and then—they must be temporarily adjourned".

In summary, then, this is a story packed with sharp detail and telling touches of irony. "Little C" points to the possibilities that are never fully realized within regularized experience.

In another short story "Company in the Wings" we see a kind of engagement with the schools of medieval philosophy defined as Realism and Nominalism.

One of the main characters Simon Frakes, although not altogether a real person, argues for an ultra-realistic description of reality. Some selections from his Trefoil Lectures are worth recounting:

> I am saying that every possible being is in actual existence always...Every possible thought has already been thought out, every riddle has been unriddled, every epigram spoken. You have only to tap them. They have been in existence for millennia.
>
> Please understand one thing: all imagined things have reality. They are not because we imagine them. Imagination is only the encounter with their reality. From the Olympian gods to Boob McNutt all are persons. To imagine the non-existing is an impossibility. All are with the billions in that limbus. All are entities in the psychic pool. I speak literally.

Simon then gives long lists of names which include characters from novels, history and comic strips. The use of the lists makes the audience uneasy:

> "Will you come to your point, Simon!" Fairbridge O'Boyle suggested...
> "I am on my point completely," Simon maintained. "One cannot give too many instances..."

This phrase may be taken as emblematic of Lafferty's whole aesthetic of abundance and plenitude. "One cannot give too many instances" because each distinct person or aspect of the physical world is brimming with meaning. That is why the long lists and litanies are significant in Lafferty.

The seeming trap of circularity is a consequence of the Fall but we have shown how we may just step out from the maze of unhappy illusions. There are new instances of things waiting in the wings. This communicative force of abundance is expressed in Lafferty through many masks and unlikely forms: the birds arguing for the "jabbering fun" of it in "And Name my Name"; Lemuel asking for his old red sweater to keep him warm in purgatory in "For All Poor Folks at Picketwire"; the rueful reflections on romance and humanity from the Blob in "The Weirdest World"; Charles Cogsworth's quote in "Through Other Eyes" affirming his knowledge of women: "I have read the prescribed texts, Gregory. I took a six-week seminar with Zamenoff. I am acquainted with almost the entire body of the work of Bopp concerning women."; chorus-like phrases in the middle of texts that seem to embed themselves in the readers' mind: "Choose us, join with us"... in "The Skinny People of Leptophlebo Street," "Preserve us this night!" in "Slow Tuesday Night"; Charles Cogsworth's belief that after the release of the Love Essence into the atmosphere in *Arrive at Easterwine* the children are, "...throwing a little bit softer rocks than they used to"; more talking birds in "Brights Coins in Never-Ending Stream" and "Groaning Hinges of the World"...

We can go on and on with instances and incidents. And that, as Lafferty believed, is the whole point.

This work © 2015 John Ellison.

John Ellison lives in England. At an early age, he selected Lafferty as a favorite author after discovering his short stories in SF magazines and anthologies in the late 1960s. John writes that at this time, Catholicism informs most of his choices in life—indeed he has shifted between the quite different milieu of Damon Runyon (he used to be a manager of betting shops) and Dorothy Day (he now works in the charity and voluntary sector). John is a frequent commenter on Andrew Ferguson's Tumblr, "Continued on Next Rock."

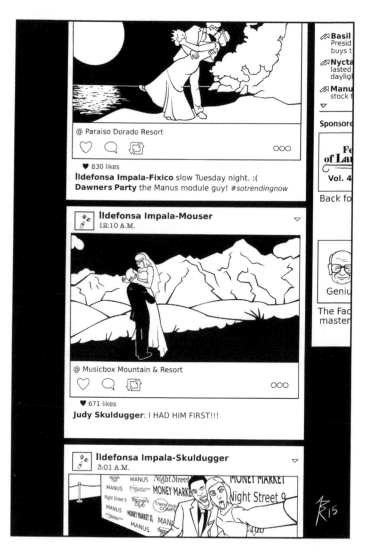

People made up their minds fast, and Ildefonsa had hers made up when she came.

R. A. Lafferty,"Slow Tuesday Night"

Illustration © 2015 Anthony Ryan Rhodes

Eudaimonism in R.A. Lafferty's *Aurelia*

by Gregorio Montejo

Kerygma (proclamation) and *didache* (teaching) are distinct yet intertwined forms of communication in the Gospel genre: they both attempt to convey a given truth, one through the witness of a life well lived according to the dictates of righteousness, the other by means of didactic preaching and other pedagogical techniques, yet these two discrete methods finally convey the same message. R.A. Lafferty's novel *Aurelia* is the tale of a fourteen-year-old girl, a student from another planet whose final stage of schooling is in the governance of worlds.[1] Each in an interstellar craft of their own devising, Aurelia and her precocious classmates embark for various distant planets in order to bring about a much-needed socio-political reformation to their chosen destinations and to get a passing grade in their last class before graduating into adulthood. Lafferty relates Aurelia's triumphs and misadventures in governorship upon her arrival in Gaea, a planet suspiciously like Earth, perhaps most evidently in its desperate need for beneficent civic leadership. In the course of the novel, the author relates a series of long disquisitions (*didache*), or sermons delivered by the title character that function as indispensable didactic accompaniments to the kerygmatic narrational arc traced by the plot. At the end of the day, the young protagonist's living example and sacrificial

---

[1] R.A. Lafferty, *Aurelia* (Norfolk, VA: Starblaze/The Donning Company, 1982). Originally entitled *To Aurelia, with Horns*, and completed the late 1970s, a copy of the original manuscript is located in Box 23, Folder 35 of the collection of R.A. Lafferty papers (Collection 1979-002) in the Department of Special Collections and University Archives, McFarlin Library, University of Tulsa. A typescript carbon with a word count in red ink of *To Aurelia, with Horns* is housed in the Iowa Authors Manuscripts Collection (Box 10) at the University of Iowa.

death both teach the self-same lesson: an understanding of human existence that finds its decisive meaning and fulfilment in *eudaimonia*, the idea of happiness as human flourishing. Neither the point of *Aurelia*'s plot nor the purpose of Aurelia's perorations can be fully understood apart from each other.

Kerygma and *Didache* in the Gospel Genre

The novel *Aurelia* displays an essentially kerygmatic structure in its broad narrative outlines. At its most fundamental, it is an account of an envoy who descends from another, more perfected region of the heavens, a place referred to as Shining World, to deliver a salvific message to a benighted world that cannot comprehend and so finally rejects the otherworldly visitor's enlightening counsel, a seemingly failed evangel that culminates with the violent sacrificial death of its heavenly messenger. The biblical *kerygma* (κήρυγμα), the core message of the New Testament, cannot be reduced to a mere enumeration of doctrines; rather, its intrinsic meaning is to be found in the entire life, mission, and teaching of Christ. In this regard, the crucifixion is the supreme instance of *kerygma* in the New Testament; the savior's sacrificial death is the foundation of Christ's salvific message as well as the hermeneutic lens through which that message must be interpreted.

The inescapable similarities between the narratives recounted in *Aurelia* and the Gospels forced Lafferty to eventually make the self-evident point that despite these telling parallels Aurelia is not, strictly speaking, a messiah, let alone *the* Messiah. Even so, in a typically Laffertarian use of comedic understatement, he acknowledged that she was indeed a "very nice girl," and regretted that his "story line required her failure and death."[2] What is significantly left unsaid in this comment is that the narrative arc of Aurelia's life necessitated her eventual failure and consequent death precisely because it so clearly traces out the telltale cruciform

---

[2] Tom Jackson, "An Interview with R.A. Lafferty," *Lan's Lantern* 39 (August 1991), pp. 49-53; at p. 50. This interview is at: http://www.sanduskyregister.com/Blog/2015/01/16/My-interview-with-R-A-Lafferty.html.

shape of a Christ-like life. Thus, even though Aurelia is undoubtedly not the Messiah, her life story is nonetheless largely messianic, thus her chronicle must necessarily conclude with a kerigmatically appropriate sacrificial death.

Historically, *kerygma* has been uniquely associated with the genre of *evangelium* (εὐαγγέλιον) or Gospel, which is literally a proclamation of "good tidings" in both word and deed that carries the promise of redemption.[3] In recent decades scholars have distinguished this evangelical *kerygma* from a didactic recitation of doctrinal elements referred to as *didache* (διδαχή) or teaching. The implication of this distinction is that the soteriological good tidings of Christ are not solely (or even most effectively conveyed) by a dry recitation of rules and regulations, but rather by the witness of lives authentically lived according to those precepts.[4]

---

[3] For a study of the way in which the kerygmatic *gospel* genre and *didache* developed out of similar oral traditions along distinctive yet parallel tracks, see Ian H. Henderson, "Didache and Orality in Synoptic Comparison," *Journal of Biblical Literature* 111 (1992), pp. 283-306.

[4] "The New Testament writers draw a clear distinction between preaching and teaching. The distinction is preserved alike in Gospels, Acts, Epistles, and Apocalypse, and must be considered characteristic of early Christian usage in general. Teaching (*didaskein*) is in a large majority of cases ethical instruction. Occasionally it seems to include what we should call apologetic, that is, the reasoned commendation of Christianity to persons interested but not yet convinced. Sometimes, especially in the Johannine writings, it includes the exposition of theological doctrine. Preaching, on the other hand, is the public proclamation of Christianity to the non-Christian world. The verb *keryssein* properly means 'to proclaim.' A *keryx* may be a town crier, an auctioneer, a herald, or anyone who lifts up his voice and claims public attention to some definite thing he has to announce. Much of our preaching in Church at the present day would not have been recognized by the early Christians as *kerygma*. It is teaching, or exhortation (*paraklesis*), or it is what they called *homilia*, that is, the more or less informal discussion of various aspects of Christian life and thought, addressed to a congregation already established in the faith... The verb 'to preach' frequently has for its object 'the Gospel.' Indeed, the connection of ideas is so close that *keryssein* by itself can be used as a virtual equivalent for *evangelizesthai*, 'to evangelize,' or 'to preach the Gospel.' It would not be too much to say that wherever 'preaching' is spoken of, it always carries with it the implication of 'good tidings'

Nevertheless, distinguishing between *kerygma* and *didache* (διδαχή) should not imply that they are wholly separate pursuits, let alone in antithetical contradistinction to each other. Rather, it indicates that they should be regarded as integrally connected constitutive elements of the same communicative action—in both theory and practice then, the messenger must embody the message, for sometimes actions do speak louder than words.

In a similar fashion, in addition to its kerygmatic narratological elements, Lafferty's novel also displays a strongly didactic or pedagogical intent. This should come as no surprise, since Aurelia's home planet was first introduced in the short story "Primary Education of the Camiroi" (originally published in *Galaxy Magazine*, December 1966), which relates the visit of a PTA delegation from Dubuque, Iowa to the Camiroi planet in order to investigate their unusual pedagogical methodologies. Among the more surprising findings are that by the second year of school Camiroi children are already being taught advanced arithmetic, while also given instruction in such unorthodox subjects as acrobatics and "quadratic religion."[5] Indeed, by the time the students reach grades seven through nine they are enrolled in courses dealing with such subjects as "Advanced prodigious memory. Vehicle operation and manufacture of simple vehicle. Literature, active. Astrognosy, prediction and programming. Advanced pankration. Spherical logic, hand and machine. Advanced alcoholic appreciation. Integral religion. Bankruptcy and recovery in business. Conmanship and trend creation. Post-nuclear physics and universals;" as well as "Cosmic theory, seminal," "Philosophy construction," "Complex hedonism." and "Laser religion," not to mention

---

proclaimed . . . . For the early Church, then, to preach the Gospel was by no means the same thing as to deliver moral instruction or exhortation. While the Church was concerned to hand on the teaching of the Lord, it was not by this that it made converts. It was by *kerygma*, says Paul, not by *didaché*, that it pleased God to save men." C.H. Dodd, *The Apostolic Preaching and Its Developments* (New York: Harper & Row, 1964), pp. 7-8.

   5 R.A. Lafferty, "Primary Education of the Camiroi," in *Nine Hundred Grandmothers*, Ace SF Special, Series 1 (New York: Ace Books, 1970), pp. 119-133; at p. 127.

"Simple human immortality disciplines. Consolidation of complex genius status. First problems of post-consciousness humanity."[6] By the time the Camiroi reach their tenth and final year of schooling, they are expected to master "Panphilosophical clarifications," "Construction of viable planets," "Consolidation of simple sanctity status," and of course "World government."[7]

In a follow-up story, "Polity and Custom of the Camiroi" (*Galaxy Magazine*, June 1967), Lafferty uses the visit of another Earth delegation to explore the socio-political and legal arrangements at work in Camiroi society. Among the most curious discoveries is the revelation that the Camiroi seem hard-pressed to distinguish between secular law and religion. "Have the Camiroi a religion?" asks one of the Terran visitors of several Camiroi citizens,

> "I think so," one of them said finally. "I believe that we do have that, and nothing else. The difficulty is in the word. Your Earth English word may come from *religionem* or from *relegionem*; it may mean a legality, or it may mean a revelation. I believe it is a mixture of the two concepts; with us it is. Of course we have a religion. What else is there to have?"
>
> "Could you draw a parallel between Camiroi and Earth religion?" I asked him.
>
> "No, I couldn't," he said bluntly. "I'm not being rude. I just don't know how."[8]

Finally, another Camiroi gives the Earthmen some insight on the matter. "The closest I could come to explaining the difference," the Camiroi said, "is by a legend that is told," as one colorful Camiroi phrase has it, "with the tongue so far in the cheek that it comes out the vulgar body aperture." The legend relates that humans were once tested on every world

---

[6] Ibid. pp. 129-130.

[7] Ibid. pp. 130-131.

[8] R.A. Lafferty, "Polity and Custom of the Camiroi," in *Nine Hundred Grandmothers*, Ace SF Special, Series 1 (New York: Ace Books, 1970), pp. 212-227; here at p. 220.

that they inhabited. "On some of the worlds men persevered in grace. These have become the transcendent worlds, asserting themselves as stars rather than planets and swallowing their own suns, becoming incandescent in their merged persons living in grace and light." The more developed of these interstellar territories are those "closed bodies which we know only by inference, so powerful and contained that they let no light or gravity or other emission escape them. They become of themselves closed and total universes, of their own space and outside of what we call space, perfect in their merged mentality and spirit." In stark contrast, there are also "worlds like Earth where men did fall from grace. On these worlds, each person contains an interior abyss and is capable both of great heights and depths. By our legend, the persons of these worlds, after their fall, were condemned to live for thirty thousand generations in the bodies of animals and were then permitted to begin their slow and frustrating ascent back to remembered personhood."[9] However, his interlocutor explains, the case of the Camiroi is altogether quite different.

> "We do not know whether there are further worlds of our like case. The primordial test-people of Camiroi did not fall. And they did not persevere. They hesitated. They could not make up their minds. They thought the matter over, and then they thought it over some more. Camiroi was therefore doomed to think matters over forever.
>
> "So we are the equivocal people, capable of curious and continuing thought. But we have a hunger both for the depths and the heights which we have missed. To be sure, our Golden Mediocrity, our serene plateau, is higher than the heights of most worlds, higher than those of Earth, I believe. But it has not the exhilaration of height."[10]

Here, in a nutshell, is the basis of Lafferty's future novel,

---

[9] Ibid. p. 220-221.

[10] Ibid. p. 221.

one in which he will explore in much greater depth precisely this question regarding the nature of the vexing relationship between revelation and legal reasoning, between *religionem* and *relegionem*, and their place within any rightly structured political system, through the medium of a kerygmatically modelled narrative, as well as a more discursive mode of teaching (*didache*). This discursive modality is given in *Aurelia* as a sequence of sermons outlining the crucial role of law in the pursuit of any meaningful form of human existence. These speeches are not a bare assertion of the law, but rather a thematically coherent set of theoretical disquisitions on the character and rationale of law itself, and they are among the least appreciated and most misunderstood parts of the novel. For example, critic David Langford has written that the "final third of the book is dominated by Aurelia's flatulent speeches to the multitudes, which use moderately simple language but achieve considerable opacity, not to mention forgettability."[11] Langford contrasts these ostensibly gaseous and seemingly impenetrable discourses with the story telling itself, which "despite confusions and disappointments," nonetheless remains "worth reading."[12] In Langford's estimation, the speeches are nothing more than an unfortunate series of irrelevantly obscure intermissions in an otherwise somewhat perplexing yet nevertheless entertaining yarn.

Aristotelian-Thomistic Eudaimonism

In a long epistolary interview conducted in the years immediately before he began writing *Aurelia* but not printed in full until several years after the novel was published, in response to the expansive philosophic question "What is your definition of the meaning of life?" from interviewer R.J. Whitaker, Lafferty responded by emphatically stating that "Using your 'meaning' in the only legitimate sense as 'purpose'

---

[11] David Langford, "R.A. Lafferty – *Aurelia* (1982)," in *Up Through an Empty House of Stars: Reviews and Essays, 1980-2002* (Holicong, PA: Wildside Press, 2013), pp. 58-59; here at p. 59. This review was originally published in *Foundation: The Review of Science Fiction* 28 (July 1983), pp. 104-105.

[12] Ibid.

or 'aim,' the meaning or purpose of life is happiness."[13] Moreover, Lafferty went on, this understanding of the purpose of life as residing in a form of ultimate happiness "was once clear to everybody in the world, and I don't know why so plain a thing should escape people now. Happiness often coincides with pleasure and enjoyment," Lafferty concluded, "but it isn't the same thing. There are many paradoxes about it, so there probably can't be any such thing as selfish happiness."[14]

This notion that life's meaning resides in a conception of happiness which cannot be conflated with mere pleasure finds its source in ancient Greek thought, and its most enduring philosophical expression in Aristotle's *Nichomachean Ethics*. Aristotle commences his inquiry into the nature of human happiness with the most basic query: What is the good for human beings? In other words, what would constitute a truly fulfilling human existence? Now, human lives are full of actions that are orientated to a variety of goods, and for each of these activities there is a corresponding end-state or purpose for which those activities are undertaken. In fact, every human action can be characterized as something that is undertaken either for its own sake or for the sake of something else, and that for the sake of which humans act must be considered as the good. This invariant orientation towards the good evinces the relentlessly teleological nature of Aristotle's ethical theory: That which we desire for its own sake and not for the sake of anything else, and for whose sake

---

[13] R.J. Whitaker, "Maybe They Needed Killing & The Importance of Happiness," in *Cranky Old Man from Tulsa: Interviews with R.A. Lafferty* (Weston, Ontario: United Mythologies Press, 1990), pp. 8-25; here at p. 13.

[14] Ibid. Lafferty goes on to point out that this notion of happiness once permeated even non-religious thought. "The secular scriptures are correct in their understanding of this. 'Oh happiness! Our being's end and aim,' Alexander Pope writes. 'It is the business of a wise man to be happy,' old Doctor Johnson wrote. 'There is no duty so much underrated as the duty of being happy,' R.L. Stevenson said, and he was sounder than was T. Jefferson in the Declaration of Independence when he wrote of it as a right rather than a duty. But being happy is a duty we owe the world and every companion of ours in it, and that is the meaning and purpose of life."

we do everything else is the supreme human good, a good that Aristotle designates as *eudaimonia*.[15]

The Greek term *eudaimonia* (εὐδαιμονία) is usually translated as "happiness," but this can lead to serious misconceptions, the most egregious perhaps being that the human good can be identified with any passing psychological state, or subjective amusement, or feeling of mere contentment. Aristotle describes *eudaimonia* as a stable, characteristically human kind of activity, a form of flourishing that can be ascertained objectively. Aristotle takes up and eventually discards a number of paradigmatic human actions, such as the pursuit of bodily pleasure, wealth, power, or honor. None of these can be the greatest human good, since they are transient or sought for the sake of some greater good. According to Aristotle, we never seek the final end in order to achieve some further end, so if there is a final end which we never seek for the sake of anything else, but solely for its own sake, this will be our *telos*, our supreme good, our final end, our *eudaimonia* or true happiness.[16]

Aristotle eventually concludes that the contemplation of truth is the most characteristic of all human activities, that which is highest about human beings, indeed our share in divinity itself. This activity is best of all human activities because with it we contemplate what is best, most glorious, and most divine. The deepest, most pleasurable, and characteristic form of human flourishing is the contemplation of eternal truth, and this is *eudaimonia*.[17] In the later Christian

---

[15] See Michael Pakaluk, *Aristotle's Nicomachean Ethics: An Introduction*, Cambridge Introductions to Key Philosophical Texts (Cambridge: Cambridge University Press, 2005); and Christine M. Korsgaard, "Aristotle's Function Argument," in *The Constitution of Agency: Essays on Practical Reason and Moral Psychology* (Oxford: Oxford University Press, 2008), pp. 129-150.

[16] Q.v. J.L. Ackrill, "Aristotle on Eudaimonia," in *Essays on Aristotle's Ethics*, ed. A.O. Rorty (Berkeley: University of California Press, 1980), pp. 15-34.

[17] Aristotle, *Nichomachean Ethics*, Book IX, § 7: "If happiness is activity in accordance with virtue, it is reasonable that it should be in accordance with the highest virtue; and this will be that of the best thing in us. Whether it be reason or something else that is this element which is thought to be our natural ruler and guide and to

tradition, the most eloquent defender of this understanding of happiness is Thomas Aquinas. For Thomas, like Aristotle, the end of human existence is also fundamentally eudaimonistic, a final end encompassing a distinctive set of human actions, the most exalted of which is the cognition and attainment of the supreme good.[18] Unlike Aristotle, however, Aquinas recognizes that this essential happiness cannot be gained through the achievement of any purely natural end, for Thomas agrees with Augustine's profound apothegm that "You have made us for yourself, O Lord, and our heart is restless until it rests in you."[19] The *telos* of all human desires, that which we never seek for the sake of anything else, but solely for its own sake, is thus God, our supreme good, an ultimate truth, a supernatural end, whose everlasting contemplation is joyous beatitude.[20]

---

take thought of things noble and divine, whether it be itself also divine or only the most divine element in us, the activity of this in accordance with its proper virtue will be perfect happiness. That this activity is contemplative we have already said . . . . But such a life would be too high for man; for it is not in so far as he is man that he will live so, but in so far as something divine is present in him; and by so much as this is superior to our composite nature is its activity superior to that which is the exercise of the other kind of virtue. If reason is divine, then, in comparison with man, the life according to it is divine in comparison with human life. But we must not follow those who advise us, being men, to think of human things, and, being mortal, of mortal things, but must, so far as we can, make ourselves immortal, and strain every nerve to live in accordance with the best thing in us; for even if it be small in bulk, much more does it in power and worth surpass everything. This would seem, too, to be each man himself, since it is the authoritative and better part of him. It would be strange, then, if he were to choose not the life of his self but that of something else. And what we said before will apply now; that which is proper to each thing is by nature best and most pleasant for each thing; for man, therefore, the life according to reason is best and pleasantest, since reason more than anything else is man. This life therefore is also the happiest."

[18] See Anthony Kenney, "Aquinas on Aristotelian Happiness," in *Aquinas' Moral Theory: Essays in Honor of Norman Kretzmann*, ed. S. MacDonald and E. Stump (Ithaca: Cornell University Press., 1998), pp. 15-27.

[19] Augustine, *Confessions*, I, 1; Augustine, in turn, is paraphrasing Plotinus, *Enneads*, VI, 7, 23, 4.

[20] Q.v. Henri de Lubac, "*Duplex Hominis Beatitudo* (Saint

It is this Thomistic iteration of eudaimonism that Lafferty explores in *Aurelia*. As he further explained in another interview, Aurelia's "striking and reasoned homilies or orations or sermons," which Lafferty hesitantly concedes "make her sound a little like a messiah," are in fact a "mini-outline of the great (3011 double column pages in my edition) 'Summa' of Aquinas," even though Lafferty cheekily concludes that it must be a "coincidence that the balanced sanity of the 'Golden World Cultus' of Aurelia's home world should parallel the 'Summa' of the Angelic Doctor."[21] The adoption of pagan notions of flourishing unto a specifically Christian theological anthropology calls for the introduction of one moral trait, namely sin, what the Bible identifies as the "mystery of iniquity" (μυστήριον ἀνομίας), that is, quite literally the

---

Thomas, Ia 2ae, q. 62, a. I)," *Recherches de science religieuse* 35 (1948), pp. 290–299; Steven A. Long, "On the Loss, and the Recovery, of Nature as a Theonomic Principle: Reflections on the Nature/Grace Controversy," *Nova et Vetera* 5 (2007), pp. 133–183; Jörn Müller, "*Duplex beatitudo*: Aristotle's Legacy and Aquinas's Conception of Human Happiness," in *Aquinas and the Nicomachean Ethics*, ed. T. Hoffmann, J. Müller, and M. Perkams (Cambridge: Cambridge University Press, 2013), pp. 52-71.

21 "Several of my novels have counterparts to specific works of theology . . . The book 'Aurelia" (Donning-Starblaze Books, 1982) has parallels with the 'Summa Theologica' of Thomas Aquinas. The fourteen-year-old girl student Aurelia (in the bottom half of her classes) is completing her tenth form schooling. The last item of her tenth form is 'World Government' in which the students must literally go out from their 'Golden World cultus' to an inferior world and take control of it and govern it for a period. If a student should fail to master and govern a world, that student would die, of course, and would also fail the course. Aurelia comes down (more by accident than competent navigation) on the world Gaea (sometimes confused with Earth). There she quickly becomes a cult figure, believed by some to be a girl messiah. She does give striking and reasoned homilies or orations or sermons that make her sound a little like a messiah. In fact, they form a mini-outline of the great (3011 double column pages in my edition) 'Summa' of Aquinas. But it is only a coincidence that the balanced sanity of the 'Golden World Cultus' of Aurelia's home world should parallel the 'Summa' of the Angelic Doctor. Aurelia was no messiah, but she was a very nice girl, and I regret that my story line required her failure and death." Jackson, "An Interview with R.A Lafferty," pp. 49-50. See it onlinet: http://www.sanduskyregister.com/Blog/2015/01/16/My-interview-with-R-A-Lafferty.html.

"hidden meaning of lawlessness" (2 Thessalonians 2:7), a notion which was wholly absent from ancient discussions of *eudaimonia*. For Aristotle, the mystery of why any humans would consciously choose to act contrary to their own highest good is discussed in terms of *akrasia*, (ἀκρασία) a disconnect between a moral agent's understanding of the eudemonistic good and the unreasoning and countervailing impulses of the emotions (*pathos*); simply put, it is a "lack of mastery" by reason over certain feelings that lead to impetuous activity.[22] But, as Lafferty explains, "Thomas Aquinas wrote that sin was an offense against happiness. Aurelia the space girl also taught that sin was an offense against happiness," hence those "who don't believe in God, or the natural order, or form, or due process, who confuse pleasure with happiness, and who aren't at all sure of being, do not accept that there are such things as sins. They are presently the majority in the world."[23] Lafferty's task in *Aurelia*, then, is to explicate the Christian Thomistic understanding of how the darkening of eudaimonistic reasoning by the effects of sin, the transgression of divine law, invariably results in a deviation from the human *telos* of flourishing.

The Aurelian Sermons

One Gaean observer of Aurelia's attempts at world governance encapsulates the Camiroi girl's entire philosophy in three aphoristic dictums, "Law is the Road-Map of Happiness. Grace is the Gift of Happiness. Justice is Happiness in society."[24] And these are indeed the most significant indicators of Lafferty's eudaimonism as promulgated in Aurelia's sermons,[25] her so-called Insights-of-

---

[22] See Pierre Destrée, "Aristotle on the Causes of Akrasia," in *Akrasia in Greek Philosophy*, ed. C. Bobonich and P. Destrée (Leiden: Brill 2007), pp. 139–166.

[23] R.J. Whitaker, "Maybe They Needed Killing & The Importance of Happiness," p. 13.

[24] Lafferty, *Aurelia*, p. 88.

[25] The parallel with Jesus' own Sermons to his throngs of followers as recounted in the Gospels are never expressly indicated, yet the implicit allusions are nonetheless present, perhaps most

the-Day which the Camiroi girl ascertains as the teachings of "Fat Tom the Sage of the Middle Worlds," a clear reference to Aquinas.[26] The first Aurelian sermon establishes the

---

evidently in relation to Christ's "Sermon the Plain" in the Gospel of Luke 6:17-49. In contrast to the longer and better-known "Sermon on the Mount" located in the Gospel of Matthew, chapters 5 through 7, the Lucan account of the Sermon, while clearly deriving from the same collection of sayings (the hypothetical Q source), nonetheless has a series of distinctive characteristics. Perhaps the most singular of these characteristics is the emphasis in Luke on Jesus' proclamation of the "Kingdom of God" as not only a spiritual event, but also a revolutionary overturning of the established socio-political order, a foreshadowing of the eschaton, which inaugurates a radical new ethic as well. See John Topel, S.J., "The Tarnished Golden Rule (Luke 6:31): The Inescapable Radicalness of Christian Ethics," *Theological Studies* 59:3 (1998), pp. 475-485, and Willard M. Swartley, "Politics or Peace (Eirēnē) in Luke's Gospel," in Political Issues in Luke-Acts, ed. R.J. Cassidy and P.J. Scharper (Eugene, OR: Wipf and Stock, 2015), pp. 18-37. Finally, it should be pointed out that in earliest Christianity the unity of the evangelical witness of Christ's life and teachings, as exemplified in the Sermons, was inextricably connected to with the tradition of didactic teaching of doctrinal truths. See, for example, Kari Syreeni, "The Sermon on the Mount and the Two Ways Teaching of the Didache," in *Matthew and the Didache: Two Documents from the Same Jewish-Christian Milieu?*, ed. H. van de Sandt (Assen: Royal van Gorcum/Minneapolis: Fortress Press, 2005), pp. 87–103. This inextricableness of *kerygma* and *didache* is also present throughout *Aurelia*.

[26]Ibid, p. 111. As G.K. Chesterton memorably wrote: "St. Thomas was a huge heavy bull of a man, fat and slow and quiet; very mild and magnanimous but not very sociable; shy, even apart from the humility of holiness; and abstracted, even apart from his occasional and carefully concealed experiences of trance or ecstasy. St. Francis was so fiery and even fidgety that the ecclesiastics, before whom he appeared quite suddenly, thought he was a madman. St. Thomas was so stolid that the scholars, in the schools which he attended regularly, thought he was a dunce. Indeed, he was the sort of schoolboy, not unknown, who would much rather be thought a dunce than have his own dreams invaded, by more active or animated dunces. This external contrast extends to almost every point in the two personalities. It was the paradox of St. Francis that while he was passionately fond of poems, he was rather distrustful of books. It was the outstanding fact about St. Thomas that he loved books and lived on books; that he lived the very life of the clerk or scholar in *The Canterbury Tales*, who would rather have a hundred books of Aristotle and his philosophy than any wealth the world could give him. When asked for what he thanked God most, he answered simply, 'I have understood every page I ever read.'" *St. Thomas Aquinas: "The Dumb Ox"* (London: Sheed & Ward, 1933), p. 3.

teleological basis of any Aristotelian-Thomistic account of human flourishing. "Happiness is both the key and the goal. Every human action must have a goal, or it will not be a human action. The 'Object of Desire' is always the Human Goal, but there are false objects and false goals."[27] Here, Lafferty is explicitly invoking Aquinas' doctrine that human actions must meet certain criteria in order to be recognized as truly conducive of the human good, and among these, perhaps the most foundational is that human activities must be goal-oriented.[28] As Thomas explains in the *Summa*, authentically human praxis is denoted by its reasoned volition (*ST* Ia IIae q.1, a.1); that is, unlike non-rational animals, human beings choose their actions according to a coherent account of what they take to be the good, and these choices are not products of deterministic causal forces, or unreasoning passion, but rather a function that must comprise both intellect and will (*ST* Ia q.83, a.3). That is, the constitutive parts of human reason must have both a cognitive and appetitive power, one which enables us to comprehend the good, and the other which elicits an innate desire for the understood good (*ST* Ia q.82, a.1).[29] This is all the more necessary, since as humans we encounter a very wide array of possible choices to make in regards to the good—what Lafferty refers to as a range of both true and false goals. As Lafferty has Aurelia say, "The will of itself is blind but it has aptitudes and powers. The intellect is powerless. The two of them together are able to give an orderly movement, which is human movement. To the extent that we ever indulge in disorderly movement, we are not human."[30]

Aurelia also follows Aristotle and Aquinas in her

---

[27] Lafferty, *Aurelia*, p. 111.

[28] See Joseph Pilsner, *The Specification of Human Actions in St Thomas Aquinas*, Oxford Theology and Religion Monographs (Oxford: Oxford University Press, 2006); Ralph McInerny, *Aquinas on Human Action: A Theory of Practice* (Washington, D.C.: The Catholic University of America Press, 2012).

[29] Cf. David M. Gallagher, "The Will and Its Acts (Ia IIae, qq. 6-17)," in *The Ethics of Thomas Aquinas*, ed. S.J. Pope (Washington, D.C.: Georgetown University Press, 2002), pp. 69-89.

enumeration of these false notions of the good which lead to disorderly movements away from true happiness: "the goal is not wealth or power or pleasure . . . The goal is happiness, which is the true object of desire, and this goal can only be attained by ordered and deliberate will."[31] The ultimate object of human desire, the supreme good, the "Final Happiness" in Aurelia's parlance, cannot be located in any of these "internal and external seducers" which deflect us from our "rational goal of happiness;" it is "neither outside nor inside, but outside-and-above. One name for this 'outside-and-above' final happiness is 'The Universal Good.'"[32] Thomas also postulated that authentic *eudaimonia* is only to be found in a supernatural *telos*, beatitude, which is only possible to apprehend in the contemplation of God's essence. While humanity is ordered to the natural goods that can be attained in this world, the natural pleasures they provide are only a *beatitudo imperfecta*, a partial and imperfectly realized sense of joy that is not true happiness.[33] Genuine beatitude entails that a human being has arrived at a state in which there is no greater good left to desire or seek, yet nothing on earth leaves us without some further desire yet to be fulfilled. Moreover, we are by nature made to seek and come to know the ultimate cause of our happiness, but simply coming to a conceptual understanding that God is the cause of happiness is not sufficient to placate the restless human intellect and will; on the contrary; the deepest human desire is to know the very essence of God, yet this innate desire for beatitude is utterly beyond what the unaided human intellect can accomplish.[34]

---

[30] Lafferty, *Aurelia*, p. 116.

[31] Ibid, p. 111.

[32] Ibid.

[33] Q.v. Anthony J. Celano, "The Concept of Worldly Beatitude in the Writings of Thomas Aquinas," *Journal of the History of Philosophy* 25:2 (1987), pp. 215-226.

[34] *ST* Ia IIae q.3, a.8: "Final and perfect happiness can consist in nothing else than the vision of the Divine Essence. To make this clear, two points must be observed. First, that man is not perfectly happy, so long as something remains for him to desire and seek: secondly, that the perfection of any power is determined by the

This proves to be the case because the vision of God's essence surpasses the "nature not only of man, but also of every creature, for every knowledge that is according to the mode of created substance falls short of the vision of the Divine Essence, which infinitely surpasses all created substance." As a consequence, Thomas concludes, neither humans, nor any other creature, can attain final happiness by their natural powers.[35] Humans need some capacity that transcends their own innate ability—a capacity that Aquinas identifies as grace, and which Aurelia calls "more-than-natural" powers— to elevate the human intellect to the point where it can come to know God essentially.

The elevating power of grace is a freely given "more-than-natural" power that perfects the human intellect and the human will by imbuing them with a steady disposition to choose and pursue the good. Aristotle identified these dispositions as *hexis* (ἕξις), what Thomas refers to as *habitus*— in other words, routine behaviors that habituate us towards

---

nature of its object. Now the object of the intellect is 'what a thing is,' i.e. the essence of a thing, according to *De Anima* iii, 6. Wherefore the intellect attains perfection, in so far as it knows the essence of a thing. If therefore an intellect knows the essence of some effect, whereby it is not possible to know the essence of the cause, i.e. to know of the cause 'what it is;' that intellect cannot be said to reach that cause simply, although it may be able to gather from the effect the knowledge of that the cause is. Consequently, when man knows an effect, and knows that it has a cause, there naturally remains in the man the desire to know about the cause, 'what it is.' And this desire is one of wonder, and causes inquiry, as is stated in the beginning of the *Metaphysics* (i, 2). For instance, if a man, knowing the eclipse of the sun, consider that it must be due to some cause, and know not what that cause is, he wonders about it, and from wondering proceeds to inquire. Nor does this inquiry cease until he arrive at a knowledge of the essence of the cause. If therefore the human intellect, knowing the essence of some created effect, knows no more of God than 'that He is;' the perfection of that intellect does not yet reach simply the First Cause, but there remains in it the natural desire to seek the cause. Wherefore it is not yet perfectly happy. Consequently, for perfect happiness the intellect needs to reach the very Essence of the First Cause. And thus it will have its perfection through union with God as with that object, in which alone man's happiness consists."

[35] *ST* Ia IIae q.5, a.

our specific teleological fulfillment as human beings.[36] Aquinas differentiated between a habitual readiness to pursue our natural *telos*, which can be attained through purely human effort, and those habitual virtues that allow us to achieve supernatural happiness, which can only be acquired by means of a divinely infused *habitus* of grace.[37] In either instance, the correctly ordered habits of the mind and heart are the only road to true *eudaimonia*: "Happiness is a habit that can be acquired. Yes, and it must be acquired by each of you or you are lost forever . . . . Is habit mere routine? Can we be happy with routine happiness?" Aurelia will ask her fair-weather followers rhetorically. "Yeah, we can. Routine means 'on the route,' on the high road . . . . the whole thing goes by free choice, and it is better to make a rational choice than an irrational choice;" indeed, "There is nothing easier and more rational than the high habits of the intelligently aimed road that knows its target. And that road takes us to the edge of the world and off it to 'Final Happiness' and to 'The Father of Lights.'"[38] Even though the journey may be "routinely" rational it is by no means pedestrian, "the most rational road will always traverse the most discovery-prone country. There will be bonus and bounty at every league of it. The air hums with activity all along the rational road. There is energy

---

[36] *ST* Ia IIae q.49, a.4: "Habit implies a disposition in relation to a thing's nature, and to its operation or end, by reason of which disposition a thing is well or ill-disposed thereto."

[37] Bad habits that lead us away from eudaimonia are called vices, while those good habits which as conducive to authentic happiness are known as virtues; cf. Bonnie Kent, "Habits and Virtues (Ia IIae, qq.49-70)," in *The Ethics of Thomas Aquinas*, ed. S.J. Pope (Washington, D.C.: Georgetown University Press, 2002), pp. 116-130. Aquinas refers to those infused habits that lead us to our final beatitude as the "theological virtues." In *ST* Ia IIae q.62, a.2, Thomas explains that "habits are specifically distinct from one another in respect of the formal difference of their objects. Now the object of the theological virtues is God Himself, Who is the last end of all, as surpassing the knowledge of our reason. On the other hand, the object of the intellectual and moral virtues is something comprehensible to human reason. Wherefore the theological virtues are specifically distinct from the moral and intellectual virtues."

[38] Lafferty, *Aurelia*, pp. 134-135.

released at every step. It is the common magic of every day."[39] The reason that we wander off that road so often, the reason Aurelia has so much difficulty convincing her listeners of its existence, is due to the fact that most humans fail to perceive that their natural desire for *eudaimonia* indicates that they are composite creatures, they are metaxic, comprised of both body and soul, made of humble matter yet destined for heavenly glory.[40]

> "A living and bodied person is a sort or arc of a circle, or perhaps of a parabola. If we continue the lines of that arc out beyond the body and the person, we come to a puzzle. The lines cannot be completed in the person's own world or context. They go over the edge. Part of the enclosed, extended person will be either ultra-natural or infra-natural—anyhow, it will be in another world, beyond the bounds of its supposed nature. We are sometimes told to become whole persons, and so we must do. But our own life and world are too small to contain our whole personhood.
>
> Well, is there any way that the circle or parabola of our persons can be completed? Of course there is . . . The reason that we are all so funny-looking, the reason that our institutions and our worlds are so funny-looking, is that this isn't all of any of them. There is more of each of us somewhere else. There is more everything of ours somewhere else."[41]

Human beings have an innate desire for a transcendent *eudaimonia*, since they are constituted for an intrinsic teleological fulfillment that resides beyond the merely

---

[39] Ibid, p. 139.

[40] For a partial analysis of Lafferty's appropriation of the idea of humanity as inhabitants of a *metaxy*, the spatio-temporal in-between or middle ground between the material and spiritual realms, from Plato via the works of Thomas Aquinas and other Scholastics, see Gregorio Montejo, "Aeviternity: R.A. Lafferty's Thomistic Philosophy of Time in the Argo Cycle," *Feast of Laughter* 1 (2014), pp. 102-114, especially pp. 110-112.

[41] Lafferty, *Aurelia*, pp. 139-140.

material. "We have an intrinsic claim to light. We have an intrinsic claim to component peace. We have an intrinsic claim to happiness. We have these claims and rights because we are human creatures . . . We can forfeit these rights and titles only by becoming something less than human creatures."[42] Yet this inherent *telos* seems to lie now forever beyond our grasp, because of "crippling that had already taken place before any of us came here," and while all humans inherit the damaging effects of this primordial calamity, it nonetheless does "not belong to our original human nature, but now it is part of our second human nature."[43] In other words, this proclivity towards counterfeit forms of happiness is now almost as deeply ingrained in our hearts and minds as that original, prelapsarian orientation towards the supreme good. And as the narrative recurrently reminds us, especially as it begins to approach its portentous dénouement, it is precisely because Aurelia not only preaches against this tragic disorientation away from the innate laws that govern our fundamental human end, but because her very presence on Gaea threatens to destabilize the crooked status quo that the "Mystery of Iniquity" has imposed since the time of the Fall, that the Camiroi girl must meet her imminent doom.

For Aurelia, the misaligned human intellect and will must be realigned once more in accordance with the essential ordered reason that regulates all being. Indeed, this is the basic content of her political platform, and the guiding light of her entire philosophy of world-governance. "Physical and moral and civil laws are all mere aspects of the universal Law of Happiness. There was one law given at the physical beginning of the universe, at the 'big-bang' moment—the Law 'Be Happy!' And the universe has been following that law ever since, with a few local exceptions."[44] This is all perfectly in keeping with Thomas Aquinas' conception of natural law, which posits that all things in creation are ruled by a universal or Divine Law which is imprinted in the their very natures.

---

[42] Ibid, p. 159.
[43] Ibid, p. 160.
[44] Ibid, p. 171.

Moreover, since all things act according to their nature, they derive their proper acts and teleological ends according to the dictates of this inner law. All things in the cosmos, particularly human beings who can discern the ordinances of the Divine Law by means of their reason, are indeed naturally governed by Aurelia's first universal axiom to "Be Happy" and seek the supreme good.[45] This insistence on the mandates of law is not a descent into a kind of Pharisaical legalism, but rather a recognition that everything in nature, above all humanity, insofar as it reflects the order by which God directs human beings through their nature for their own ultimate flourishing, reflects the universal law of *eudaimonia* inscribed within their own natures.

"In the Ante-Room of the Real World"

In any event, human laws, the sorts of statutes, regulations, and decrees that civil authorities can legislate, even when they mirror a higher universal law, are not the sole meaning and purpose of governorship. Humanity was not created for the sake of the law. Mankind was created before

---

[45] *ST* Ia IIae q.91, a.2: "Law, being a rule and measure, can be in a person in two ways: in one way, as in him that rules and measures; in another way, as in that which is ruled and measured, since a thing is ruled and measured, in so far as it partakes of the rule or measure. Wherefore, since all things subject to Divine providence are ruled and measured by the eternal law; it is evident that all things partake somewhat of the eternal law, in so far as, namely, from its being imprinted on them, they derive their respective inclinations to their proper acts and ends. Now among all others, the rational creature is subject to Divine providence in the most excellent way, in so far as it partakes of a share of providence, by being provident both for itself and for others. Wherefore it has a share of the Eternal Reason, whereby it has a natural inclination to its proper act and end: and this participation of the eternal law in the rational creature is called the natural law. Hence the Psalmist after saying (Psalm 4:6): 'Offer up the sacrifice of justice,' as though someone asked what the works of justice are, adds: 'Many say, Who shows us good things?' in answer to which question he says: 'The light of Thy countenance, O Lord, is signed upon us': thus implying that the light of natural reason, whereby we discern what is good and what is evil, which is the function of the natural law, is nothing else than an imprint on us of the Divine light. It is therefore evident that the natural law is nothing else than the rational creature's participation of the eternal law."

the giving of human law, and then laws were created in order to help mankind flourish, but the people of Gaea misunderstand this about Aurelia, whose world-governance is not primarily aimed at finding political solutions to humanity's problems. "The old word 'to steer a ship' is the same as the old word 'to govern.' But the best steering of a ship isn't political steering, and neither is the best government of the world."[46] The depths of Aurelia's true understanding of governance is perhaps best captured in a curious phrase she relates in one of her later sermons—"Obey the Law and Do as You Please," which the young Camiroi envoy closely associates with another saying, "The Law is the Lantern to Light People Home."[47] The former phrase, of course, evokes a witty play on the words of Augustine's celebrated adage, "Love, and do what you will."[48] But it is more than just a clever rephrasing, for its echoing parallelism with Augustine's earlier moral axiom subtly underscore the fact that Aurelia came to Gaea not to impose an outward legal norm, but rather to reorient the hearts and minds of her listeners back to the all-but-obliterated internal dictates of the Law of Happiness.

As the appointed hour of her increasingly destined death nears, Aurelia gives one final sermon. "If we are well enough disposed," she tells her remaining followers, "the passage from life through death to fuller life would be no more noteworthy than the passage from one day to another," although this is not to "say that it is not noteworthy at all; for the passage from one day to another should always be the walking from one delightful mansion to another." In preparing herself and her listeners for her coming passage from one transient mansion to another, more permanent domicile, Aurelia recalls scenes from one of her favorite

---

[46] Lafferty, *Aurelia*, p. 173.

[47] Ibid, p. 171.

[48] Augustine, *Homily VII on the First Epistle of John*: "This is what I insist upon: human actions can only be understood by their root in love. All kinds of actions might appear good without proceeding from the root of love. Remember, thorns also have flowers: some actions seem truly savage, but are done for the sake of discipline motivated by love. Once and for all, I give you this one short command: love, and do what you will."

childhood collections of fairy tales, a book full of "multi-colored wonders" and the "excitement of strangeness," including "persons of incomparable beauty and pleasantness, companionship where each one takes the heart from his breast and exchanges it for the other, music that makes the mountains break open like doors, the enchantment of *sanctified flesh*, and the ship that sails on the river named 'Forever.'"[49] But, can these thing be real, do they actually exist? Of course, Aurelia readily answers. But where or when? Why, here and now, for these "are the things that happen and exist every day in the real world. And here and now we are at least in the ante-room of the real world." Most importantly, the "right key that opens the door in the wall" to this more glorious place is "called on one side of it 'Grace' and on the other side 'Love a-burning,'" and it still opens the door "even if you use it upside down."[50]

After this final summation, it only remains for Aurelia to die an apparently meaningless death, be buried in an unmarked tomb, and then quickly be forgotten by the very people she had attempted so assiduously to enlighten. "After Aurelia had been dead for a year, an ailanthus tree"—also known as the 'tree of heaven' (*Ailunthus altissima*)—grew upon her grave without a gravestone. "It did smell funny, but it was pretty. It was the tree that should have reminded people of Aurelia, but there was no memory of her left to be revived."[51] Despite these vicissitudes, including the stupefying amnesia of her unfaithful disciples, neither Aurelia nor her teaching were given in vain, for in the end Aurelia's edifying *didache* is inseparable from her life, mission, and death. Indeed, it can only be rendered meaningless if that teaching is irrevocably sundered from the lived witness of her *kerygma*. She descended from Shining World to proclaim the ineradicable human desire for true and everlasting happiness that remains imprinted in our innermost being despite our capricious memories and the ravages of sin, and the seemingly

---

[49] Lafferty, *Aurelia*, p. 175.

[50] Ibid.

[51] Ibid, p. 182.

fruitless conclusion of her mission, along with her tragic sacrifice testifies to the truth of that transcendent desire's certain fulfillment only in the "outside-and-above." Her message, as given in both words and deed, reveals that we are merely sojourners in the antechamber of the real world, a transitory place where only grace can unlock our innately given potential for beatitude by means of a radical transformation of our reason and volition, a freely-given instrument of deliverance that evinces the ardent ardor of "The Father of Lights" for us to rejoin him in our true home, the dwelling-place of *eudaimonia*.

Gregorio Montejo is a professor of Historical Theology at Boston College. His research interests include Thomas Aquinas, Christology, and Trinitarian Theology. Montejo is a member of the Catholic Theological Society of America and the Society of Biblical Literature. Most recently, he gave a presentation on "Re-imagining God's Apophatic Form: Aquinas, De divinis nominibus, *and the Pauline Corpus" at Villanova University's Patristic, Medieval, and Renaissance Conference (PMR).*

Outside the Cathedral
by Kevin Cheek

> "I don't see him as a religious writer, but rather a writer who was religious."
> -Paul Rydeen

There is a place in New Mexico that has tremendous personal significance to me. In the village of Chimayo, there is a Catholic mission church called the Santuario de Chimayo. It is by no means the oldest church in the state, dating only to the early 1800s, but it is among the most beautiful. It has become a tourist destination over the decades, for its beauty, for its astonishing example of 19th century Spanish colonial artwork, and primarily for the deep sense of reverence, history, and spirituality that pervades it. Make no mistake, this is no museum of Spanish colonial mission history, this is a living Catholic church with several services a week, weddings, funerals and baptisms. It is full of the life and death and hope and trials of the small mountain community it serves.

I am not Catholic (I grew up largely without any kind of religion), yet I visit the Santuario often. I look reverently at the retablos. I even visit the small room in back and take a pinch from the pit of miraculous healing earth in hopes that it may help my various ills, though they are too minor to really warrant a miracle. I believe I go there because it is a beautiful place and because the sense of history and reverence and the sense of community all resonate strongly with me. Even though I do not share the particularly Catholic mysteries, the joy in experiencing mystery is a part of me as well.

R. A. Lafferty was a devoutly religious man. There can be no real argument with that statement. His erudite and devotional Catholicism was a fundamental and guiding element in his life. It informed his writing and added a level of depth and mysticism to his stories.

However, his writing appeals to a very broad audience— much broader than the audience for religious fiction or

Catholic fiction. I have spoken with Lafferty fans whose faiths are Hindu, Zen Buddhist, Jewish, Atheist, and perhaps many others.

I first discovered R. A. Lafferty as teenager. As I recall, I was talking with a friend's mom about the possibilities of future Human evolution. She stopped me, put a copy of *Nine Hundred Grandmothers* in my hands, and told me to read "Ginny Wrapped in the Sun" before continuing the conversation. I did, and found reading "Ginny..." a disturbing but intriguing experience. I was also delighted by "Narrow Valley," all of the Institute stories, and several of the other gems in the collection. And I was hooked on Lafferty for life.

I have returned to "Ginny Wrapped in the Sun" many times, and have never been completely comfortable with it. Many—perhaps most—of Lafferty's stories are deeply informed by his Catholic faith. In some of the stories the religious influence is nearer the surface, as it is in this story. The story takes its name from a line in Revelation 12:1. "A great sign appeared in heaven: a woman clothed with the sun, and the moon under her feet, and on her head a crown of twelve stars." The biblical story concerns a woman who gives birth to a miraculous child. The child is then swept up into Heaven while a dragon pursues the woman. This helps usher in the final war between Heaven and Hell at the end of the human world. (I am not well versed in Revelation, so please forgive any inaccuracies in my summary.)

"Ginny Wrapped in the Sun" tells the story of the end of humanity and the reversion of the "contingent mutation" that gave us our humanity. It tells the story of a four-year-old girl, Ginny, who becomes pregnant at 4 and is the seed that gives rise to a new form of humanity that lives only a dozen or so years, essentially as howling monkeys. It also tells the story of the scientist who is delivering a talk on how some recently discovered fossil skeletons of a group of early hominids are all of 4 and 5 year old specimens, indistinguishable from modern human, but more similar in grouping to howling monkeys, and how those were our origin and our destination.

As I said, I have always been uncomfortable with the story, not so much because of its religious allegory, but because of the cavalier way it treats the pregnancy of a four-year-old child and the murder of another. What the religious references do give it is a framework upon which to hang these uncomfortable elements—a sense of depth and profundity that allow one to look past the difficult elements to see what the story is saying. Essentially "Ginny Wrapped in the Sun" is telling us that the dinosaurs ruled the earth for over 50 million years, while we've only been here for fifty to a hundred thousand. And then it asks us what makes us think we will last?

My favorite Lafferty story refers to religion, but perhaps does not have religion as its main point. In "Days of Grass, Days of Straw" the main character finds himself in a fog wondering what kind of day it is. The premise is that prophets, people of great strength, virtue, and above all vitality can wrestle with God in the form of a mist. If they win the wrestling match, they get to determine what kind of day it is, and call for days of increased joy and vigor—days of grass, days of sage, even days of ice and fire. However, God will not record these days on the regular calendar, and they slip from our memory in the regular days, the days of straw.

In another parallel storyline, in a regular day of straw, the main characters hold a symposium to discuss the possibility of the days out of count.

> "This gets out of hand now," Vincent Rue protested. "It is supposed to be a serious symposium on spatial and temporal underlays. Several of you have turned it into a silly place and a silly time. You are taking too anthropomorphic a view of all these things, including God. One does not really wrestle with God in a bush or a mist, or ride in wildly on a pony and count coup on God. Even as an atheist I find these ideas distasteful."
>
> "But we are anthropoi, men," Adrian proclaimed. "What other view than an anthropomorphic view could we take? That we should play the God-game, that we should wrestle with a God-form and try to wrest lordship of days from him, that we should essay to count coup on God, I as a theist do not find at all

distasteful."

OK, so perhaps religion really is at the core of the story, or more accurately man's relationship with God and the Universe rather than the practice of religion. Lafferty seems to be telling us to take a greater hand in our fate. His heroes and heroines (Lafferty is one of the few SF authors to unselfconsciously write really strong female characters, by the way—but that is a topic for another essay, or even a full semester course of study) respect God, but also challenge God, joyously, unhesitatingly, even jubilantly.

What the religious aspects in this story give us is a framework for the tricks of the narrative to work. This is a tale of parallel time streams or parallel realities, an often-tread trope of SF. In "Days of Grass, Days of Straw" it is not the scientists finding a door into an alternate plane, or time travellers creating multiple time streams, but individual heroes wrestling with God for control over which time stream a given day belongs to.

There are plenty of Lafferty stories where he is in a more overtly religious mode—stories like "And Walk Now Gently Through the Fire" and "Horns on Their Heads." I am less comfortable with these stories. However, what I am most uncomfortable with in these is how he sets up a world of exaggerated hippie ideals but sets it up as a straw man that he can then systematically knock down. I know that my own worldviews (slightly liberal, sharing much with hippie idealists in my belief that we really can make a better world for all and that war really is a pretty stupid solution to problems of diplomacy) are often in his crosshairs. I feel uncomfortable when I feel that he is misrepresenting those views in order to make them easier targets.

One of the greatest Lafferty stories with strong religious and philosophical underpinnings is "Old Foot Forgot." This story is a cry for individualism and a master class in accelerated worldbuilding. He builds a complete world and its philosophical system in just a few pages, mainly through ritual and reverential mention.

Now he stacked some of the needful things from the clinic, and Lay Sister Moira P. T. de C. took others of them to her own giolach house to keep till the next day. Then the Dookh-Doctor ritually set his clinic on fire, and a few moments later his house. This was all symbol of the great nostos, the returning. He recited the great rhapsodies, and other persons of the human kind came by and recited with him.

"That no least fiber of giolach die," he recited, "that all enter immediately the more glorious and undivided life. That the ashes are the doorway, and every ash is holy. That all become a part of the oneness that is greater than self.

"That no splinter of the giuis floorboards die, that no glob of the chinking clay die, that no mite or louse in the plaiting die. That all become a part of the oneness that is greater than self."

He burned, he scattered, he recited, he took one glob of bitter ash on his tongue. He experienced vicariously the great synthesis. He ate holy innuin and holy ull. And when it was finished, both of the house and the clinic, when it had come on night and he was homeless, he slept that renewal night under the speir-sky.

Notice how he invokes the idea of a religious order by naming some of the characters with religious positions as in "Lay Sister Moira P. T. de C." It was decades before I learned that stood for Pierre Teilhard de Chardin.

Having painted that idyllic world, Lafferty then stands it on its ear and rails bitterly against it:

Everybody now knew that it was the last week in the life of the Dookh-Doctor, and everyone tried to make his happiness still more happy. The morning jokers outdid themselves, especially the arktos. After all, he was dying of an arktos disease, one never fatal to the arktos themselves. They did have some merry and outrageous times around the clinic, and the Dookh-Doctor got the sneaky feeling that he would rather live than die.

He hadn't, it was plain to see, the right attitude. So Lay Priest Migma P. T. de C. tried to inculcate the right attitude in him.

"It is the great synthesis you go to, Dookh-Doctor," he said. "It is the happy oneness that is greater than self."

"Oh I know that, but you put it on a little too thick. I've been taught it from my babyhood. I'm resigned to it."

"Resigned to it? You should be ecstatic over it! The self must perish, of course, but it will live on as an integral atom of the evolving oneness, just as a drop lives on in the ocean."

"Aye, Migma, but the drop may hang onto the memory of the time when it was cloud, of the time when it was falling drop, indeed, of the time when it was brook. It may say 'There's too damned much salt in this ocean. I'm lost here.'"

"Oh, but the drop will want to be lost, Dookh-Doctor. The only purpose of existence is to cease to exist. And there cannot be too much of salt in the evolving oneness. There cannot be too much of anything. All must be one in it. Salt and sulphur must be one, undifferentiated. Offal and soul must become one. Blessed be oblivion in the oneness that collapses on itself."

"Stuff it, lay priest. I'm weary of it."

"Stuff it, you say? I don't understand your phrase, but I'm sure it's apt. Yes, yes, Dookh-Doctor, stuff it all in: animals, people, rocks, grass, worlds and wasps. Stuff it all in. That all may be obliterated into the great—may I not coin a word even as the master coined them?—into the great stuffiness!"

"I'm afraid your word is all too apt."

And later, a bit more strongly:

"I would rather burn in a hell forever than suffer happy obliteration! I'll burn if it be me that burns."

What the use of religion gives the broader audience in this story is a set of expectations or archetypical reference points that let him build the world and its spirituality with a few short strokes. Here we have a world where unity with all life is celebrated over individuality, and death is embraced as a returning to "the oneness that is greater than the self." To readers well versed in the writings of Pierre Teilhard de Chardin, it probably also provides a scathing critique of his philosophy. That the story can serve so well on both those levels shows the power of Lafferty's Writing.

"Old Foot Forgot" is a joyous call to arms for the individual against the trends in society that demand us to become anonymous.

I have mentioned the word "joyous" many times. I think that is the single greatest appeal of Lafferty's writing to readers of all faiths and backgrounds. Lafferty's Catholic faith was a joyful faith. In *Fourth Mansions* he scathingly condemned the people of Washington DC as "Those who do not have the faith, and would not have the fun." For Lafferty, faith was fun—wooly, raucous, dangerous fun. His faith informed everything he wrote, and his joy in his faith infused his writing with fun. That fun is contagious and can be felt by all readers, from the conservative Catholic to the liberal atheist and all other points on the spiritual compass.

Even though I do not worship at the cathedral, I can still appreciate its beauty, its community, its sense of joy and wonder. And even from the outside, the view of the cathedral is amazing.

Kevin Cheek is a technical writer living and writing in California. He has been exhorting his friends, family, coworkers, and random passersby to read Lafferty since the early 1980s, and sincerely hopes you will do the same.

"Santuario de Chimayo" © 2015 *Anthony Ryan Rhodes*

Copyright, Copyleft, Copyfuture
by Rich Persaud

In response to a heartfelt one-liner on a quandary familiar to Lafferty fans of 2015 A.D.

? created Man
Man created Art
Man died
Man created Payment Systems
Payment Systems died
Art lived on
Man created new Payment Systems
Payment Systems died
Art lived on
Art created ?

One day, we will have Payment Systems which separate payment from distribution. A future Lafferty fan will bake a special, one-of-a-kind, unrepeatable cake and will deliver it to a future Locus office. Locus will license the cake-making human to view seven holograms derived from *The Books of Sand*. One hologram will be created by the hitherto unknown grandchild of Lafferty and an Oklahoma Native American, whose appearance will cast confusion and excitement upon Lafferty rights, lefts and futures.

First illustration from "Hill's album of biography and art" by Thomas Hill, pg.151, published in 1857. Photo is courtesy of the Internet Archive Book Images collection on Flickr, www.flickr.com/photos/internetarchivebookimages/1480483 4873/. No known copyright restrictions.

Second illustration from "St. Nicholas: An Illustrated Magazine for Young Folks, Volume XXXVII" by Mary Dodge, pg. 394, published in 1910. Illustration by W.J. Scott, courtesy of the Internet Archive Book Images collection on Flickr, www.flickr.com/photos/internetarchivebookimages/1459667 5598/. No known copyright restrictions.

Rich Persaud created www.ralafferty.org to introduce new readers to Lafferty's works. He writes at www.symspaces.com.

"Papa Garamask," Chavo chortled in a booming giggle from above, "fear you nothing. I will roll boulders down on Sinek and kill him."

R. A. Lafferty, "Frog on the Mountain"

Illustration © 2015 Anthony Ryan Rhodes

Lafferty and His Monsters - Part 1: The Early Works

by Daniel Otto Jack Petersen

Introduction: Lafferty's Cartography of Monsters

This essay on Lafferty and monsters completes a trilogy of sorts on Lafferty and the non-human more generally. Like some infamous movie franchises of late, however, this 'third' and 'final' installment got too big and has to be presented in two parts. This is, you guessed it, part 1. For lack of a better organizing principle (something monsters tend to defy anyway), we will quest chronologically through the monsters in Lafferty's works. Rather than seeing this approach as a colonial safari or menagerie or "cabinet of curiosities," let's try to think of it more as a sort of Bestiary Errant, an adventuring after the morphology and meaning of Lafferty's monsters in semi-encyclopedic fashion. (That said, this two-parter is a mere primer, I'm afraid, and by no means exhaustive.)

As with objects[1] and animals,[2] Lafferty's engagement with the monster is so ubiquitous that it might go somewhat unnoticed at first. Yet, once you become aware of the teeming presence of monsters in his fiction, Lafferty seems to convey that the monstrous is not a reality found off the maps, encountered only after you enter the uncharted zone marked "Here Be Dragons." Rather, they're not only on the maps, but, in a sense, for Lafferty monsters are the maps. As we'll see, he depicts humanity navigating through shifting 'monsterscapes' or 'dragon-scapes'[3], interior and exterior, dangerous and vital. In Lafferty's narratives, the monsters may be diabolical or holy

---

[1] See my essay in *FoL* volume 1.

[2] See my essay in *FoL* volume 2.

[3] R. A. Lafferty, *Fourth Mansions*, 1969, Ace Publishing Corporation, New York, p. 219.

or strange mixtures, but we cannot do without them. They will destroy us or make us whole, depending on whether we give them their proper place. (And note: to be eaten up by monsters isn't necessarily to be destroyed. With Lafferty, we shouldn't be surprised to find, resurrection is always on the cards.

Lafferty in the Horror Magazines and Anthologies

In Lafferty's fiction, horror is a key category in general. His oeuvre is replete with gruesome happenings and grotesque imagery[4], mixed though these aspects usually are with laugh-out-loud humor. The laughter, in fact, often only increases the discomfort of some grisly detail. The horror mode that Lafferty wove into his tales was obviously detected by editors, for he was published in Robert A. W. Lowndes's *Magazine of Horror* a number of times in the 1960s and then repeatedly published in anthologies of horror fiction in the 1970s. This publication history is briefly but intriguingly enumerated. All of the following are first publications of the stories unless otherwise indicated. Lafferty's story "The Man Who Never Was" was published in the Summer 1967 issue of *Magazine of Horror*; "The Ultimate Creature" in the November 1967 issue; "Cliffs That Laughed" in the March 1969 issue. "Ghost in the Corn Crib" was published in *The Haunt of Horror* June 1973, the lone volume of Marvel Comics' ill-fated attempt at a print-only anthology series. "The Man With the Aura" was published in the 1976 *The Year's Best Horror Stories: Series IV* (the story was first published in 1974 in *Witchcraft & Sorcery* # 10; both series were edited by Gerald W. Page). "Oh Tell Me Will It Freeze Tonight" was published in 1976's *Frights* edited by Kirby McCauley. Lafferty twice placed very odd, creepy, and experimental stories in anthologies edited by modern horror master Ramsey Campbell: "Fog In My Throat" in 1976's *Superhorror* and "The Funny Face Murders" in 1980's *New Terrors 2*. His story "Splinters" was published in the 1978 initial volume of Charles

---

[4] Ghosts and the ghostly in Lafferty is a topic in its own right, one that looms so large and central that it deserves its own separate treatment. It will not be covered in this essay or its sequel.

L. Grant's *Shadows* series of horror anthologies. (In the latter two books, *New Terrors* and *Shadows*, Lafferty shared the pages with some of the earliest anthologized short stories of the then rising Stephen King.)

Monsters in Lafferty's Early Tales

Given this early association with the modern horror genre, it won't surprise us to find that Lafferty did not shrink from the recurring depiction of monsters in his fiction. Even in some of his most well-known tales, monsters lurk. The titular 'pseudo-ursine' demi-god of the story "Snuffles" (1960) is an unforgettable example. There's also the tentacled and hooved version of a husband and the giant arachnid version of his wife in Lafferty's multiple reality story "The Hole On the Corner" (1967). And these monsters have bite, to say the least. Each of the tales just mentioned features a denouement of devourment.

As for xenobiology in the earlier short fiction, there is the alien blob of "The Weirdest World" (1961), the porcine alien of "Pig in a Pokey" (1964), the gargoyle aliens of "Name of the Snake" (1964), the insectile aliens of "The Pani Planet" (1965), the goblin-esque aliens of "Ride a Tin Can" (1970), the frog-ape aliens of "Frog On the Mountain" (1970), and the arachnid aliens of "Once On Aranea" (1972).

Fairy tale creatures often feature as well, especially as woven into the language of Lafferty's prose. Just recall how many times characters (the aliens listed above as well as various humans) are referred to as giants, goblins, witches, ogres, and trolls. And there are persistent references to dragons and sea-monsters as well (the celebrated Ktistec Machine Epikt often takes on such a form, usually comically, yet in a gigantesque way that still packs some awe).

The early tales certainly begin to give hints of the contours of Lafferty's monsterology: e.g. monsters help us name both ourselves and our Others, often in hybridity with non-human ecology; they are likely to eat us, often as a judgment on our failure to engage fully with reality, and sometimes even for our betterment; and these stories simply begin to suggest Lafferty's burgeoning thesis that the quiltwork of existence is rife with monstrosity, implicit and explicit. Monsters feature even more so, however, in Lafferty's early novels, and have much more to reveal to us there. To these we will now turn at length.

Monsters in Space Chantey

Space Chantey (1968)[5], in addition to ovine and Circean transmogrifications, asteroids that are living cattle, and giant spaceship-swallowing "Megagaster birds," features a monstrous innovation on the episode with the Sirens in Homer's Odyssey (the ancient Greek epic upon which Lafferty's entire spacefaring novel is fast-and-loosely based). On the oceanic planet Sireneca, with its single island continent, the explorers find a mountain covered with blonde beauties singing a rousing song that rises to, but, maddeningly, never reaches, its musical climax, the finishing note that would resolve the tune. Through a hilariously grisly little episode of "scientific induction" that costs the lives of several crewmen, the adventurers confirm their notion about the mountain:

> "The mountain itself is the creature," said Captain Roadstrum. "The scree and the boulders are part of its hide, and it shivers its hide like a World horse. The whole thing is alive. The blonde maidens are but tentacles of the thing."
> "May I tangle with such a tentacle!" said Crewman Crabgrass. (69)

It's a pleasingly creepy innovation, mixed, as usual for Lafferty, with a note of piquant humor in the language and imagery. Rather than maidens with tentacles, such as you might find on gorgon-esque or Scylla-like creatures, here the maidens are the tentacles of a larger being.

Deciding to rid the spaceways of this waylaying and death-dealing menace (the tentacle-maidens burn to a crisp the men they embrace, in addition to the mountain driving them mad with its permanently unfinished song), the men

---

[5] All quotes from the 1968 Ace Double version, Ace Books, New York.

enter the inside of the "mountain-animal" (71) reckoning they "must go inside the creature and kill it interiorly" (72). Inside of it, they find the being stranger still:

> It is a big rambling spider-form inside here and the mountain is a living shell it has built for itself, for it's a mixed creature. (72)

It's hard to say what Lafferty may be doing consciously or unconsciously here with the Woman as Monster tradition, whether he is deepening such fears by showing a scarier monster behind the women, or whether he is subverting such fears by making the women mere facades. In the latter case, there is nothing authentically female about the monster (indeed, a few paragraphs down it is referred to by male pronouns). It only preys on male fear and desire with its deadly stereotyped maiden-protuberances. Considering the fact that Lafferty's fiction features so many powerful and memorable female characters (Margaret the Houri is one such in a later chapter of this novel, taking the men for rides on her shoulders, as many women characters do throughout Lafferty's tales) and considering Lafferty's take-downs of corporately greedy hyper-masculinity (e.g. "Nine Hundred Grandmothers"), I suggest that Lafferty is (perhaps somewhat unconsciously here) subverting the Woman as Monster tradition in this mutation of the Siren myth.

Captain Roadstrum and his men next realize that the words of the mountain being's tune are a repeated cycle of Monday and Tuesday and Monday and Tuesday that slaves once sang at their work in an Irish cycle - until a savior delivered them by coming and saying "And Wednesday too," thus breaking the charm that bound them to their masters, the "puca" (shapeshifting creatures from Celtic folklore). The monster is thus seen to be made not only of mixed ecological[6],

---

[6] There seems to be a persistent tradition throughout the ages of conflating monsters and mountains, which will have to be explored eventually in regard to Lafferty as the singing-spider mountain here in *Space Chantey* is by no means his only monstrous mountain. See also, for example, his short stories "World Abounding"

but also mixed mythical, elements intruding into this Homeric material. Captain Roadstrum, as he announces that he will play the savior role of the Irish legend, notices yet more myths woven into the thing:

> I will set a Wednesday-term to the monster. But there are other elements in this. Is not the climbing up of the giant spider and the slaying of it an Arabian-cycle thing? And did not Hans Schultz, in the green-island cycle, have a dream of the same thing? Upward, men; we are onto a great kill! (72)[7]

Just as all of Lafferty's work in general is a rambunctious sampling of folklore, legend, archetype, and myth from various parts of the world mixed together with his own personal mythologies, so too are his monsters comprised. This "mixed creature" thus exhibits the hybridity, "category crisis," and "transgression of boundaries" often noted by theorists as a central feature of the monster.[8]

Lafferty provides more description of this monster than perhaps he is usually wont to do, given his characteristically summarizing style, as the monster slayers go about their objective:

(1971; featuring another monster-mountain from Lafferty's oft reprised Interplanetary Romance mode) and "Oh Tell Me Will It Freeze Tonight" (featuring his native Oklahoman Winding Stair mountains in his more regional folkloric mode). For instances from his novels, see the Thunder Mountain of Astrobe in *Past Master* (another extra-terrestrial example, which I do not go into below) and the "magic mountain" Nanih Waiya that mystically superimposes itself onto the mountains of Oklahoma in Lafferty's historical Choctaw novel *Okla Hannali* (1972). I will be comparing these and others with the equally ubiquitous orological monsters of Cormac McCarthy's fiction in my doctoral work.

[7] Even with the ever resourceful help of the East of Laughter Facebook crew, I haven't been able to identify either of Lafferty's mythological references in this passage. Please do write to us if you know to what they refer.

[8] Cf. Weinstock, Jeffrey Andrew (2014), Editor, *The Ashgate Encyclopedia of Literary and Cinematic Monsters*, Ashgate Publishing Limited, Farnham, p. 517.

> Hawsers, cables a meter thick they climbed—and these were but the fine silks of the giant spider. The hairs on its toes were even thicker, and the men blasted them, beginning the attack. A note of alarm crept into the mountainous singing now. The creature knew that it was invaded but did not know how or by what. The creature sent tremors through its webs that threatened to dash the men down to their deaths. (72)

This interior adventure takes place in a garish red light, the source of which is now revealed:

> The mountainous interior spider had nine outside eyes and one great glowing interior eye by which he liked to contemplate himself. This was the spookiest light ever seen; and was the spookiest place, but one, in all the universes. (72)

So to the Siren myth's theme of the maddening temptation of unfulfilled desire, Lafferty adds the hidden motivation of a self-gazing monster.[9]

And yet further nature of its structure is grasped, evincing the narrator's irrepressible wonder for even such a monster:

> It was now seen that the entire mountain-creature was one single instrument, and the whole planet was its sounding box. The blondie-orifices were but small reeds of this amazing organ, the giant web-threads were quivering strings. (73)

That such creatures are "amazing" is a theme common to all of Lafferty's representations of monsters. There is always something fascinating about them, even if they are deadly or evil. A certain respect and awe toward monsters is a given with Lafferty.

---

9 Possibly making it a powerful image for the age of social networks and "selfies."

There are then encountered "quivering stalks," which receive the same (farcical) scientifically inductive experimentation the tentacle-maidens had received earlier, this time to see whether the stalks "emit a very strong digestive juice" (73). The result is similarly grisly, adding comic gore-horror to the monster-horror:

> "Touch one, Crewman Cutshark," Captain Puckett ordered. "Observe the data, Crewman Bramble."
> Crewman Cutshark touched one of the stalks, and he dissolved. The flesh was whisked away from him like vapor. He was only rather dirty white bones, and then the bones also dissolved.
> "What did you get, Crewman Bramble?" Captain Puckett asked.
> "Eleven million dissolution units at a base of—"
> "Leave off the science stuff or I'll clamp you all in irons," Roadstrum warned. "Upward, men, to the big kill." (73)

This is not that kind of science fiction. Lafferty meta-fictionally warns us off such "science stuff" through Captain Roadstrum's command. This is not about "hard sciences" but about desire, monsters, myth, and chthonic catharsis. Thus the narrative's appropriate method is "soft science, the science of the shadow areas and story areas" as a storyteller says in Lafferty's short story "Cliffs That Laughed" (noted above as being published in the *Magazine of Horror* in the '60s).[10]

Continuing their invasion of the creature's interior, Roadstrum and cohorts reach its ocular essence:

> Ah, the baleful red-glowing inner eye of the monster, which was also its soul and its mortal center. It blazed with red and black fire, and crackled and stunk. (73)

The mountain's tune becomes "hysterical with horror,

---

[10] For a discussion of the "science of story areas" as the project of Lafferty's entire career, see Andrew Ferguson's invaluable Master's Thesis "Lafferty and His World," p. 52ff. This is available at

giddy and gibbering, hate-hopping, and yet quite the best thing of its sort ever done" (73). The men leap into the spider-monster's great red eye and it finally resolves its truncated tune in its death agony. "Then the whole mountain died" (74). The men emerge from the monster and the monster diminishes:

> Roadstrum kicked the mountain open and they all went outside. The mountain was smaller as though the air were being let out of it. [...] The blondie appendages had become broken dolls.
>
> All loaded into the hornets for further adventures. It was early Wednesday morning. (74)

Clearly, there are appropriate occasions for monster slaying in Lafferty's narrative world. In this episode it would seem to be a symbol of breaking a repetitive cycle of slavery, setting a Wednesday term to the monster. This episode also seems to be about seeing through mere appearances of what the nature of a given monster really is, discovering its interiority and confronting it in that spooky inner space.

Yet Lafferty is not setting up as an "eternal conflict" between monsters and humans. The received wisdom of monster theory goes like this:

> From cosmological encounters and wars between monsters and gods and later between monsters and men, as in the stories of Odysseus's wanderings among the Sirens and adventures with creatures like Polyphemus, developed an archetype of reason and beauty in eternal conflict with the irrational and the chaotic. The earliest cosmologies associate monsters with chaos and unreason, out of which form itself emerged and on occasion, as with Medusa and Scylla, this chaos is tied to the primal female nature.[11]

---

https://www.academia.edu/329007/Lafferty_and_His_World.

[11] Friedman, John Block (2013), "Foreword," *The Ashgate Research Companion to Monsters and the Monstrous*, edited by Asa Simon Mittman and Peter J. Dendle, Ashgate Publishing Limited, Surrey, p. xxviii.

Whether or not this is an accurate portrayal of ancient and medieval monster-ology, Lafferty is certainly rambunctiously playing with all these dialectics, muddying the paired oppositions. For one thing, Lafferty takes even the monsters that ought to be slain as monsters that are nevertheless needed in the narrative landscape, not repressed but confronted, and, just as importantly, confronted in the right manner, which is not "scientific" in a narrow sense, but something deeper. The monster of desire and self-gaze here is defeated not by pure reason, but by more shadowy methods of affective and intuitive heroism. And, as I've briefly argued above, I think Lafferty in his own way is debunking the historical tendency to make monsters "tied to the primal female nature" as well.

Furthermore, there are monsters and there are monsters in Lafferty, as we'll see. The monsters can be beautiful in their way, yet still in need of slaying. Or the monsters can be chaotic in isolation, when they have no accepted place in the world or in our hearts. Lafferty aims to give them that place, demonstrating that monsters are needed as a central feature of creativity and spiritual progress.

Monsters in *Past Master*

Past Master (1968)[12] features an array of colorful, gruesome, and lively horrors. Its band of misfits encounters a feverish series of monstrosities and grotesqueries, along with wonders and glories, during their tour of the ostensibly utopian planet Astrobe. The novel shares some of the raucous adventuring quality of *Space Chantey*, but is overall a much more overtly philosophical and theological novel, inclusive of many speeches and discussions toward that end. The historical figure of Thomas More is brought from the past to this future in order to facilitate just such debates about the nature of utopia and human being... and monsters. So here there are not only graphically gnashing and thrashing monsters but a fair amount of monster exposition as well. This involves the novel

---

[12] All quotes from the 1999 Wildside Press POD version, Wildside Press, Gillette.

in a more complex view of monsters that, whilst it includes conflict, also goes beyond it.

Ouden the Nothingness Monster

From the opening pages we are introduced to the ogre-faced, thorax-and-lorica-bodied "mechanical killers" that enforce the utopian planet's thought policing. Though these "devils dressed in tin cans" (46) are trotted out throughout the novel almost as plot-props, their presence can in certain moments make for some atmospherically menacing imagery (reminiscent of Samuel Delany's baroque style from around this same era). In Thomas More's first visit to the grotesquely non-utopian city Cathead, we witness this scene:

> The Killers were milling around outside, and the air was full of sullen electricity. There was fear and anger like soot in the air. Bot-flies were spluttering and roaring about the slippery blood in the roadway outside and in the common room itself. There had been carnage, and the atmosphere spoke of more to come. (45-46)

And moments later:

> The mad goat-man was crooning a little song. The killers were thronging and gnashing in the roads like the iron dogs they were. (47)

And shocking carnage does indeed follow.

But the recurring presence of the mechanical killers furnishes but skirmishes with the greater entity that lies behind them and controls them. Fairly early in the novel we hear of their ultimate master, the ultimate monster, "the monster Ouden, the open mouth of Ouden," and have its name translated directly: "Ouden means nothingness" (35). Ouden is introduced as the problem with utopian Astrobe. In a later scene this nothingness monster numinously visits Thomas and his friend and ally Paul: "Then the monster Ouden came and sat in the middle of them and encircled them" (50). That encircling was not easy to bear: "They shriveled together in his presence, and their bones grew hollow" (51). This monster's message to them is true to his nature: "I will annihilate you" he informs them baldly. Resistance by the protagonists only brings out the monster's eloquence in the form of a persuasively disturbing little meditation:

> "I deny you completely," said the Paul-Thomas. "You are nothing at all."
>
> "Yes, I am that. But all who encounter me make the mistake of misunderstanding my nothingness. It is a vortex. There is no quiet or static aspect to it. Consider me topologically. Do I not envelop all the universes? Consider them as turned inside out. Now everything is on the inside of my nothingness. Many consider the Nothing a mere negative, and they consider it so to their death and obliteration."
>
> "We laugh you off the scene," said Paul-Thomas. "You lose." (51)

The men are trying to put a brave face on it, and in Lafferty's worldview, where "cosmic laughter" is the true ultimate[13], they're on the right track in trying to laugh off the persuasive rhetoric of nihilism. But with their every riposte the Ouden monster's aggressive oratory mounts:

> "[...] Your own mind and its imagery weakens; it is myself putting out the flame. Every dull thing you do, every cliché you utter, you come closer to me. Every lie you tell, I win. But it is in the tired lies you tell that I win the most toweringly."
>
> [...]
>
> "I eat you up. I devour your substance. There was only one kindling. I was overwhelmed only once. But I gain on it. I have put it out almost everywhere. It will

---

[13] See Andrew Ferguson's interpretation of R.A. Lafferty's short story "Nine Hundred Grandmothers" for the view that Lafferty advocates "cosmic laughter" as the essential creative force behind the universe: http://antsofgodarequeerfish.blogspot.co.uk/2011/09/thoughts-on-nine-hundred-grandmothers.html.

be put out forever here."

[...]

"Never will I leave. Not ever in your life will you sit down that I do not sit down with you. And finally it will happen that only one of us is left to get up, and that will be myself. I suck you dry." (52)

This suffocating, despair-inducing magniloquence has a long pedigree in literature, including the likes of Milton's Satan, Weston the Un-man in C. S. Lewis's Perelandra, and Judge Holden and Anton Chigurh in Cormac McCarthy's novels Blood Meridian and No Country For Old Men respectively. But here, the great Nihil is stripped of its seemingly human forms, or even a directly demonic persona. It's as if one of Lovecraft's Old Ones - or more accurately, the sum of all Old Ones and the indifferent universe they symbolize - were given voice here. The imagery (or non-imagery) of total devouring, of all-encompassing darkness, and of sucking vortex is the face (or non-face) of raw and unmasked nihilism for Lafferty, the Ultimate Monster of Nothingness. Yet notice: despite the great monster's own speechifying, he reveals that it is dullness and cliché and tired lies that are his true language, and the pathway to his victory among people. Ouden towers by making people and the world flat and grubby and vapid: flameless, snuffed, sucked dry.

Rimrock the Eutheopathic Seal-Man

Woven around these encounters with Ouden are the introduction of a semi-anthropoid oceanic monster of sorts who joins Thomas's company as guide and companion and co-combatant. A telepathic, shapeshifting man-animal or animal-man native to Astrobe, Rimrock is something of a mythopoeic character, often the occasion for a sort of psychological poetry, a lyrical emissary of the unconscious. Yet he has his monstrous aspects, for "Rimrock the ansel, of that most gentle species, had nevertheless slicers three feet long" (19), tusks or sabre-teeth it is hard to tell which as his form is often in flux, but powerful enough to do battle with mechanical bears in an early scene in the novel. And though undoubtedly a noble creature, toward his enemies "Rimrock was a devious fellow"

(19). This monster is made of wise-as-serpents-but-gentle-as-doves stuff. Thomas first meets him in this manner:

> "A communication center is approaching, on two feet or on four," Paul said. "He can put anybody into contact with anybody."
>
> "Aye, I feel him. [...] It is Rimrock the oceanic man!" [...]
>
> And Rimrock, the oceanic man, came in, on no legs at all, then on four legs, then on two. And he shook hands with Thomas with great friendship. (49)

Rimrock is an emotive and intuitive monster, the kind of monster you feel approaching even before you see it. We are given some explanation as to his no-foot, four-foot, two-foot approach:

> An ansel is in appearance a little like a seal of old earth. It can slither with great speed along the land, just as though it were swimming in water. It can walk passably, as a man or as an animal. And it has curious mental powers. (49)

Thomas clasps Rimrock in immediate friendship just as he grasps intuitively something of his nature:

> "My friend from the green ocean," Thomas boomed. "You of the rubbery black hide and the tufted ears! You bound or you walk, and you talk inside men's minds and make appearances. Read me the meaning of this damnable world, Rimrock." (49)

And Rimrock will indeed at least help Thomas read the meaning of Astrobe, for as I have said, he is creature of the unconscious (or subconscious), and the unconscious is the missing element in the Astrobean utopia.

In this encounter we are again reminded: "Rimrock the ansel was much larger than any earth seal, and the slicing mouth on him was a meter long" (50). As a shapeshifting seal-man, he draws in part on the Celtic folklore of the selkie. Yet he is a seal-man of a particularly monstrous variety with the repeated reminders not only of his shifting multi-form but also of the tremendous slicing capacity of his mouth, a comparatively tiny but sharp resistance to the allegedly all-encompassing "mouth of Ouden".

As a being that is "eutheopathic"(200), he represents mental, empathic, and theopathic (God-affective) depths that have been suppressed in humans, ecology, and the cosmos by the flattening schema of the Golden Dream of Astrobe (as the planet's utopia is referred to by its architects). There is a scene where Rimrock informs Thomas of the ansels' evolutionary mythology: "Our legend is that we are the people who climbed all the way to the sky, broke holes in it, and climbed out into a strange world that is above the sky" (88). In a lengthy, beautiful passage, pocked with humor, Rimrock describes this journey of ascension to Thomas, and then tells Thomas ruefully that humans don't feel the awe of this ascension as ansels do because humans have forgotten such origin myths buried in their own "underminds". Rimrock remonstrates: "But how can you forget that you live on the top of the sky?" (89). Claiming that he himself is one of the "primordial heroes" of his people who first broke through the sky in ages past, Rimrock exclaims: "May the sense of wonder never leave me!" (90). This oceanic monster-man, then, is a harbinger of the wonder of deep origins. Whereas Ouden sucks dry with cliché and non-think, Rimrock rehydrates with myth and mystery and meditation. But - beware! - the deep waters he and his kind supply to the vanishing human psyche are lively and populated.

It is the claim of the social architects of utopian Astrobe that one of the perfections of people who embrace the Golden Dream is that they themselves no longer dream. The telepathic Rimrock demurs: "I have walked through many thousands of those dreams myself" (87). In fact, Rimrock points out that his rather numinous race works to preserve the place of much-needed monsters in the human psyche by their presence in people's dreams:

> "Regular people have sealed off the interior ocean that used to be in every man," Rimrock said. "They closed the ocean and ground up its monsters for fertilizer.

That is why we so often enter into peoples' dreams. We take the place of the monsters they have lost." (90)

As I've said, there are monsters and there are monsters. For Lafferty, even though some totalizing monsters may be out to deceive and devour us, yet to have *no* monsters in our own subconscious is to be dehumanized. (As we'll see below, this theme will be picked up in full in his novel published in the following year, *Fourth Mansions*.)

Hunting Monsters in the Feral Lands

This replenishment of lost monsters by counter-forces happens not only interiorly on Astrobe, thanks to the ansels, but also exteriorly in a region apart from the utopian cities, and even apart from the non-utopian cities of squalor (many Astrobeans choose to live and suffer in the latter rather than participate in the depth-deprived utopian dream). Thomas and his band of primordial rebels go through a lengthy tour of the Feral Lands in chapters six and seven. Though this monstrous region is not within the purview of the "rational" Golden Dream, the utopians realize it is necessary in its way. Thus they isolate it so that it will not contaminate their even-keeled society. They banish their non-utopian ideas and entities to this wild realm. For some, a very small subset of the millions who live wretchedly in the non-utopian cities, this fierce place is a depth-renewing hunting ground and playground, a space to both kill and create monsters, activities which are left out of the sanitary utopian psychology.

The very ground of the Feral Lands is itself monstrous: "in plain fact there was no ground itself, nothing that could be called the surface, the fundament" (100). Those travelling through the region couldn't tell if they trod a meadow or were "working through the tops and middle heights of trees" (100). This is a place of dank psychic depths exteriorized:

> Another plain fact was that there were no trees themselves. One could not say that this was one tree and that one was another. They were not individuals; they were one creature. As well say that this is a grass, and that is a grass. They were entangled. In the thick

going if you climbed down far enough into the sleek darkness you still would not find firm ground. Water rather. And even in this fundamental bottom water it was possible to go down still more hundreds of feet through the growing plants and roots, never finding any bottom except a growth too dense to permit further descent. (100)

Into this bottomless muck-scape the adventurers go. There was no other way to traverse it but to involve yourself with it, enmesh yourself in it:

> And yet the party walked and scrambled and stumbled along pretty well, going up and down; now on a good matted surface, now along a sparse skeleton of green girders; sometimes skirting large aereal ponds that had been built by the kastroides[14]. Some of these ponds were more than a hectare in area, quite deep, and of a lively surface both from creatures and from the effect of the swaying support. (100-101)

Significantly, Rimrock finds himself very much at home in these undulating wetlands and leaves the group for the time being to travel more quickly down inside the reedy depths. Deep monster calls to deep monster.

The Feral Lands are also home to a number of monstrous fauna, including the dire wolf (which can take an ox's head - horns and all - in one bite), the still larger "lazarus-lion" (which can do the same to an even larger species of ox), and largest of all, the "porche's-panther," which hunts and eats all the other predators. The habits of a giant bird species of the region provide a macabre image of how un-utopian this space is. Paul tells Thomas:

> A rational man has no business here. I know a cliff not a half day from here where there are a thousand skeletons hung up on thorn bushes. The rouks[15] fly

---

[14] Prehistoric giant beavers.

[15] Probably a variation of "rook" from Lafferty's deep

down and kill people for fun. They carry them up and hang them there for a warning. Most of those bones have old black meat still clinging to them. You told me that in your time on Earth men killed wolves and hung them on fence rails as warning to other wolves. This is the same. There is even the tale that the King Rouk pays a bounty to each rouk who so kills and hangs up a man. (102-103)

The human here is both hunter and hunted. Thomas says that being a hunter here would yield "an intense and rewarding life" (103). Paul, a hunter in the Feral Lands himself at times, affirms this.

Yes, the life is intense. The rewards are intangible, but for some they are deep. But those who follow the trade do not live to a great age. But those men have a certain flavor to them. I suppose the lazarus-lion thinks so too. (104)

Hunting monsters gives one's life flavor. We will all be the prey of Death, so we might as well taste good to the old bastard when we go, jokes Lafferty. Only a life lived full and deep, in the company of monsters, can acquire that kind of seasoning.

The one hunting (or rather, fishing) scene we're given here is when the group joins a green-robed monk, a black[16] priest, in hunting the hydra of the region. It's perhaps the most vivid scene of the novel. The monk dives into the water

---

linguistics; a corvid bird, of the crow family, thus adding a traditionally spooky element to this depiction.

[16] The monstrosity of racial otherness is a huge category in Lafferty's work, one which, unfortunately, I don't go into in this article. Next to the frequent and beloved American Indians populating his fiction, Syrian characters show up perhaps next in frequency. There are also a number of stories that feature aboriginal peoples of the southwestern Pacific ocean, where Lafferty served during World War II. Lafferty, as a self-professed "ruddy Irish Catholic," didn't even consider himself uncomplicatedly "white." This is undoubtedly one of the topics in Lafferty Studies that could be given a book-length treatment.

with a harpoon, resurfaces, and hauls up a churning creature from the bloody water.

> It was a fat discoid thing, black and quivering, and one third of its circuit was angry-toothed mouth. It weighed a hundred and fifty kilograms and it could have snapped a man in two through the trunk. (107)

When Thomas expresses his awe and admiration for the monstrous catch, he is informed "it's but the grasshopper that one catches in his palm to use on the hook. This isn't the fish. It's the bait" (107). As this bait thrashes half in and half out of the bloodied water, the real prey begins to manifest its approach: "There was something else now: great wings, as it were, deep under water and gathering for the pounce upward, the greatest wings ever" (107).

Evita, the young witch among the group (and thus herself a monstrous figure), begins taunting the rising water monster with demented rhymes while the monk slashes the bait so that it "bled in spectacular fountains of dark rushing red that exploded with the lustful smell of rampant iron and stripped green wood and battlefield stink" (107). And finally, the sought-after monster breaches:

> The green-robe leapt clear from his bait-creature at the last possible second. Then the great thing swooped and struck upward: a thousand kilograms of center bulk that swallowed the trussed creature in a single gulp, thirty-meter-long tentacles that reached blindly for more prey, the big eye in the middle mad and livid with malevolence. The Devil! The main bulk was clear out of the water with the speed of its upward surge smashing the surface. It was but a lightning instant, but many things were observed simultaneously in that instant, not the least of which was the lightning itself—the corona-like discharge and blinding aura of the great sea-creature.
> It was the hydra taking the bait. (108)

It's a fantastic aquatic monster that sits well alongside

Tolkien's Watcher in the Water, Lewis's Hnakra (in a not dissimilar hunting scene on the seas of the planet Malacandra), Gene Wolfe's own 'batfish'/devil-fish attack in *On Blue's Waters* (1999), and no doubt others. (I wonder, for example, if there is anything comparable in Edgar Rice Burroughs's Mars or Venus tales, and I have heard there are tentacled terrors in William Hope Hodgson's seafaring horror tales.)

Paul, Evita, and the green-robed monk leap for the creature's great eye[17] in an ecstasy of violence:

> They went with snake-like knives for the hydra eye and the brain behind it, feverish in their haste before the terrible tentacles could be brought to defend and to attack. Hysterical battle, hooting challenge, high screaming triumph.
>
> The hydra trumpeted with an anger and agony that stabbed through the whole feral region, killing small birds by the very pitch of the scream. It submerged with the crashing fall-back from its great surge; and the three attackers stayed with it, cutting and hacking in near hysteria. (109)

The monster re-emerges and the frenzied attackers finish it off:

> The huge tentacles lashed and writhed, but no longer with great power in them. The green-robe and Paul and Evita were through the giant eye and into the brain, cutting relentlessly and furiously. Evita had the head and most of her inside the big eye, and her chant came out of that cavity: "Devil, Devil, boom and bell! Watch Evita give you Hell!"—the weird voice of a small child gone mad.
>
> The hydra-devil groaned with an echoing hollowness that shook the whole region.
>
> And then it died. (109)

---

[17] Sharing, as it does, a singular livid eye and tentacles with the spider-mountain of *Space Chantey*, suggests that Roadstrum and crew confronted yet another manifestation of the Devil.

Thomas, shaken with the passion of the performance - in fact, more than he would like to admit, for he is not yet a believer in the feral things as these strange people are - immediately grasps that this is no mere adventure, but rather "hunting in depth," to borrow a phrase from Lafferty's short story "Frog On the Mountain" (1970). "Why, this is allegory acted out before my very eyes," he exclaims (109), and the monk enjoins him to enjoy it for it is "high and roaring comedy" (110). When Thomas asks for further elucidation, the monk expounds:

> Why, it's the killing of the Devil, good Thomas. The Devil must be killed afresh somewhere every day. If ever he is not, then our days be at an end. Say, he is a big one today, isn't he? He's not always a hydra, you know. Some days he is a mad dire-wolf. Some days he is a porche's-panther gone musk. The Devil has his several forms, but we must kill him every day to limn his limits. (110)

In this land of psychic depths, they do defy the Ouden monster, but they do not deny the existence of the demonic. Rather, they delimit it and limit it, at great risk, but also great enrichment, to themselves.

Indeed, the brains of the devil-fish will provide invigoration for the band: "Evita had finally emerged from the monster, glistening with blood and gore, and bearing a great arm-load of Devil brains" (111-112), which the group proceeds to cook and eat. Many readers will balk and Lafferty is wryly ready for them: "You ever cook any Devil brains yourself? Don't knock it if you haven't tried it" (112). Still, he grants dryly, it's not for everybody. "With dishes of this sort, you like them or you like them not" (112). Thomas again surprises himself when he finds that he is among those who like this dish.

> They entered into him. Ah, the salt and the sulphur of them would stand him well in his crux hour when it came. By eating its brains, he would always have a certain mastery over this enemy. (113)

The Feral Lands are a space where you not only may be eaten by monsters, but where you may also *eat monsters* yourself. Getting into monsters and getting them into you, even the dangerous and evil ones, are part of Lafferty's strategy for recovering lost depths.

Playing Monsters in the Feral Lands

Lafferty is even modeling his monster theory for readers by the sheer creation of so many monsters throughout his works. It is important that they not only be present but that we take ownership in the creation of many of them. And it is important that we play with them.

This sense of ludic monstrosity is a central feature of the Feral Lands and part of what makes this region "the psychic power-house of Astrobe" (125). The monsters that utopians have "ground up for fertilizer" reappear here as "animals or creatures or beings ripped out of their context and set to wandering" (124). And they "are real, and many of them are angry at their misplacement" (124). The presence of these misplaced entities combined with the fact that the "psychic force, the libido, is completely rampant here" (124) means imaginative play in the Feral Lands is going to yield startling results. After a comically gruesome manifestation and discourse on ghosts in the region, we are informed:

> If three persons of the feral strips imagine a thing strongly enough (however monstrous it may be), *they can bring it into being*. They can create a contingent body for any thing they imagine, and it will be inhabited by certain unbodied spirits here. I have seen it done. I have helped do it. When children of the feral strips play "monsters," they make monsters that can be seen and smelled, and which on occasion have eaten them up. (125, italics in original)

There's an interesting play here between monsters as psychological constructs and monsters as real beings existing in the world quite apart from our imaginings. Most monster theorists I have encountered in my research so far seem to conceive of monsters strictly as being of our own making, even when they are something in the real world that we label "monster" (such as deformity or a man-eating predator). I, on the other hand, am exploring the idea that the category we call "monster" pre-exists us and that features of the real world summon us to name them as such (by whatever linguistic and conceptual apparatus we bring to bear upon them).

This may be something of what Lafferty is getting at as well. For him, the ontological interiority and agency of objects and animals that I explored in the first two essays of this series, together with the existence and influence of angels and demons and ghosts (and perhaps other otherworldly beings), and the existence and formation of our own immaterial souls, all stretch our categorizations to breaking point, hybridizing the known with the unknown, forcing us to acknowledge that existence just *is* monstrous in warp and woof.[18] We may try to isolate the reedy, meshy, grotesque, and invigorating Feral Lands and the monsters that populate such regions, but they are always near and returning and ultimately, contra Oudenic utopians, unsubjugable and ineradicable. And indeed, they are dangerous. Yet we must hunt them and play with them even though they may well eat us up.

This discourse doubles back on the earlier hunting and we understand that the "roaring comedy" of the hydra scene was a ludic pastime too, part of what it is to "play monsters" in the Feral Lands. For now, on Astrobe, all "irrational" monstrosities find a home in the feral strips:

> Yes, here are all improbable persons and animals, spirits and half-spirits, clean and unclean; the archetypes of folk dreams; they are here alive, and often fleshed. Here there is superstition (the beyond-belief or over-belief) as a shaggy and pungent thing that leaves footprints and fang-marks. Every thought or inkling, suppressed as irrational in rational Astrobe,

---

[18] I.e. existence is itself a "harbinger of category crisis" as Jeffrey Jerome Cohen defines the monster, "embodying a relentless hybridity that resists assimilation into secure epistemologies." Cohen, Jeffrey Jerome (2013), "The Promise of Monsters," *The Ashgate*

comes out here and assumes flesh. Why, there is a stock-breeder here who breeds, improves, and slaughters for profit a creature that had its origin in the nightmares of Golden Astrobe. It was banned there by group therapy. It came out here and became physical fact. (125)

Therapeutic banishment of nightmare monsters will only work for so long, Lafferty avers. Plan on seeing them again. It is much better to learn to hunt and play with them, to face your monsters, even if it kills you. With Lafferty, after all, as I said at the opening, resurrection is always on the cards (rising from the dead being yet another monstrous mode of being not disallowed by Lafferty's open universe).

Monsters in Fourth Mansions

Fourth Mansions (1969)[19] is something of a theological, metaphysical, and political treatise on monsters, and an idiosyncratic psychological cartography of monsters to boot. Men and women throughout the novel almost kaleidoscopically slip in and out of various animal modes of themselves: fish, snake, badger, falcon, toad, spider, cat, dog, bull, and so on. These transmogrifying zoomorphisms occur mostly through Lafferty's lyrical prose and at a vivid psychic level, but occasionally in a marvelously alarming physical display as well. These are all symbols for inner states that make their way into the vivid exterior of the story making it feel, at times, something like a phantasmagorical animated cartoon. Based in part on the mystical theology of St Teresa of Avila's *Interior Castle*, the novel is a rambunctious quest for ontological integration and spiritual mutation. It is a quest and a question: will humanity take the next step out of the "Fourth Mansions" the human soul currently occupies in its stages of drawing near to the "theocenter"[20], and, importantly,

---

Research Companion to Monsters and the Monstrous, p. 452.

[19] All quotes from the 1969 Ace Books version, Ace Publishing Corporation, New York.

[20] To borrow a phrase from Gene Wolfe's Book of the New Sun. Wolfe, Gene (1994), *Shadow and Claw: The First Half of the*

a step *up* into the "Fifth Mansions"? If it can, then it will enter a greater level of maturity and revelation and wholeness for humans and the world.

Fountain-Devils and Walking Tentacles

Freddy Foley, the "everyman" or "everylout" protagonist of the story, is a newspaper reporter who on several occasions meets up with primordial beings called Patricks. In a shifting ecomonstrous[21] Texan landscape he is shown hidden wonders by a Patrick called O'Claire. There he witnesses a "primary fountain," a source of freshness and creativity for the world. It is an awesome sight and sound and smell:

> Musical thunder of the fountain. Climbing churning water that was golden or white or green or blue or thunder-color. Height above height of it, fountains bursting out of fountains, castles of water piled on top of castles. Whole nations of spirits living in the towering columns of foam. The living airy shocking sudden smell of fountain water, salt and sulphur and iron, and fresh. And the vast bottomless lake of which the incredible fountain was center. (72)

The preternatural fountains seem not unlike the Feral Lands of Astrobe, except that they are a guarded resource of the ordered world that feeds and freshens it rather than a suppressed and isolated element that haunts it against its will.

Freddy is informed that this fountain and its lake are also full of fish, and "full of shellies, full of grandpappy frogs and big turtles" (72). And Freddy, with a start, sees something more even than these:

> "It's full of big blacksnakes too," Freddy growled, "big ones, five or six there."

Book of the New Sun, Orbit Books, New York, p. 66.

[21] For a brief outline of the theory of the "ecomonstrous," see my essay in *FoL* volume 2, pp. 28-31. For a fuller explication and application, see my undergraduate honors dissertation now available: https://www.academia.edu/13205984/Ecomonstrous_Environments_in_the_Fiction_of_R._A._Lafferty_and_Cormac_McCarthy.

"Sometimes they are seven, sometimes eight, sometimes nine," O'Claire said, "but they aren't snakes. They are all the tentacles of one amorphous creature. I believe that every primary fountain has one. This one tries to escape, and if he ever escaped into the world there would be disaster beyond telling. He leaves the center sometimes and tries to climb out on the shores. Then I beat him back. That's the main reason I am here." (72-73)

Even here, in one of the world's fountains of creativity and psychic health, monsters are included and necessary and even central. They find their home here, unruly work though they make for their numinous guardians. Though O'Claire boasts "the tentacled fountain-devil has never slipped me once," he admits that those in other primary fountains "do slip into the world from time to time" and wreak havoc (73). The monster is utterly dangerous if not rightly placed in the scheme of things, but it is nevertheless a part of the grand scheme.

Later in the novel, O'Claire seeks out Freddy in his native Oklahoma to inform him that his fountain monster has in fact escaped him and is loose in the world. Then he points to none other than Freddy's girlfriend:

> "There is a walking tentacle of the damnable world-eater itself, and nobody rises to kill it or confine it! She's one creature of it, one snake of it! Get back in your place, creature, or I'll beat you back!"
> "I will not get back in my place!" Biddy Bencher sparked, for she was the walking tentacle of the world-eater. (99)

She is not in fact the only devil-tentacle abroad in the world. Biddy's fellow brain-weavers, who psychically form an invasive group mind that Freddy too is touched by and made a tangential part of, are each a tentacle un-fountained and out of place. As the novel progresses, two of the most powerful of these, James Bauer and Arouet Manion, are locked in an epic psychic combat. In their minds they shift through vivid dreamscapes, battling as bulls on the edge of a primordial cliff and as snakes trying to eat one another's heads and so on (some of the best scenes of the novel). But in the flesh, they are in an opulent upper class home, tranced before one another:

> James Bauer and Arouet Manion still continued their teetering on the edge of the world battle. They fought through arena after arena. Bauer still sat, ponderous and purple-swollen and glassy-eyed, breathing like thunder. Arouet still stretched dragonlike on the stone floor, shuddering with final sickness, poisonous to the last. They were two arms of the deadly hydra[22], tearing and killing each other. It is only for this reason that the abominable creature, recreated so many times, has never demolished the world: it mistakes its own tentacles for other things and battles them to the death. (226-27)

Thankfully, the fountain monster, when out of its rightful place, does provide some check on itself by being self-destructive. Still, several members of their "weave" are actually murdered by them before they do each other in, so the monster is still harmful.

It Looks Like a Good Year for Monsters

In chapter four, tellingly titled "Revenge of Strength Unused," Freddy Foley (whilst in the guise of one Doctor O'Claire) is told:

> "Doctor O'Claire, it has been said that a heresy is the revenge of a forgotten truth. I say that every monstrous appearance or movement is the revenge of a strength or variety unused, of a vitality untapped in us. And it looks like a good year for monsters." (107-108)

---

[22] Our third instance of a tentacled devil monster, obviously a central symbol in Lafferty's schema. Lafferty and tentacles (and sea monsters more generally) will have to await another study. It would be especially interesting to see how his work relates to Weird and "New Weird" fiction's exaltation of the tentacle.

There are echoes of *Past Master* here. The monsters are the vengeance of our own neglected depths and resources. But the stranger speaking to Foley here doesn't represent the full truth about monsters for Lafferty, I think. Monsters are not *only* the "Return of the Repressed" (to use a Freudian phrase popular in monster studies), but are also things already always in us and in the world, even (especially!) when things are in harmony. For Lafferty, it's not a question of monsters or no monsters, but rather of *what kind* of monsters, constructive or destructive.

Battling Beautiful, Arty Dragons

When the monsters are wrongly exteriorized, however, we must do battle with them. Yet we must be careful, for we are ourselves mixed up with them. In a certain sense, they come out of us and so they are not completely Other to us. Thus it is reflected about one character:

> One who battles a dragon must watch that he be not ensorceled by the beauty of any part of it. Dragons are sometimes iridescent in some of their limbs and appendages. They are curious and arty and there is a sort of rousing music in their bellowing and fire-snorting. Richard Bencher had him a battle; so many parts of the opponent were also parts of his own curious self. (145-46)

Lafferty, unlike Tolkien, and more like Le Guin (both of whom writers Lafferty had his issues with), mixes humans and dragons ontologically together rather than keeping them strictly apart as mere exterior adversaries. Consistently with Lafferty, the end game of the battle with monsters is not vanquishment but integration.

We Are the Abiding Monsters, And We Are Real

In a question and answer session during a psychic lecture, yet another Patrick, called Croll, asks the psychic lecturer: "Who are the monsters who still trouble the world, now that you fine-haired dudes have it all fixed up so fine?"

(200). The lecturer takes up a position not unlike the utopians of Astrobe, admitting only a dispensable and vanishing role for monsters:

> The thing to grasp about the monsters of my questioner is that they are not exterior but interior. They neither guard nor assault the world for the reason that they are not there. They are but unconscious remnants in some persons. It was once believed that we had need of these symbols. If we had once, we have not now. (200)

He then outlines the "four menaces" that have been the subject of the entire novel, factions of primordials tied to four quadrants of politics: the Toads, Pythons, Falcons, and Badgers. He connects them to the cherubim described in chapter one of the prophet Ezekiel in the Bible, angelic beings beneath the throne of Yahweh that had four faces: that of a lion, ox, eagle, and man (as well as being six-winged and covered in eyes). Lafferty thereby ties the whole discourse to *holy* monsters, but in a very contaminated form considering the earthly representatives of these heavenly monsters are so compromised in motive and action.

The lecturer continues to disavow the reality of the monstrous. Yet the very person who had asked him the question was one of the monsters, for the Patricks are the Badgers in the fourfold schema. The lecturer, one Michael Fountain (note the irony of his surname), continues:

> "Some, however, believe that these are valid symbols in our unconscious, and that by them our unconscious is trying to tell us something: as though we had cut some needed element out of ourselves and these symbols were warning us to bring it back in. I do not accept this view. [...] There is polarity in the world, but it isn't so storied and allegorical as that. [...] There are no exterior monsters who trouble the world either in attacking or defending it. They are not real."
>
> ("Old Gaffer, we are real," Croll said, giving the hissing growl of a very badger. "We are the abiding

men, we are the abiding monsters, and we are real.")
(201)

The monsters abide beneath the monster-denying rhetoric.

Now, at this point, if this discourse on the reality of monsters seems very abstract, note two things. First, lesson number one in monster theory ought to be that monsters are valuable in and of themselves, whether or not we can explain or decode them, whether or not we can make any human "use" of them at all.[23] Lafferty's monsters, like all monsters, bring us out of ourselves and humble us, whether we value that or not. So, in a certain sense, I would say don't ask for the purpose of monsters, just surrender to them. Still, monsters do have meaning for our lives. So, secondly, I would say try this: pay attention to everything going on around you in people's lives, work, news, etc. this week and see who's denying monsters and who's acknowledging them, at various levels - as sources of potent creativity, replenishing interiority, exteriorized menaces, etc. Which ecologies, politics, philosophies, theologies, social and civic institutions, families, media, careers, economies, etc. are hunting and playing with monsters and which are suppressing them to some other region[24] It is not my project here to apply Lafferty's

---

[23] In the monster studies I have read so far, this does not seem to be grasped clearly enough. Most monster theories seem to rely wholly on *interpretation* of monsters, sometimes even against what their own definitions of the monster explicitly state. It is a stunning irony that what ought to be one of the purest studies of the non-human is so thoroughly anthropocentric. I think this is inevitable if we start with the premise that monsters come strictly out of our heads and have no basis in extra-mental reality. Given this premise, monster theory is just a back door to anthropology. No doubt some would gladly acknowledge this. I think it is damning.

[24] And if we learn anything from Lafferty, it's that this will inevitably be tricky: for example, not every TV show or movie that features monsters (such as ubiquitous werewolves, vampires, and zombies) will be straightforwardly on the side of preserving the monstrous. Some monster shows are themselves attempts to grind up or otherwise subjugate the monstrous and make it serve some

monsterology into contemporary culture. But this can (and hopefully will) be done.

We Cannot Live Without Monsters' Blood Coursing Through Us

The penultimate chapter of *Fourth Mansions* opens with an instance of Lafferty's ubiquitous verse, including this stanza:

> I feed on elementals like a cloud
> Though buried in constraining earthy room
> Where now I harvest lightning in my tomb
> And integrate the monsters for a shroud. (208)

Integrate the monsters before they disintegrate you. That seems one way to sum up Lafferty's monster theory.[25] Not only must we resist the temptation to deny their reality, we must positively step into the monstrous ontology and unify the monsters. That death and the tomb may have to be an inevitable part of this integrative process is no surprise coming from Lafferty whose fiction often, in one way or another, evinces the cry: "I want a death and resurrection of the thing" (*Past Master*, p. 8).

The Patrick Croll had asserted the persisting reality of monsters like himself in the last chapter. Here he declares monsters an outright theological category:

---

utopian programme or other. And, of course, some monsters, in fiction and otherwise, are only devil-tentacles let loose in the world because something is out of place in our souls and/or our metaphysics. I don't think Lafferty necessarily encourages our "Othering" of one another, trying to make one another out as the bad monsters or the equally bad monster-suppressors. But I do think a deep reading of Lafferty engenders a humility by which we may ask ourselves and our societies the tough questions about the reality of monsters.

25 Or, in the memorable phrase of our fearless editor: "Better to exercise your monsters than exorcise them." See this thread in the comments section at *The Ants of God Are Queer Fish*: http://antsofgodarequeerfish.blogspot.co.uk/2011/07/some-initial-thoughts-on-r-laffertys.html.

"There is a holiness in a whole person or a whole world," the patrick Croll said. "The veriest monsters inside us may be sanctified. They were put there by Him who is 'Father of Monsters' also. What right have we to cut them out of us? Who are we to edit God? We cut strong things out of ourselves and suppress them, and the rocks and clouds will give birth to them again. We dry up our interior fountains and they gush out again, exteriorly and menacingly. We cannot live without monsters' blood coursing through us. Only to the whole person is life worth living and death worth dying. Here in Fourth Mansions we must be whole or we must be nothing." (208-209)

The above, Croll says, is a recited passage from "the manual," a kind of catechism it would seem. Once again, the theme is that monsters must not be excised but rather sanctified. It's fascinating that Lafferty seems to be making a reference to none other than the ancient Greek monster-god Typhon, who is regularly referred to as "Father of Monsters," claiming here that the God of Catholic belief is *also* a Father of Monsters. Presumably we are to understand that the God of Lafferty's Christianity is progenitor to different kinds of monsters than Typhon's brood, which includes Cerberus, Hydra, Chimera, and Sphinx (and, of course, that God fathers monsters in a different mode altogether - not through coupling with goddesses or mortal women). What's of note is again how Lafferty battles monsters with monsters. In Greek mythology Zeus seeks to vanquish Typhon as he does all other monsters, interestingly enough, by means of his thunderbolts.[26] Here Lafferty is harvesting lightning from clouds as well, but not in order to cut such things out of the universe or ourselves but to sanctify and integrate them, make them part of holy (and wholly) living, make them the strength in our very blood, "tainting" humans with monstrous genetic makeup, and thereby, paradoxically enough, making us fully human, and making the world itself whole as well.

---

[26] Cf. *The Ashgate Encyclopedia of Literary and Cinematic Monsters*, p. 549.

The Integrated, Fully Conscious, Holy Monster-Man

The title of the final chapter of *Fourth Mansions* forecasts victory, not vanquishment, for monsters: "And All Tall Monsters Stand". As the action commences, Freddy cries out to his fellow resistors: "You battle your monsters and I'll battle mine! There *will* be dimensions - in me, or in the world" (231). But it's very interesting to note that their method of battling at this point - murdering evil monster-men, the Returnees, not unlike staking vampires - doesn't succeed. The denouement here shows a different way: death to self.

Freddy has a holy office bestowed upon him and we are told his secret. It is very simple. Indeed, it is simplicity itself: "He was Everyman. He was Everylout" (251). Unlike a Herculean hero that goes about vanquishing Typhonian monsters (even unlike Roadstrum and crew in this respect), Lafferty gives us an 'everylout' hero who is blessed with grace to integrate the monsters within himself. Almost every character throughout the book is grasping for power, for themselves and for their faction, and in so doing unleashing destructive monsters rather than harnessing creative monsters. Freddy is described at the very beginning of the novel thus: "There was a young man who had very good eyes but simple brains. Nobody can have everything" (7). And again: "Good eyes but simple brains, that was Foley. He really could see at levels where many folks cannot" (10). Freddy follows the grace of his gift and his limitation, and also follows his reporter's nose, refusing to be corrupted by various temptations along the way, uncovering what scraps of truth he can. By these peregrinations he ends up unjustly incarcerated and drugged in a mental institution, yet receiving all the powers into himself:

> Nobody else, coming in simplicity, had ever partaken of all four Monsters. Nobody else had had such good eyes, had ever been able to see on all the levels and into all the worlds. No person else had ever integrated all his archetypes and become fully conscious - even while tumbling into needle-induced unconsciousness. (251)

The word "partaken" signals almost a eucharistic note,

Freddy feeding on the monsters for spiritual sustenance, coming fully awake as a human being, fully conscious even as the doctors drug him to sleep. The four monsters - Toads, Serpents, Falcons, Badgers - by themselves could not evolve, but coming together in this humble, chosen man they trigger the transformation they had sought for themselves:

> He had been called, as the patricks had not been, as the Harvesters themselves had not been, as none of the exterior creatures had been of themselves. The Harvesters, the persons of the weave, had not themselves truly mutated. They couldn't have done it; they hadn't the holy simplicity for it. Theirs was a false and premature mutation. It was Fred Foley who now became the first of the new mutation, the special sort of man. (251)

For now, Freddy is in the tomb, his integrated monsters his shroud. This is his second day of entombment, for he had sojourned in this mental hospital earlier in the novel as well. But the third day is coming, when All Tall Monsters Stand. Freddy will rise and all the many monstrous facets of the world and humanity will rise in him.

It is a potent and musky mixture that Lafferty outlines swimming and flitting inside Freddy (and almost all the symbols and references here have been pretty thoroughly unpacked and manifested throughout the novel; these are summarizing tokens here of imagery replete throughout), the new man as he awakens to glory:

> And in the morning—
> (Green-mottled humor in him, helical passion, saintly sex-fish, ashen death-joy, cinnamon cookie for Cerberus—
> Pride of patricks in him, Black Patricks of New York and Nairobi, Yellow Patricks of Moscow and Lhasa, Brown Patricks of Batangas and Tongareva, Nobility of Metropolitans and Simplicity of Crolls, the Exarch of Yerevan and the Aloysius of Dublin in him—

Oceanic ages in him, insane flitting reptilian wraiths that have a random gift that isn't given to proper creatures, a new interior guest from that returning jewel-headed toad people—

Flight of falcons in him. "You can command the falcon, Freddy, when you wake to it," came the underground voice of Miguel. "You can even command the falcon to furl its wings again."—

Unweaponed simplicity in him that could burst every bond. Every under-thing rooted in him now—

The ashen Letitia herself had just borne a child who was truly beautiful and full of light, somehow, in a manner and place that we do not know the names of. So—

Letitia-gladness in him. Gobbled devils in him—)

—and in the morning he would come out of it all: a new element that the returnees had not calculated in adjusting the cyclic trajectory. (Returnees also in him.) (251-252)

Lafferty's vision of a fulsome humanity—of real people with real depths in them, authentic interiority—is a strange one. And why not? Are we not strange creatures? Is it not an odd world we inhabit and that inhabits us? Lafferty spent his career trying to convince us this is so. He seems to say: if we will not be monsters, then we will not be men and women. He would seem to agree with monster theorists that "identity is networked, hybrid, monstrous, fragile."[27] Note all the eco echoes in Lafferty's imagery of the new man here, all the mythic resonance, carnival sensuality, shifting zoomorphisms, pageantry of religious orders, racial plenitude, otherworldly impingements, spiritual resources, recovered joy, the bodily fruitfulness that eats up demons. Such a hybridized and networked vision of human being may not be safe and secure, but it is large. The integrated monster-man is expansive rather than reductive, because "monsters open up more possibility

---

[27] Cohen, *The Ashgate Research Companion to Monsters and the Monstrous*, p. 464.

than they foreclose"[28] and thus stand tall.

Almost all of Lafferty's novels end on an ambiguous, and usually beleaguered, note. Yet he tried to inject each of those teetering endings with a powerful shot of genuine hope. *Fourth Mansions* is no different.

> On so small a new module it might depend. What would be the shape and direction of it now: still the repeating cycle, or the ascending spiral?
> Would the next Mansions be the First again? Or the Fifth? (252)

In a way, you could say that Freddy's fragile upward-yearning mutation here is the biologist's theory of the leaping "hopeful monster" taken to mystical and cosmic levels. It seems to be a trope or theme that Lafferty returns to again and again in his fiction.

Monsters Missed, Monsters to Come

In closing I can merely mention a few more novels from this era that we haven't covered but that we could under this topic. The goblin-esque alien Puca children in *The Reefs of Earth* (1968), especially with their intended worldwide murder spree, are monsters of a sort, of course. Indeed, they are perhaps the strongest manifestation and most sustained treatment of the wild ghostly/beastly quality that Lafferty's children always display in his tales. In this regard, note chapter five's title: "A Child's a Monster Still Uncurled." As *The Encyclopedia of Fantasy* notes: 'the actual children in RAL's stories [...] are undoubtedly monsters, though in a state of grace.'[29]

The theme of *The Devil is Dead* (1971) is that we are trapped in the monstrous and wonderful archetypes, howling to get out; and that there are "nearer monsters" than extra-terrrestrials, under our skin, in our blood. *Okla Hannali* (1972) repeatedly refers to the larger than life protagonist Innominee as a giant, magical "monster man;" and there are other

---

[28] Ibid., p. 452.

[29] http://sf-encyclopedia.uk/fe.php?nm=lafferty_r_a

elements of the monstrous including the mystic mountain mentioned above and Innominee's morally horrifying nemesis Whiteman Falaya, who seems to be something of a monstrous force of evil and/or nature, not unlike Cormac McCarthy's Anton Chigurh in *No Country For Old Men*.

So, in Lafferty monsters are irrepressible and necessary for human and cosmic wholeness, dangerous but also enriching. We can't truly live without them, even the ones we must slay every day in order to limn the devil's limits. The very fabric of existence—the human psyche no less than the ontic ambient—is a kaleidoscopic raftwork of cascading monster shapes (shown probably most vividly and densely in *Fourth Mansions* out of all these early works). There's no escape from the monsterscape. If you put one foot in front of another, one thought in front of another, you are traversing monsterland, in which we all live and move and have our being. So, it seems to me, says Lafferty. To go further into interpretation of Lafferty's monsters requires a thorough unmasking of all the symbolic layers with which he has constructed them. I will be doing some of this more detailed work in my doctoral research and I hope others will join me in these fecund fields.

Rich with monstrous minerals as these early works are, however, Lafferty's oeuvre contains so very much more monstrosity than even this brief survey of his most known work suggests. The latter half of his output features wry and sometimes profound takes on creature feature mainstays such as vampires, werewolves, and muck-monsters as well as more original and comically grotesque inventions. The later novels see the monsterscape become more implicit, yet almost more replete, throughout the narrative tapestry, with still some overt moments of the rearing up of specific monster presences. To those we turn in the sequel to this essay and the conclusion of this "trilogy" next issue, monsters willing.

Daniel Otto Jack Petersen is a PhD candidate at the University of Glasgow. His doctoral thesis is an 'ecomonstrous' reading of the fiction of Cormac McCarthy and R. A. Lafferty.

"And be careful you don't let go of it till after you're dead."

R. A. Lafferty, "Ghost in the Corn Crib"

Illustration © 2015 Anthony Ryan Rhodes

The Annals and Ace; or, The Textual History of an Historical Text

by Andrew Ferguson

Annals of Klepsis was the last of Lafferty's works released by a major publishing house (New York: Ace Science Fiction Books, 1983), and the manuscripts from his Tulsa archive relating to this book provide insight as to his methods of composition and also about the uneven editorial decisions made while bringing the novel to press.

There are three complete drafts of *Annals of Klepsis* in the archive:

1. First draft (dated 9/25/80–10/28/80), typed single-spaced on wide-rule notebook paper, with extensive markup — additions, deletions, interpolated passages handwritten on the back of pages,[1] and indiscriminate marks across the text in Lafferty's usual manner of indicating a defunct draft [Ms. II:1:31. R.A. Lafferty Archive, University of Tulsa];

2. Second draft in carbon-copy (completed 11/11/80), typed double-spaced, with corrections in author's hand and word count [Ms. II:1:32];

3. Production copy (undated, but a date of 6/5/82 would accord with his other filekeeping), typed double-spaced with copyeditor's and typesetter's marks and notations [Ms. II:2:1];

There are also two small sheafs of pages marked as replacements for the pages of the same number, made in response to editorial requests [Ms. II:1:33]: one sheaf, dated 7/2/82, is sent to Ace Books editor Beth Meacham; the other, dated 7/5/82, is sent to Lafferty's agent, Virginia Kidd, to

---

[1] Compare the statement within the book that "It is illegal in all the worlds to write on the reverse side of a paper," bringing the riposte that the writer in question "had a lot of illegal habits" (114).

replace the pages in the ms. copy she still held.[2] (Confusingly, the two sets of papers do not match exactly, though the differences are slight.)

This progression of drafts accords with other of Lafferty's works in the archive for which multiple drafts are extent: a first draft produced rapidly and then extensively revised (and often finished) in longhand; a second draft incorporating these revisions and adding chapter headings, epigraphs, and a table of contents; and a final draft in which he incorporates changes either requested or required by the editor, sometimes strengthening but just as often weakening the final work. *Annals of Klepsis* is unusual in the preservation not only of the patch pages Lafferty wrote in response to the editor's queries (more often the changes are made silently between typed draft and print publication), but also in Lafferty's correspondence with his editor about these queries.

An exhaustive collation of the book is beyond my scope here; instead I will detail one particularly bothersome alteration, and then touch on a few other, potentially beneficial changes made in the patches (and several other matters Lafferty refused to change), before tackling the tangled question of the ending. In the book, a peg-legged historian, Long John Tong Tyrone, travels to the pirate planet Klepsis, a "world without history," for the purpose of writing it one. After witnessing a coup, marrying (somewhat to his surprise) into the royal family, and setting sail with the powerful ghost who in life founded Klepsis, Tyrone finds his fate — and that of the cosmos more generally — bound up in the "Doomsday Equation," which posits an impending apocalypse that threatens the "Particular Universe" (Lafferty's construct of seventeen habitable worlds in four different systems) with extinction.

In the original draft, the particulars of this Equation are

---

[2] These letters are likewise held in the University of Tulsa archives; the Meacham correspondence is filed under "Ace Books" (Ms. I.1.2). The letter to Kidd is Ms. II.6.5; sadly much of the correspondence between Kidd and Lafferty about *Klepsis* does not seem to have survived.

given in a lengthy quotation by one "Karl Sayon"[3] as an epigraph to Chapter 10 (of 13 total), with short insertions indicated in Lafferty's hand, and a longer one on the back of the preceding page; in the second draft, this passage incorporates all the additions but otherwise remains unchanged. Between the second draft and the production copy, this quotation is moved to the front of the book to serve as a preface for the whole. This change was at editor Meacham's behest, one of a series she requested that Lafferty consider in the course of bringing the book to market. Specifically, an early mention of the Doomsday Equation would keep it from being a surprise to the reader when later it becomes a major focus of the work: "Everyone else seems to know about it already, so why should the reader be left out?"

In the July 2 letter that accompanied the sheaf of pages sent back to Meacham, Lafferty notes that "These will get rid of some of the difficulties, [and] give an early awareness of the Doomsday Equation..." [Ms. I:1:2]. But this "early awareness" disrupts the pacing of the entire novel: instead of the Equation being something hinted at early on and definitively established only once it is an immediate threat, it is left to hang over the preceding action, casting in a lesser light the nine chapters in between the passage's old and new locations. The result is a novel shaped more in accordance with the genre conventions of SF — the world-destroying threat is established early and fought against throughout the book, even if this central battle is often placed in the background to allow for the development of other episodes. Had it been published to Lafferty's original schema, *Annals of Klepsis* would have more clearly resembled the structure of the historical accounts his title suggests: an annal, in this case, that would document the beginnings of history (if not an entire year's worth) on a planet previously without one.

Moreover, it disrupts a typical Lafferty pattern in which immediate and intimate knowledge about every narrative situation, however sudden, is granted to every character, save

---

3 A clear parody of Carl Sagan, for whom Lafferty held no great love—another indication that the statement likely shouldn't serve as prelude for the whole.

one—that one being most often the protagonist. Think here of Dana Coscuin or Aurelia in their books, or Freddy Foley in *Fourth Mansions*, or Constantine Quiche in *Where Have You Been, Sandaliotis*; it's a Lafferty-standard narrative trick, taking any confusion the reader might (and probably does) feel at his gonzo narrative logic and channeling it into the one character who is likewise hanging on for dear life and following all those who seem to be in perfect rapport. Here the fish in too-deep water—as he is continually reminded by even incidental characters—is the undistinguished historian Long John Tong Tyrone, suggesting both the difficulty of the task he has set himself, and also his own unsuitability for that task. To answer Meacham's question: the reader should be left out because Long John is left out, and the book's pace is established through him.

Fortunately, several other of Meacham's suggestions proved more productive, albeit mostly in minor ways. The most other immediately evident shift is also at novel's beginning, right after the newly-ensconced Sayon quote, in that striking opening: "*Remember these words, burn them into to your mind, think of them always*" (1, italics in original). While some of the information that follows was given also in the earlier drafts, it was credited there to the "penny philosopher" Fairbridge Exendine, a member of the odd crew that takes to odder seas several times in the novel. Exendine's statement is on the number of habitable worlds, and the question of what it means to be "habitable"; the cast of characters, however, is not given at all, nor is the final directive to remember. This new start to Canto One is far sharper and more urgent than the draft; here Meacham's advice to give here a "statement of theme" (comparable, she notes, to that prefacing *The Fall of Rome*) produces an improvement similar to that seen between draft and publication of another Ace book, *Past Master*, after Terry Carr counseled Lafferty on the importance of hooking the reader right away.[4]

Several other of the patch pages add slight character depth to two of the female crew members: one, cryptography

---

[4] The Lafferty-Carr correspondence may also be found in the Ace Books folder. Ms. I.1.2.

student and probable spy Conchita O'Brian, makes a strong impression in Canto One but is killed by the tyrant Prince Henry soon after; Meacham asks if she could either be toned down at the beginning, or if there could be some "qualms" shown about her execution. Lafferty, of course, never being one to tone anything down, inserted the passage where three code-talking parley birds request the inscription of "cult words" on the memorial of their "cult figure" Conchita, for they have (Lafferty writes, appropriating from Meacham), "cold qualms about her dying so lively and so young" (84). The other character given additional lines is Terpsichore Callagy, introduced as a student of art, specifically "art whose colors bark and howl at you" (4). Yet though she fares better than Conchita, in the draft her quest for art is given no further attention. After Meacham rightly calls attention to this oversight, Lafferty uses Terpsichore to accentuate particularly lurid or outré moments, gushing her admiration over the "raw art, primitive art, art with all the hair on it" in Long John's whipping (39), the "soul of art itself" in the chests of gold in the Klepsis pirate hoard (84), and the "undying, eschatologic" and "consummate art" of Aloysius Shiplap's flaming hair and the prospect of lightning death at novel's end (212).

All of which brings us to that ending page, one which seems to have given Lafferty trouble even as the scene remains consistent throughout: the planet (and Universe) stands to be destroyed by Doomsday Lightning, which will fall on the final toll of the En-Arche bell, as the Doomsday Equation is completed. Aloysius Shiplap and a nameless slave-mathematician race against that clock to establish a counter-equation that would evade Doomsday and its Lightning. The slave finds a solution, only to be struck and rendered mute and handless; Aloysius tries to reconstruct the slave's work, is struck himself, but presses on with his hair on fire. Even in the original draft, Terpsichore is present up to the last moment, though solely to point out to the Institute member that his hair is on fire; he seemingly solves the equation but the lightning is gathering up one last strike, and the novel "ends" with an em-dash and the fate of man and world still in question.

The patch page gives Terpsichore much greater

involvement, as she exults in the "scarlet murder as high art" around her (211); here though even Doomsday gets in on the art kick, "snak[ing] down a jagged and erratic bolt of garish lightning that was sheer art—if you like the eblouissant in art." Here Lafferty closes off em-dash and novel both with a curious direct address, almost an apology for the flaming-haired éblouissant (that is, dazzling, or stunning) aesthetic that went before. While Lafferty is no stranger to anticlimax and the undercutting of narrative events, it's highly unusual for him to undercut the narrative voice in this way. In the production copy of the draft, this phrase has been excised; whether this was Lafferty's or Meacham's work is unclear, but the end (if such it be) is much the stronger for it.

There is much more to be said about the book, which has always been one of my favorites but appears to me more and more central to his work each time I return to it. There is one bit of unfinished business here, though: the change Lafferty rejected outright, a relative rarity against the many, often questionable changes to his work he incorporated or approved in his eagerness for publication (especially for novels). Meacham grew particularly fond of the overeager voluntarism of Becky Breaksticks, and wondered if she might be brought into the book earlier. Lafferty replied that this was impossible, primarily because Becky did not enter the book till late on, among the media rushing to cover the Klepsis story; but also because "her volunteerism and pushiness is intended to represent modernism coming to Klepsis, as it would go against the nature of the old Klepsis people of pirate blood to be grabby in any way." Lafferty raises the possibility here of seeing *Annals of Klepsis* as a fable of modernism itself, bringing with it a beginning of history that also marks an end of much else—something Klepsis has held out against for long (this being in the year 2200 or thereabouts), but can no longer resist. It's a possibility that echoes much of Lafferty's earlier works, but resonates particularly strongly in the strong series of novels he wrote in the early 1980s: *Klepsis* first; then *Sindbad, the 13th Voyage*[5]; *Serpent's Egg*; and *East of Laughter*.

---

5 Already mentioned in *Klepsis*, among the Tarshish storyteller's repertoire (73).

Much, as ever, remains to be done.

This work is © 2013 Andrew Ferguson.

Andrew Ferguson is a Ph.D candidate at the University of Virginia. He wrote on Lafferty for his MA thesis in Science Fiction Studies at the University of Liverpool, and is now building on this work for a biography in the University of Illinois' Modern Masters of Science Fiction series. His blog, "Continued on Next Rock," is at ralafferty.tumblr.com.

From Russia with Laff: A Very Brief Report on R.A. Lafferty's Russian Translations

by Niyaz N. Abdullin

Say one thing for me as a writer, say that I've never written anything that could be published. Except maybe once, but it was a long time ago. So, no high art and poetry here, just plain words and phrases, sorry, folks.

Say one thing for me as a translator, say that I'm omnivorous. I translate almost everything, because it is my job, and I rarely do anything for pure fun. (However much I like my job.)

Say one thing for me as a translator of Lafferty, say that I'm one crazy dude who agreed to take his *Arrive at Easterwine* as my first Lafferty-related assignment. It was not like I was being choked with options, but the editor, Sergey Gontarev (who, by the way, did a hell of a job in the field of translating Lafferty), honestly warned me about its complexity. He said something like it was one really tough piece of literature. On reading that comment, I thought something like this: NOTHING – CAN – BE – TOUGHER – THAN – WILLIAM – BURROUGHS. Well, you want to say a thing for W.S. Burroughs, say that he was just a kid, who only tried to learn how to speak and write something new and humorous. That's what *I think* (after dealing with Lafferty's texts), at least, and I'm not here to speak about W.S. Burroughs, nor to blacken his name. Sorry if I did offend somebody.

So, where did I stop? Ah, yes, Sergey asked if I could translate any of two (or three? sorry, can't remember properly) pieces by Lafferty. I said O.K., why not? Yes, that was a simple "O.K. why not?". No *my-God-what-a-chance*!-s. I'd never heard about Lafferty before. Perhaps that ignorance spared my brain and psyche from greater damage. And, I believe, it saved the prettiness of the future translation as well, for when you know that you deal with some famous thing, you are almost certainly doomed. It's better not feel over-responsible for something great in your hands. Well, if only just a smidgen, so that you're not totally cold to it. Just keep calm and do your job. You try to feel it, process it in your mind, and then express it in your language. In the author's manner, of course. That's how I work, at least, and pardon me for my lack of modesty, it is doubtful, really, that someone else could write in Lafferty's manner. But I try, I try hard, trust me. Especially I had to walk a good long mile in Lafferty's boots, when it came to translating the very title of *Easterwine*. In Russian, it would sound oddly and lose its sense, "paskhalnoe vino". I had to invent it almost totally anew, and I turned out *Krestinvin*, or "krestilnoe vino" (baptismal wine). There are some other examples, but I don't want to make a linguistic research of it, I mean not now, not here.

When I first tried *Easterwine*, it felt like some unknown part of my mind awakened. Some crazy part, really. Perhaps, while reading these lines you can feel it, see it. Sorry, if you do, but Epiktistes turned out to be a highly radioactive (in a literary sense) machine. He, Epiktistes, didn't kill my mind, but made something different of it. Something of his mobile-extension-kind of different. It is hard to describe what I feel and what I think of it, so I just keep translating Lafferty's things trying to do my best, and that perhaps is some proper way to show my attitude to the author. Maybe – just maybe – if I were some scholar, I then could say something very, very smart, but I'm just a translator, who is like a minesweeper crawling along a mine-field full of literary mines. When I feel that a mine is close – real or imaginary – I write to Andrew Ferguson, thanks, thanks, tons of thanks to him for his answers! I also consult the folks from *East of Laughter* Facebook-page. Tons of thanks to them, as well! As for *Easterwine*, when I didn't know about those two brilliant sources of help, I relied on my super-editor, Alexandra Pitcher. Suppose, it's enough to say, that without her help the book in Russian would be short of a great deal of its literary and cultural allusions.

Ah, allusions. They could be a topic of a separate article, I believe, but, as I've already said, I'm not a scholar, I'm just a minesweeper of a translator, ever threatened to lose a limb or two. Sorry for a cruel metaphor, couldn't think of anything peaceful. But sometimes Lafferty seems to be way too joyful in his manner of depriving his characters (however unimportant) of their lives. On the other hand, it's better to say a quick goodbye to a character when their job is done, I think. But enough with poetic notes. Having received a magic kick in my butt from Alexandra, I used this tremendous experience while performing an editing of a *Past Master* translation. You know, I'd never thought that I would want to strangle a colleague of mine, or to tie a rope with a heavy stone over my neck, and... (I hate it when anyone, especially someone who has not a smallest notion about the principles of translation art, criticizes a translation. And I myself try to understand another translator's motives when I see some strange tropes in a translated text, not to criticize them.) Yes, I'm just joking, the translation was decent. However, the text bristled with dubious passages, and the original translator never bothered to highlight any allusions and made no footnotes. It took a special agreement with Sergey, that I delete, or change, or do anything that I believe to be appropriate to make the text correspond to its original source. And in the process I surprised myself having found lots of allusion-mines. As they say, all things are difficult before they are easy. It's true. And *Past Master* turned out to be some kind of a... I don't know. Some kind of walking another good long mile in someone else's boots. These boots made my legs and feet stronger, having not killed them, but I strongly doubt that I will accept another such a walk suggestion soon.

Sorry, but I've chosen to write about these two pieces only, because they have been real challenges for me. I never neglect translating short stories, whenever Sergey asks me to do it. They are great, but they are rather simple and easier to translate them.

What else can I say? I keep translating Lafferty's things. And I like it. I like the texts; especially I love the folks from Institute for Impure Science. Aloysius is my hero! (Don't ask why, I just love his Shiplapishness.) Though, my favorite short story is "In the Turpentine Trees." And I like the process of translating, though it is sometimes a real pain in the... well, you know. But it is fun for me, as well. A rare possibility to pamper my professional ego, to work with greater dedication.

Niyaz Abdullin was born on May 31, 1983 in the city of Naberezhnye Chelny in the Tatarstan Republic, Russia. After graduating from school he studied in the Tatar American Regional Institute, and received two advanced degrees in linguistics. He writes that "until my third year I couldn't even dream of becoming a translator in the field of fiction, until Prof. Dmitry Bobkov, our instructor in the practice of translation, gave us a passage from C.S. Lewis' Narnia to try to translate. From that moment on, I can say, I knew I would be a translator of fiction." Abdullin has now been working as a professional translator for approximately nine years. In addition to Lafferty, he has translated works by such authors as Connie Willis, Philip Dick, Robert Silverberg, Harry Harrison, Robert Sheckley, William S. Burroughs, Kurt Vonnegut, Mike Resnick, and Christopher Anvil.

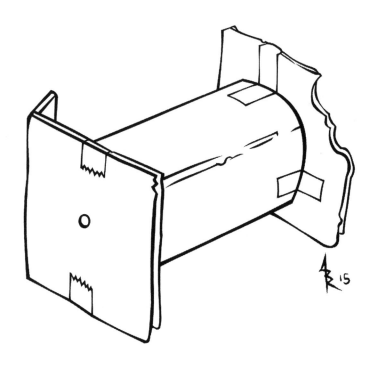

- Class IV Disappearer -

"You'd better try it on something else. Dishes cost money."

    R. A. Lafferty, "Seven Day Terror"

"Class IV Disappearer" © *2015 Anthony Ryan Rhodes*

R. A. Lafferty: Effective Arcanum

by Don Webb

> Take the wordies
> from hind brain
> tell of weirdies
> in a great word-rain
> —Grimorie of Aloys

Blurbers (those who blurb) say two contradictory things about the work of R. A. Lafferty. Often both poles will appear in the same blurb; blurbers do not aim for consistency, but instead for creating a mood that will induce the sensory-overloaded reader to purchase the book. The first remark is how familiar Lafferty's work is—he is either compared to Twain (or some likewise wholesomely American figure) or to the folktale, ghost tale, or talltale. The opposite pole stresses the uniqueness of his work—unique, quirky, one-of-a-kind. It would seem that either the blurbers have indeed read the work, and are hard put to find words to explain the effect of Lafferty's prose on their psyches, or they are merely quoting other blurbers.

I wish to argue that Lafferty deliberately creates the mythic effect through a technique I call effective arcanum, and that rather than examining his work with the conventional tools of science fiction criticism, we need to examine his system—firstly for our pleasure, and secondly so that we may recreate it (because the sign of an authentic religo-magical system is the power of the followers to reproduce the results). It may seem strange to think of Lafferty's writing in terms of religious phenomena, but if you consider the devotion that the small press world has shown, you'll begin to see what I mean. Behold, now I speak prophetically: with Lafferty gone there will be (unfortunately) a lot of bad Lafferty pastiche—not because of the commercial viability of such writing (Lafferty being one of the least commercial writers we have) but because of the desire of the writer to recreate the effects of Lafferty's writing on his or her psyche.

In this (and a few other ways as well) Lafferty is very similar to H. P. Lovecraft. Let us examine six ways in which Lafferty's fiction creates the Unknown rather than the Known, and then let us give some consideration to the strengths and weaknesses of the method (and its reception and lack thereof in the world of Science Fiction and fantasy). Hopefully some later, more qualified writer than I will begin the task of putting Lafferty into the bookshelf of literature, where he belongs. By the way, each of these points can be expanded into a dissertation—and no doubt will be in the fullness of time.

I. Lafferty uses textual devices to estrange the reader in a hypothetical time before the beginning of the narrative. He comments on the method himself in one of his created texts:

> "Atrox Fabulinus, the Roman Rabelais, once broke off the account of his hero Raphaelus in the act of opening a giant goose egg to fry it in an iron skillet of six yards' span. Fabulinus interrupted the action with these words: 'Here it becomes necessary to recount to you the history of the world up to this point.'
>
> "After Fabulinus had given the history of the world up to that point, he took up the action of Raphaelus once more. It happened that the giant goose egg contained a nubile young girl. This revelation would have been startling to a reader who had not just read the history of the world up to that point: which history, being Fabulinian in its treatment, prepared him for the event."
>
> THE FALL OF ROME, Auctore."
> (From East of Laughter.)

By   creating   a   text   of   seeming   antiquity,   the

defamiliarization of the world is seen as something that already happened before the narrative. The story doesn't have to explain the strange state of affairs it begins with or ends with. This runs counter to the paradigms of Science Fiction, in which texts which are cited are real (or presumed to deal with the hard factual world), and provide a springboard for the Man With A Plan to demonstrate his cleverness based on the facts of the matter. Likewise it violates the paradigms of horror (our everyday world with one intrusion or anomaly which can be isolated or at least explained), and of fantasy (another world with its own consistent laws). Lafferty uses created texts, either created out of whole cloth—such as the frequently-cited *The Back-Door of History* by Arpad Arutinov or *The Fall of Rome*, an actually published Lafferty book ("auctore" simply being Latin for "by the author")—or partial cloth, wherein Laffertyisms are attributed to the Psalms, or reference made to Aristotle's *Beard in Essential* and *Beard in Existential*. These are legitimated by the actual quotations from actual people mixed into the stream. Therefore reality is carefully displaced, sometime somewhere before either writer or reader has anything to do about it. This is an extremely effective modification of the fairy tale formula of *in illo tempore*. But instead of the "Once upon a time," where we know what the different laws are—Lafferty just convinces us that the laws are different.

2. Lafferty makes use of dead language words to play upon our collective unconscious. Mainly Hellenisms work their unconscious magic upon us; although like Joyce he combines his Greek with Irish—note the Puca in *The Reefs of Earth*. Consider the following examples. In *My Heart Leaps Up*, Lafferty's "autobiography" from Chris Drumm, the lead character is named Helen Anastasis. We may sense the rightness of the name, but unless we know Greek, we don't realize Anastasis = against inertness. Likewise, in "Continued on the Next Rock" the hero's name of Anteros = "One who loves in return" sadly sums

the hero's love and the girl's obstinacy (which are seen as a **mechanism** of their reincarnations—reminding one of the strangely Greek-named heroes of the *Mummy* films—Kharis, whose name means "gift," and Anake, whose name means "necessity"). Lafferty's use of Greek, Latin, Irish, and Hebrew tags is not merely demonstration of his vast erudition. It is a technique used by magicians for centuries to give their spells potency. Whereas he directs most of his narrative at our conscious—using simple daytime language—he also directs the same tale at our unconscious achieving a form of meta-communication. This is one of the most subtle forms of displacement. We feel early on in the Lafferty story that more is going on then we know, and at the end of the story that more has gone on than we can know. The use of foreign tags and the use of rhythm discussed below are good tools in displacing the narrative.

3. Lafferty plays upon our subconscious in another way—the use of rhythm. Yevgeny Zamyatin developed the concept of a "prose foot" as a way of internal pacing of fiction. He saw it as a kind of rhythmic device that by causing the reader to remember an earlier part of the narrative became a force for a choral (as in pertaining to choruses) cohesion that bound the story together in a different way than plot mechanics. This method, which I can't detect in Zamyatin's works (since Russian is Greek to me), is the core of Lafferty's work. He has invented the postmodern equivalent of the Homeric epithet. Now that I've told you what the magician's about to do, see if you can catch the trick the next time. Oops, went past you! A couple of examples will suffice. In the short story "The Transcendent Tigers," the device of a rhyming couplet to destroy a city of the world is used throughout the story. We become so in rhythm with the words that Lafferty doesn't have to provide the name of the city when the last half of a couplet ends the story—"Knife and Fork—and the reader provides "New York" thus having his own imagination and language complete the terrifying little tale. Likewise, rhyming nonsense is the

way a character may enter the world of the Shelni in "Ride a Tin Can"—perhaps more significantly, the understanding of the nonsense can turn you into a Shelni.

4. Lafferty uses the image of the wonder child to evoke a past that never was. This is the emotional equivalent to the intellectual process mentioned in #1. Unlike Bradbury, who invokes some kind of Norman Rockwell past by visual detail, Lafferty invokes the very rapid sense of childhood as we remember it. His heroes in "Lord Torpedo, Lord Gyroscope," Karl Riproar and Emily Vortex, are typical Lafferty wonder kids who do everything very very fast. His children as well as his hard-drinking young men move in a world that has been condensed by memory, and so we match with our own perceived fast and fleeting moments of childhood. Otherwise his children possess special powers, which, unlike the typical mutant of SF or demon-possessed horror kiddo, are never explained. These powers can be anything from the ability to make things disappear, in "Seven Day Terror," to—perhaps the greatest Lafferty trick of all—remaining perpetually four years old. This is a wonderful assertion of the fictive impulse—instead of appealing to our memories, he appeals to the type of story we told each other at that age and combines that appeal with the nostalgia we have for our youths. A careful blend, there; we read and feel nostalgic for realities that never were. And if we feel nostalgic for realities that weren't—we are displaced before the narrative happens.

5. Lafferty denies the uniqueness of the spectacular events, and by so doing once again displaces reality. The most outrageous situations are either ignored (as "In our Block," wherein the presence of a group of beings who can make anything instantly and in any quantity—a favorite Lafferty motif—is simply explained away as there are lots of odd people in the world), or a figure shows up claiming to have previously done the deed, but

in a different way. The latter role is usually filled by Willy McGilly. In "Seven Day Terror," he marvels that current kids use a beer can to make a disappearer, when he had used an oatmeal tube. In "Thus we Frustrate Charlemagne," he points out that all he needed to kill historical figures was a dart, rather than huge computer. And so forth. By denying the uniqueness of a spectacular event, Lafferty simultaneously accomplishes three things. One, he postulates that the world (at least this fictional world) is actually much, much stranger than our own. It is not only broad enough for the strange event—it is broad enough to hold the laws which permit the strange event. Two, he postulates that, in general, people's memory of wonder is so poor that they generally have forgotten the true marvels of the age. The truly successful people in Lafferty's works—the true geniuses and *Übermenschen*—are Those Who Remember the wonder of the world, such as Willy McGilly. Three, he once again dislocates reality before the narrative starts. The reader is not presented with a world that he or she knows with one anomaly to puzzle out; the reader is presented with a world that he or she has never known. Or, to create a more dreamy distancing effect—a world that he or she has forgotten. Which leads us to:

6. Lafferty uses the feeling of estrangement, of "I think I've forgotten something," as a mood to displace the narrative. We've all had those haunted days when we felt that we should've known something more than we knew. Lafferty often invokes that mood as the voice of a tale. Although not the only writer to do this—Robert Pinget comes to mind—Lafferty is certainly the only popular English writer who pulls off this particular trick. Two examples come quickly to mind. In "Thus We Frustrate Charlemagne," the history changers at the Institute for Impure Science decide to change history, but they will have an objective reference to the world before the change, so they can see if their attempt worked. Of course—following a long established tradition in Science Fiction—the change changes their memories and their

external object. Now this is more than commonly interesting, because the Institute for Impure Science is here doing to itself what Lafferty does for his readers— changing the rules at some time before the action begins (this is one of the many uses of self-reference which haunt Lafferty's work). A second example would be "What's the Name of that Town?", in which Epikt (note the wonderful Hellenism: Epiktistes means "The Equitable One," a great name for a calculating device that takes all elements (*Stoichae*) **equally**) sorts his facts to discover that something must be missing. The missing thing is Chicago, and when Epikt pronounces the hidden name, no memory results. Here's a primary Lafferty formula. Even when all the facts point to the mysterious nature of the matter, people simply can't remember the mysterious (except the Epiktistes—who as his name implies takes all facts equally, from padding in Hungarian dictionaries to Little Willy jokes about blood and chewing gum—and the most inspired genius of the day, Gregory Smirnov, who has tingles of memory). There is a Platonic theme in much of Lafferty's work: the world would no longer seem so dreary if we could only remember it. He even points out the two methods suitable to induce memory: the precision of Epiktistes, which he himself shows in researching and coining such names; and the inspiration of Smirnov, which Lafferty shows doubly strongly.

There are two benefits and two drawbacks to Lafferty's use of techniques of estrangement. The first drawback is that since his work doesn't fit the paradigms of Science Fiction, Fantasy, or Horror writing, the publishing world approaches it with great reluctance. I have never seen a second edition of any of his works, very few have made it into hardback, and, with the decline of the short story as a commercial medium, his work more and more has become the province of the small press. The radical openness of his texts, which, although they may offer a solution to the particular situation, leave that world more open by suggesting that such have happened before and will happen again, have clearly prompted editors to request new endings of several stories. Pick up any collection of Lafferty's shorter works and look at the ends of the stories. Note how many of them have the four or five paragraph ending (in another voice) that in a humorous and off hand fashion undercut the narrative. The lack of satisfactory endings reflects the need to comply with genre restrictions.

The second drawback is that since Lafferty's use of structure and displacement techniques place him outside of the paradigms of science fiction, and his venues place him outside the scope of academic criticism, very little is said about his work. Although we live in an epoch where the bold academic adventurer is like to go into the Venusian swamplands of SF, such academic probes are looking for SF in its pure state and will regard sports (particularly those infused with humor) as anathema. Those individuals looking from within the SF world may lack, or simply disdain, the linguistic and critical skills needed to begin to reveal that in Lafferty's work there is much more going on than meets the eye. The brave individuals who have attempted to do so have either merely produced fulsome praise or attempted to classify Lafferty's writings on the basis of superficialities (i.e., calling him a surrealist). Lafferty's use of displacement is not unique, but so few writers have consciously attempted the process, and their works are so varied, that there are no unifying articles, no language for the critic with a day job to draw on. Some bright lad or lass (with the appropriate dignifying letters following their names) may read this and look for the method of displacement in H.P. Lovecraft, James Joyce, Robert Pinget, Gilbert Sorrentino, Flann O'Brien, R. A. Lafferty, Howard Waldrop, and R.A. Wilson. Now there's a book worth reading. The astute observer will note that all the names on the list are Irish, saving those which are not.

The first benefit is the sheer memorability of R. A. Lafferty stories. The techniques of displacement, which work well on the shorter work, tend to over-weary the reader trying to hold it all in the longer pieces. However, any of the shorter pieces, once read, can be recalled because the effect that his work has on the psyche is ongoing. We may think of some classic SF tale such as Asimov's robot stories and use it to illustrate a point, but people recalling Lafferty tales do so with wonder. As an experiment, try to start telling any Lafferty story you know to anyone who has read any SF at all. Notice how early on they say, "I read that. It was neat." This is markedly different from the purely nostalgic reaction we have to E. R. Burroughs or Bradbury. I deem Lafferty's stories effective arcanum, since they clearly continue to work the soul once read.

The second benefit that Lafferty's stories have is that they give the rest of us something to shoot for. Over my writing desk I keep a copy of the Russian critic Victor Shlovsky's remark, "The technique of art is to make objects 'unfamiliar,' to make forms difficult. To increase the difficulty and length of perception is an aesthetic end in itself and must be prolonged. Art is a way of experiencing the artfulness of an object, the object itself is not important." Shlovsky wasn't writing about Lafferty, but I doubt if many writers could so clearly be an example of art as Shlovsky defines it.

Don Webb, freelancer writer, speaker and teacher, has over 250 published stories, four hardback novels, and damn near 2000 Google hits that are really about him. He usually says very funny things for his bios, so why ain't you laughing now?

He saw the whole world with garish orange eyes now.
R. A. Lafferty, "The Ninety-Ninth Cubicle"

Illustration © 2015 Anthony Ryan Rhodes

A Sound of Lafferty

by Roman Orszanski

[This paper was originally presented as a talk to Critical Mass, Adelaide South Australia's Science Fiction Literary Discussion Group, at a meeting held in February 1989, and subsequently published in the *Australian Science Fiction Review*, Second Series (March 1989), Vol. 4:2, Whole Number 19, pp. 14-18. Mr. Orszanski's piece was one of the first essays to explore the thesis that Lafferty could be best appreciated as an oral storyteller of folk tales, rather than a modern-day literary artist who writes predominantly for the printed page. Interestingly enough, we know that Lafferty himself possessed a photocopy of this article, which is now housed in the Lafferty archive at the the University of Tulsa McFarlin Library. For the twenty-sixth anniversary of its original presentation, Roman Orszanski reprised his talk at a meeting of Critical Mass in October 2015. A recording of that presentation by Orszanski is available online at http://doxa.podbean.com/e/a-sound-of-lafferty/. Once again, the reading demonstrates the importance of orality and the oral tradition in Lafferty's written work. This essay has never been reprinted and is now quite difficult to obtain, but it is republished here by the kind permission of the author.]

> It Is the secret river that not only greens the soul but also runs under walls and gains entrance to all fortified and walled places of the world and of the mind. Regard your own estate and case. Is your own town not built on two rivers which are separated by a firmament between? One of them is the impossible river by which all things may enter anywhere. We'd be robbed of our celestial birthright without it.
>
> (Ignace Wolff, The River Inside quoted by R. A. Lafferty in "Rivers of Damascus")

Lafferty's words belong to such a river: an ancient, invisible river which nourishes and greens our imagination. The river made up of storytellers' voices, ancient and modern, weaving myth and legend, whispering ghost stories and telling folk-tales. An oral tradition which stretches from cave mouth to radio studio, from the Halls of Asgard to the main street of Lake Wobegon.

R. A. Lafferty is not recognized as the brilliant fabulist he is because he belongs not to the literary tradition, but to the oral tradition. If his stories were recorded, or broadcast on radio, he would have a huge following and would be kept constantly in print (on tape?). Instead, he is appreciated by a select few, and most of his work is out of print.

Because Lafferty follows the form, style and content of the oral tradition, he is not appreciated in print. I suggest that his work is sadly undervalued, and deserves to be reassessed. I contend that he has been neglected because of a literary bias towards the written word, and a proper appreciation requires placing his *oeuvre* in the appropriate context.

Why place Lafferty in the oral tradition?

The first clue is the language: it rolls trippingly off the tongue. Sentences are short, and straight. Reading a story aloud sounds right, and is easy to do.[1] The stories are often written in the first or second person, either narrated by one of the characters, or directly by the author himself. Consider these passages from the start of one of his tales:

> But here is the heroine, a live one, perhaps a lively one. Should she not be a platinum woman, scatter-ornamented and beautiful, according to the norms? Or a shining ebony or a creamy chocolate? Should she not be adjusted and legal? Flowery and scatter-eyed? Should she not be of the multiplexity, nonlineate, a Scan, an Agape Apple, a Neutrina, a Pop Poppy? A Poster Coaster at the very least? Should she not be a Happy Medium, a Plateau Potato, a Twanger, a Mime,

---

[1] Rhip Baldridge and Ira M. Thornhill founded Corroboree Press in Minneapolis, Minnesota to publish the work of R. A. Lafferty. At Aussiecon II, Rhip mentioned that they proofread R. A. Lafferty aloud to each other, and enjoy this thoroughly. Looking back on Lafferty's work, I realized also that the author is typically speaking directly to the reader. This conversation triggered the thought which led to this article.

a Dreamer, and Enhancer-Dancer? Are these not the aspects of a heroine?

Nah, she wasn't like that at all. She was a Morning-Glory which is illegal. She was a Gown-Clown, which is also illegal. She was not flowery, not scatter-eyed. She wasn't even quite beautiful though she rather wished that she were. And yet perhaps she was, in another way, in an old and almost private way.

[...]

Here is the hero. Should he not be a Swing, a Slant, a Cut, according to the norms? A Spade, a Buck, a Whanger? Should he not be a Head, a Flash, an Etch, A Neutrino yet, a Burn, a Vein, a Flower? Yeah, but he wasn't like that. He wasn't that kind of hero at all. He was a Dawner, he was a doggedly pleasant man, he was even a sort of battler ("He saith among the trumpets, Ha ha; and he smelleth the battle far off" - Job), he was friendly; he was even intelligent on some subjects and murderous on others. He was big enough and thick enough; his hair was brambled but short. The people said that he would be the father of Ishmael. He didn't know what they meant; neither did the people. He was a moving man with cat-springs in him. He was a yellow-card street-sweeper, and his name was Morgan Saunders.

He was making his rounds, cleaning up after the swingers. He growled when he came to the twisted and grubby woman who was very young and very dead.

("Ishmael into the Barrens," *Golden Gate and Other Stories*, pp. 99-101)

Next, observe that Lafferty follows the form of folk tales with their design for the listener, not the reader. The story, as well as the language, is linear. We don't have complex flashbacks, multiple viewpoints and convoluted conversations. We do have asides to the listener, reminders of other events in a larger cycle of tales, and the repetition of detail that are common to stories told. We also have the repetition traditional to folk tales: the structure which allows for anticipation on the part of the listener (e.g., Three Little Pigs, Three Brothers, Four tasks, etc.). Consider these two passages from "Days of Grass, Days of Straw":

> Christopher Foxx was walking down a city street. No, it was a city road. It was really a city trail or path. He was walking in a fog, but the fog wasn't in the air or the ambient: it was in his head. Things were mighty odd here. There was just a little bit of something wrong about things.
> [...]
> Christopher Foxx was walking down a city street. Things were mighty even here, mighty neat. There was just a little bit of something wrong about their rightness. The world was rubbed, scrubbed, and tubbed; it was shaved, paved and saved; it was neat, sweet and effete.

How about this extract from "Brain Fever Season" (*Ringing Changes*), as Barnaby Sheen and colleagues are trying to find out why one of the hottest new items in the porno stores is an 1834 grammar of the Tibetan language? Naturally, Sheen suspects his *australopithecine* houseboy, Austro.

> "Austro, do you know why an obscure Tibetan grammar should suddenly become a hot item in the porno stores?"
> "Mr Sheen, you know I'm not old enough to go into the porno stores."
> "No, but you're old enough to avoid a direct answer to a straight question. Austro, if this little puzzler were handed to you, what first step would you take toward finding an answer?"
> "Carrock, I'd triangulate in on it. I'd find where the puzzler originated and where it spread from. Oh, oh, oh, why don't I learn to swallow my tongue? Why do you ask me questions? I'm just a twelve-year-old kid. Got to go right now!" and Austro ran down the stairs and out of the house.
> Barnaby Sheen phoned Roy Mega at his

mysterious number at his mysterious room. Nobody was sure where Roy Mega lived, but Barnaby Sheen believed that the young man had a room in that very house. Barnaby's was a big and junky house (most persons know how many rooms there are in their houses and where they are, but not Barnaby), and Roy had a cavalier way with space, and with telephones. Barnaby was sure that he was paying the phone bill on Roy's mysterious phone at least.

"Roy!" Barnaby barked into the phone. "Do you know why an obscure Tibetan grammar should suddenly become a hot item in the porno stores?"

"Do you believe me the sort of young man who goes to the porno stores?" Roy's voice asked out of the phone. "I'm hurt. Besides, it isn't obscure any longer. Got to hang up now. Got to go down to the lab and work on a hot new idea."

[...]

"Roy, if you were asked to solve the problem of Tibetan grammars suddenly becoming hot items in porno stores all over the world, where would you start?"

"I'd start the same place as any other problem. I'd find out where it starts. Then it's easier to find out what it means. I'd triangulate in on it and find out who created the situation and started the problem to rolling around the world. Oh, oh, oh, I've got to invent an automatic guardian for myself! We hadn't decided what we wanted to do with it yet. Why do I say these things? Got to go now! Got to go down to the lab for one of those brilliant sessions."

Many stories have an explicit prologue in which the characters are introduced, the action foretold (not always in all detail, sometimes teasingly).

Such presage is typical of folklore (or theatre): warnings occur early in the story (beware of the Big Bad Wolf), chants and verses warn of events to come, or cycles of events which repeat themselves. The world in Lafferty is constantly remade, patterns of events re-occur.

And what about the stories themselves?

Lafferty's stories typically deal with mythic themes - we hear of long-forgotten times, mighty deeds and forgotten heroes. Lafferty tells us of a rougher world, a livelier place, with characters painted in bold colors, not all of them visible to the human eye.

This mythopoeic style is not in vogue; the magic realism of Borges, Fuentes and Marquez has only recently (last decade) enlarged the popular market. Sf remains firmly wedded to the naturalistic style of the 'thirties (with, thankfully, a few exceptions) and Fantasy is trapped in the endless series of barbarians, wizards and quests, or a naturalistic style slightly extended. (One ordinary day, with unicorns ...)

Cyberpunk moves further into the realm of gritty realism. And, to cover such themes in a humorous and witty manner! Very Irish, but not in vogue in the genre. Perhaps the closest genre worker was Cordwainer Smith - equally poetic, but far more serious. And his universe didn't shift as much as Lafferty's.

What makes up Lafferty's world? The R. A. Lafferty universe has more in common with that of the twelfth century, before the scientific worldview: when all manner of beings and objects were endowed with life and intelligence; when secrets were all about, waiting to be discovered. Many of his characters possess abilities beyond ours: they have extra, or sharper, senses; they have multiple personalities, they know of multiple events. They have tricks and skills which are rarely explained, but taken for granted—bi-location is such a handy skill ...

R. A. Lafferty's characters inhabit a wider, richer, more densely populated world. Consider the beings which populate Lafferty's stories! Many are of the first race, the one with six fingers, or the demigods fashioned of clay, or *Australopithecus*. Some are the essence of character—such as The Detective, or The Master Forger. Archetypes? No, the archetypes are based on these characters. Some have ancient histories, all are extraordinary. Lafferty doesn't pretend these are normal people: they just are, and inhabit the world.

And, of course, there are many tales: it is taken for granted that there are multiple histories of the world. Or perhaps the world is born eternally anew, and Events are foretold, to recur again and again. We are never sure if the current version is real, or imagined, or stable for the length of the story.

In *Apocalypses*, we have the curious tale of an extraordinary forgery. Listen as our Master Detective, Constantine Quiche, consults the World's Greatest Forger, Angelo DiCyan:

" ... How big, Angelo? That is my first question. How big a forgery could there be?"

"Oh, as big as the biggest figure that could be written on the biggest tab that the customer could lift. There is no other limit. I could forge this very world that we are on, and I could forge it convincingly enough for your most astute planet buyer. All I would need is money enough for the project and a place to set my fulcrum."

"Yes, all right" Constantine said. "I didn't know it could be done quite that big, and this isn't a question of it. As big as a country or a realm, yes, but not as big as a world. Then there is the other part of the inquiry. How about a forgery - how shall I say this? - a forgery of which there is no original."

"Oh, certainly, certainly, there are instances of that, Constantine. That is almost too easy sometimes. To do it best, one has to reject the 'too-easy' and 'too-cheap' solutions. Then you have really quality forgeries of which there are no material originals. This thing is difficult only because it places the forger on his honor, or at least on that forgery that he may delegate to serve as his honor. It is so hard to check it when there is nothing to check it by, and the commissioning of such a thing might be subject to abuse.

"And there is another detail which not-quite-master forgers sometimes overlook in doing forgeries-without originals. There is one small thing that must be done. One must make a slight change in the world first: a silent, slight, adaptive change in the world itself so as to produce such a world as would accommodate this missing masterpiece. But we all of us change the world continually.

"Nor let us be misled by such a term as 'missing original.' That is not the same thing as 'no original'. I have in mind one of my own nearly perfect forgeries, the 'Weeping Hermes of Praxiteles'. I made this forgery of an unavailable original. I made it very much as Praxiteles would have made it. And I made it as good as Praxiteles could have made it. The original had been the Landmark Greek Sculpture of the fourth century B. C., and I made it to be so. But I had already rambled through the mind of Praxiteles by means of many of his other sculptures, which is what made my forgery-without-an-original such a superior one. But it wasn't as if there had never been an original. There had been. I could study the missing masterpiece by its effect on all later works. I could study the written descriptions of ·rt that have come down to us. Really, I already had the impression, as it were, from the mud in which it had lain. I had only to pour the mud mold full of molten marble.

"Incidentally, I have found the missing Praxiteles, the 'Weeping Hermes' itself, and I am ruddy foxed if I know what to do with it. It isn't as good as my version which is now accepted as the original. Even as one of my 'authentic' forgeries, it would lower my reputation a bit. But I will keep it awhile, and then I will find a way to turn it to best advantage.

"But you are talking about the forgery of something that never was, and yet could have been?"

"Yes I am, Angelo," Constantine said. "And perhaps that could-have-been context would have to be, maybe has already had to be, forged also."

"Oh well, many things are able to grow their own contexts about them. Sometimes a thing will seem right for a while, and then it will seem just a bit wrong. Like yourself."

"Like myself, Angelo?"

"Yes. Weren't you absolutely secure and sure of

yourself as the best detective in the world for a while? And, in the last eighteen hours or so, haven't you come to feel that there was something just a little bit wrong with you in that role, with you in any role?"

"Yes, that's so Angelo. What of it?"

"Maybe you here present are only a forgery of Constantine Quiche. Maybe I forged you."

Oh well, at least Quiche would then be a *masterly* forgery. Somehow this passage always reminds me of Welles's *F for Fake*. Lafferty's work belongs firmly to the tradition of folktales and myths: many of his stories not only deal with the traditional themes (complete with morals!), but they fall naturally into a cycle of tales.

Let us consider some of his works

Archipelago and Finnegan

What could be more Irish than tales of Finnegan and the Devil? Their story is told in a trilogy of novels: *Archipelago, The Devil is Dead* and *More than Melchisedech*. Only the middle one of these has wide circulation (Dobson SF '71); the first was published in 1979 by a small press, Manuscript. As far as I know, the third is as yet unpublished.

And they also tell the story of Papadiabolous the Devil and his company, and of two of the hidden lives of Finnegan; and how it is not always serious to die, the first time it happens.

Here is one man who was buried twice and now lies still (but uneasy of mind) in his two separate graves. Here is another man who died twice—not at all the same thing. And here are several who are disinclined to stay dead: they don't like it, they won't accept it.

Given here, for the first time anywhere, are the bearings and correct location of the Terrestrial Paradise down to the last second of longitude. You may follow them. You may go there.

Here will also be found the full account of where the Devil himself is buried, and the surprising name that is on his tombstone boldly spelled out. And much else.

(The "Promantia" of The Devil is Dead)

The Men Who Know Everything

Barnaby has a curious collection of folks at his place:

(Austro, the houseboy and bartender of Barnaby Sheen, was one of the genus *Australopithecus*, which is either ape, or ape-man, or man, the middle one of these being impossible. The genus was supposed to be extinct long since, but Austro was proof that it wasn't.)

(Loretta Sheen was a life-sized, sawdust-filled doll: Barnaby insisted that this object was the undead body of his real daughter Loretta. We had all known Barnaby well all our lives, yet we couldn't remember for sure whether he had ever had a real daughter or not.)

(Mary Mondo was a ghost, the schizo-personality of a girl named Violet Lonsdale whowas long since dead. But Mary Mondo was not dead.)

("Animal Fair," Through Elegant Eyes*)*

Roy Mega (as we saw above) may also be one of Barnaby's guests, but we don't quite know. Austro, incidentally, also produces a curious, yet popular (at times prophetic) comic strip—chiselled into stone!

Barnaby Sheen and his friends, the Men Who Know Everything, Dr George Drakos, Harry O'Donovan, Chris Benedetti and R. A. Lafferty (who admits his lack of knowledge in some areas has been somehow overlooked by his companions) keep inventing things and getting into trouble. The stories appeared in the 'seventies, and are collected in *Through Elegant Eyes* (Corroboree Press, 1983) and also some in *Ringing Changes* (Ace, 1984).

The Institute of Impure Science

The institute and its members appear in a wondrous novel, *Arrive at Easterwine: The Autobiography of a Ktistec*

Machine. Since the entire story is told by the machine, we're never sure if the shifting events and constant changes in History actually happen, are a delusion of the machine's, or are enacted in some simulation of a parallel world within the machine. Many abstract qualities become measurable:

> "...this extension [of the EP locator] will locate habitats of love and benignity without fully understanding what they consist of. The device scans, and ultimately it records in myself all human locations in the world where authentic benignity and love obtain.
>
> "I have most of them now. Have them all unless unsuspected ones should turn up in supposedly unpeopled wastes of Antarctica. And those loci that I have do not add up to very many: Only seven towns in the world, each of less than a thousand persons; no more than a hundred hamlets; not over half a million families, and about as many singletons.
>
> "We will discover, if we may, just what is to be found in these special loci," Aloysius said, "and then we will imitate the special thing in our own persons, to the extent that we are adequate persons to compass it."
>
> "What we will do," said Gregory, "is extract the special essence that is to be found in these places. Then we will put it through every test possible, inside and outside of Epikt. When we have it analyzed completely, we will synthesize it. We are now able to synthesize anything we can analyze. And when we have it synthesized, then we will manufacture it on a large scale; and we will spew it out into the world in overpowering quantities. By this, we will change the world, as nobody has known how to change the world before."
>
> "Aw, coot's foot, it won't work," Aloysius said. "There is a barrier between such things and others."
>
> "You yourself, Aloysius, have in other experiments shown the barrier between tangibles and intangibles to be a semipermeable membrane,"

Gregory Smirnov stated. "Glasser has proved emotion to be an electromagnetic phenomenon; Valery has shown group feeling to be a chemical affinity; Cogsworth has measured the velocity vector of several of the intuitions; you yourself have demonstrated that grace has both weight and valence; I have done valuable work on the in-grace and out-of-grace isotopes of several substances, proving the materiality of grace. Everything has a material base. There is nothing the matter with matter. Life is no more than a privileged form of matter. Love is no more than a privileged form of life. It is an all-one stream flowing along forever. If we did not believe this we would be false to the very Idea of the Institute of Impure Science."

(Arrive at Easterwine, *1971*)

Lafferty's themes and concerns are those you'd expect from a mythmaker. His Roman Catholic background permeates his work, imbuing his stories with fantastic characters.

Themes include the discovery of ancient magic; the creation of the world, and its inhabitants; hidden (ancient and forgotten) knowledge; the eternal struggle between Good and Evil.[2]

For all of the reasons suggested above, Lafferty's stories are tales to be told and retold: they are designed to be read aloud and enjoyed. Lafferty is an extraordinary fabulist and myth maker. He deserves to be as famous as Cordwainer Smith, but isn't treated seriously because of the humor in his tales.

Also, the form of his work doesn't suit the written word; he is continuing the oral tradition in a modern setting. If it weren't for our bias toward the written form and naturalistic narrative, he would be recognized for the Irish-American genius he is. There are hundreds of his tales as yet

---

[2] I wonder here if Lafferty is guilty of the Nestorian or Albigensian Heresy; at the very least he would be sympathetic to the view of the Bogomils, that the Devil created the world—but that's another article, for that way madness or a PhD thesis lies.

unpublished, but unlike P. K. Dick, his genius won't suddenly be discovered after he dies: his agent has orders to destroy any unpublished stories. Luckily, some fans in the US have started a programme to collect and publish all of his works in a small press format (Corroboree Press, 2729 Bloomington Ave South, Minneapolis, Minnesota 55407 USA); please contact them for further information.

Finally, you might want to put Lafferty to the acid test: find a friend and read them some stories aloud.

Treat them to the *sound* of Lafferty.

Bearded broadcaster, cyclist, urban ecologist and SF fan, Roman Orszanski lives in a 2 story straw bale house in a sustainable community in the center of Adelaide. In his spare time he produces and publishes fanzines (doxa!), as well as podcasts (http://doxa.podbean.com/), writes articles and reviews, and works with a team to produce The Environment Show on local community radio. Archives of older shows can be found at http://enviroshow3d.tumblr.com

R. A. Lafferty: The Function of Archetype in the Western Mystical Tradition

by Dena C. Bain Taylor

Mythology is not a static art. It is solid, grounded in traditions that go back beyond memory; yet it is always capable of transformation and continuously subject to reshaping. Raphael Aloysius Lafferty is a shaper of myth who in a dozen novels and over one hundred stories bases his mythological pictures on the mystical tradition of the West, and on the attempt of man to transcend the rational and expand his perception of the cosmos.

In the now-familiar terms of Jungian psychology, mankind shares a common and inborn unconscious life—not limited to the experience of any one individual—which is expressed in dreams, fantasies, and mythologies in the forms of archetypal images and symbols. In the works of R. A. Lafferty, however, the archetypes of humanity are not incorporeal symbols—they appear in the flesh as characters intimately concerned with shaping the course of human history. To Lafferty, the mystical Christian archetypes of good and evil represent the eternal struggle between forces of darkness and light in a dualistic universe, and he creates out of his own beliefs an ethic as well as a cosmology. This essay examines the nature and function of Lafferty's archetypal embodiments in adding what he calls "the yeast of the immaterial" to mundane reality in two of his novels, *Past Master* (1968) and *The Devil is Dead* (1971).[1]

In both Eastern and Western mysticism, the mystical

---

[1] All quotations from the works of Raphael Aloysius Lafferty are from the following editions: *The Devil is Dead* (New York: Avon Books, 1971); *Past Master* (New York: Ace Books, 1968), hereafter DD and PM respectively.

experience is a direct intuition of ultimate reality: a Supreme State in the East—Tao, for example—and a Supreme Being in the West. Lafferty, though habitually unwilling to be interviewed or to divulge information about himself, has nonetheless expressed very openly his conviction of a Supreme Being and his strong adherence to the tenets of the Roman Catholic Church. He describes himself as a Catholic of the "out-of-season or conservative variety" in Harlan Ellison's introduction to one of his stories in *Dangerous Visions*.[2] For Lafferty, the word "faith" is synonymous with inescapable logic, complete clarity, order, and certitude as well as with the Church, the Indwelling of the Holy Spirit, and the Body of the Lord. He sees faith as a science, defining science as "a branch of study concerned with observation and classification of facts, especially with the establishment of verifiable general laws, chiefly by induction and hypotheses."[3]

Lafferty's philosophy is strongly reminiscent of medieval Church mysticism in his attitude toward faith as a science; in his dualistic conception of the universe under the control of the emanations that proceed from a transcendent yet immanent God; and in his fascination with language, a fascination that connects very closely with the Cabala, the medieval system of Jewish mysticism which exerted a strong influence in the development of Christian mysticism in the thirteenth century.[4] In Lafferty's mythos, the emanations of spiritual energy are in constant motion. Mankind's function is not to balance the elements and thus negate their effect, but to work out the eternal flux between the positive and negative on the physical plane through its assumption of the responsibility of free will, while never, by divine design, resolving it.

---

[2] *Dangerous Visions,* ed. Harlan Ellison (London: David Bruce and Watson, 1967).

[3] Paul Walker, "R. A. Lafferty: An Interview," *Luna,* No. 67 (Spring 1977), p. 6.

[4] For discussions of this influence, see Thomas Katsaros and Nathaniel Kaplan, *The Western Mystical Tradition* (New Haven: College and Univ. Press, 1969); and Hilda Graef, *The Story of Mysticism* (London: Peter Davies, 1966).

Lafferty's novels are not generally well known, although his short stories are common in science fiction anthologies. It is perhaps only fair to provide short summaries of the two novels to be discussed—for readers unfamiliar with his work—before proceeding to develop the thematic concerns sketched above. These "bare bones" cannot, of course, convey any idea of the wit and humor of Lafferty's style, but if they encourage the reader to look further, so much the better. I feel that Lafferty has suffered neglect as a writer that he does not merit.

Past Master is essentially the story of the dystopia that results when the archetypes of the divine in all their forms are consciously—in this case, physically—divorced from the human collective unconscious. The novel takes place on the golden Planet Astrobe, an Earth colony that has grown to overshadow its parent world in the five hundred years of its settlement. Astrobe is the perfect materialist utopia and is based on the *Utopia* of Thomas More, who appears as the revenant hero of the novel. Every possible luxury is provided in the planet's magnificent cities, and all luxuries are free to the beautiful, cultured Astrobians. Machines that were designed by other machines to do all of the work have now evolved into Programmed Persons having equal rights with humans and their own Inner Circle of Masters matching that of humans. Most important, a limitless supply of Programmed Killers can instantly sense dissatisfaction with the Golden Astrobe Dream and relentlessly pursue and destroy those who become their lawful prey by acting or even thinking contrary to the Astrobe ideal. As the novel begins, the planet faces an unprecedented and incomprehensible crisis because humans have relinquished all responsibility—and thus all power—to the Programmed Persons.

In fact, there is very little physical difference between humans and mechanicals. They can intermarry and cannot be distinguished by sight. Only one difference remains. Despite the overwhelming emphasis on the material, humans still retain some connection with their collective unconscious mind and its manifestations: religion, superstition, psychic phenomena—in short, things supernatural and nonmaterial, things of the soul, not the body. The Programmed Persons have reacted in two ways to this phenomenon they cannot share. On one hand, they pass laws making any sort of imaginative, metaphysical, or even consistently individualistic thought a crime against the Astrobe Ideal, and the Programmed Killers become a true and totally merciless thought-police. On the other hand, in their envy they seek a god for themselves. Searching the histories of Astrobe and Old Earth for a god, they settle at last on an old mechanical toy excavated from one of the Egyptian pyramids, when the Ouden—the Nothingness that envelops all the universes and is the enemy that swallows all life—comes to them and proclaims itself their god and king. It seems inevitable that humanity will die at the hands of the perfect materialism it created. It valued so little those things that made it truly human that it did not build them into its utopia and thus left them vulnerable to destruction.

Several things, however, work against the Ouden and the Programmed Persons. Increasing numbers of people choose to leave the ease and opulence of the golden cities. First thousands, then millions flow into Cathead, Barrio, and Wu-Town—hellish slum cities which sprang up overnight. Killing work, squalor, and rampant disease combine to destroy even the hardiest within a month at most. Yet, by the same principle that makes a man smash his hand against a wall to prove to himself that he is awake, the inhabitants of Cathead and Barrio choose a life of misery over a living death of ease.

Second, on Astrobe, unlike Old Earth, the archetypes of the collective unconscious are able to assume physical reality. The harder the civilized Astrobians try to dismiss them as irrational and impossible, the more they manifest themselves in Cathead and Barrio and the feral wilds that surround all the cities. A group of these archetypes play a major role in the novel in working against the sterile Astrobe Dream: Evita, the ageless and beautiful child-witch; Rimrock, the ansel (a race of Oceanic men native to the planet); Paul, warrior-guardian of Thomas More; Walter Copperhead, the necromancer who reads the entrails of devils and planets; Father Oddopter, a green-robed priest of Saint Klingensmith, in whose company Christ walks on Astrobe; and the Second Adam, a boy who is always present to die gloriously in righteous battles.

Archetypal function is more important in Lafferty than the actual correspondences between humans and specific archetypal figures, such as can be discovered in the gods in human form that abound in the works of Roger Zelazny, for example. Although correspondences are fruitful in examining the major characters—Thomas More and Evita in *Past Master*, Finnegan and Anastasia in *The Devil is Dead*—such analysis becomes futile and misleading in the case of the plethora of partly archetypal, partly heroic, partly human minor characters. Their function as a group is, however, very important. The cosmos in Western mysticism exhibits a continual dialectical conflict between the forces of creation and destruction which are manifested in the natural process of growth and decay. In *Past Master*, all of these minor figures are manifestations of the natural forces of Astrobe. Indeed, the psychic forces that created the archetypes of Astrobe, like the ones that did so on Old Earth, are the strong inner powers of the planet on which the civilization of the Golden Astrobe Dream is a thin yellow froth. As Father Oddopter tells Thomas More: "Here [in the primordial wilds of the feral strips] are all improbable persons and animals, spirits and half-spirits, clean and unclean; the archetypes of folk dreams, they are here alive, and often fleshed" (PM, p. 99).

The third element working against the Ouden and the mechanicals precipitates the action of the novel. At its beginning, three members of the Inner Circle of human Masters decide to send for a leader from the past to help them solve the crisis of mass desertion from the Astrobe Dream that threatens to destroy it. They choose Thomas More, a man who would be popular with the people and who had, at the end of his life, one completely honest moment. It is not for his honesty that they want him, however, but for his popularity. They plan to present him to the people as the Past Master and to use him as a figurehead in their own schemes. But Thomas More, the fisher-king revenant who died once because he would not be a king's rubber stamp, is prepared to do so again. Initially, he is captivated by the reality of what he says he wrote as "a sour joke," horrified by the misery of Cathead and Barrio, and doubtful of the existence of the fleshed archetypes of the feral wilds. He allows himself to he used as a figurehead by the human Inner Circle and as a tool by the Inner Circle of the Programmed Persons and their god. At last, however, he takes his stand, allies himself with the rebels of the slums and the group of archetypal figures, and refuses to sign a bill banning the last vestiges of religion and "the Beyond" on Astrobe. As in his first life, he is maneuvered into giving up his life to maintain his integrity, and his death at the end of the novel triggers the revolution that will destroy the world and bring about the birth of a new order. In *The Devil is Dead*, the archetypes of the collective human unconscious are again capable of physical manifestation, and two archetypal groups of dark forces fight for domination of humanity, with Finnegan, the hero, standing between them and belonging, like Thomas More, to both and to neither. The novel opens when Finnegan awakes on a sidewalk with no memory of the past few months. He is immediately hired by the millionaire Saxon X. Seaworthy to fill a berth on his yacht, the *Brunhilde*, once occupied by a crew member who was murdered mysteriously. Although Seaworthy tells Finnegan that the *Brunhilde* is about to embark on a global pleasure cruise, the ship is actually on a mission for one of the two groups of dark forces. This group is descended from other-world beings, whom humans traditionally call daemons and who come to Earth approximately once a century to impregnate human women. The children of these unions, satyrs—demons and devils—have formed a formed a conspiracy of evil. Seaworthy's group, ostensibly under his leadership but actually commanded by Papadiabolous, a son of the Devil, sails around the world during the course of the novel, spreading the technology of war, a plague that they hope will cause humanity to destroy itself. A highly confusing alliance exists between Seaworthy's group and representatives of the second archetypal group, who have managed to infiltrate his crew: Anastasia, the mermaid; Joe Cross, younger brother of a king; Manuel, the stowaway, who is also a distinguished and weary old nobleman; and Don Lewis, the prince who fails in his quest: "They were an exiled royalty, exiled for thousands of years, and returning and returning again and again. They were timeless, and they were alive and vigorous" (DD, p. 79). This group, though they have no love of modem or "new recension" man, is of human descent. They belong to the Elder Race (or old recension man, as Lafferty also calls them) contained in the myths of many cultures and given fleshly life in the novel.

The novel follows the ship on its deadly journey around the world until the alliance between the two groups breaks apart and they begin to fight each other. Finnegan allies himself with the Elder Race, from which he is descended. The book ends as the final battle between the Devils and the Elder Races is about to begin. Both groups will be destroyed, but both will rise again, to fight each other and humanity once more.

Examining the nature of these archetypal groups, we find that the mythological tradition of an Elder Race, a race of giants, demigods, possibly extraterrestrials, as in the tradition of the Dogon tribe of Africa,[5] is reflected strongly in *The Devil is Dead*. Humanity in the novel is distinctly divided into two lineages—old and new recension humans, with the old recension an element that runs furtively through the blood of younger race and produces small groups of people that revert to the ancestral type every few thousand years. It is the only way the Elder Race can survive after the sound defeat it received at the hands of the new in primordial times, and it looks for ways, including a temporary alliance with the completely evil forces of whom Seaworthy's group is a part, to achieve its revenge and return. Finnegan, who bears the mark of the old recension, a scar just under the skin of the left wrist, is puzzled that the Elder Race is remembered in Genesis as a race of powerful giants: "There were giants on the earth in those days, and also afterward, when the sons of God had relations with the daughters of men, who bore children to them. These were the mighty men of old, the men of renown" (Gen. vi. 4).

Lafferty's sources tend to be buried and sometimes mixed beyond recognition by his style, which is good-humored and

---

[5] The belief of the Dogon that beings from Sirius B, the companion star to the Dog Star which has been discovered only recently by astronomers, came to Africa five thousand years ago to instruct humanity, is meticulously examined in Robert K.G. Temple,

light-hearted, and which echoes the Irish folktale. It is incongruent with the deeper concerns of his mythos. This can and does create a great deal of confusion, which no amount of reflection can alleviate, in the relationship between the Devils and the Elder Race and between these two acting as a combined force and the new recension. The relationship between the old and new recensions is much more clearly a statement of the mystical dialectic, and Lafferty's use of the passage from Genesis is a reflection of the Old Testament myth of the mating of daemons (i.e., angels) with humans, and the degeneration of the resultant race until its almost total destruction by the Flood. Lafferty also puts this relationship into anthropological terms wherein the old recension is Neanderthal man, who was overcome in an incredibly narrow instant of time by the taller, stronger Cro-Magnon man and absorbed by him to create the mutation known as modern, or new recension man. The Cro-Magnon forebrain and consciousness is dominant in us, but we also inherit the poorly understood back-brain of the earlier race, which is "partly the seat of the unconscious, we know; of the subliminal, of certain psychological manifestations, of what we can only call ghostliness . . . . It was the 'other people,' the 'Ugly' people who gave to us whatever ghostliness we have, and whatever imagination" (DD, pp. 206 -7).

Lafferty often uses dreams in his works to show the conflict between the archetypal groups, and he mixes waking and dreaming realities so fluidly that the terms tend to lose their distinction, as do the concepts of "past," "present," and "future." Lafferty's use of Western mysticism creates a situation wherein time is a function of the conscious mind, and the unconscious mind, which recognizes no such temporality, is revealed through dreams. The worlds of dream and myth are alike in this creation of an eternal present, and also in other respects. As Ira Progoff says:

> Dreams and especially myths are a primary medium for intuitive insights into the ultimate nature of human experience . . . . In general, dreams are that

The Sirius Mystery (London: Sidgwick and Jackson, 1976).

aspect of the symbolic dimension that is experienced in personal terms. When the symbolic dimension is perceived in transpersonal terms, in terms that pertain to more than the subjective experience of the individual reaching to what is universal in man, whether the experience is in sleeping or waking, myth is involved. It is myth because it touches what is ultimate in man and in his life, expresses it symbolically, and provides an inner perspective by which the mysteries of human existence are felt and entered into . . . . They [dreams] are patterns of symbolism that pertain to mankind as a whole.[6]

Thus, in *Past Master* a phenomenon known as Hopp-Equation Travel makes it possible to travel the five light-years between Astrobe and Earth in less than a month. However, the Law of Conservation of Psychic Totality will not be broken, and the full five years of psychic experience must be compressed into one month. It compresses itself into self-contained, perfectly timed ninety-second dreams, and Paul, the space pilot sent by the human Inner Circle into the past of Old Earth to retrieve Thomas More, calculates that he has at least twenty thousand of these dreams during the passage from Astrobe to Earth: "There is a great lot of psychic space debris, and when one enters its area on Hopp-Equation flight one experiences it. Every poignant thing that ever happened, every comic or horrifying or exalting episode that ever took place, is still drifting somewhere in space. One runs into fragments (and concentrations) of billions of minds there; it is never lost, it is only spread out thin" (PM, p. 23). Once the mind is open to these passage dreams, moreover, they return continually once the passage is over; and throughout the course of the novel, Thomas has frequent passage dreams that tell him of the past or the future, of the true natures of the people with whom he deals, of the progress of the conflict in

---

[6] Ira Progoff, "Waking Dream and Living Myth," in *Myths, Dreams, and Religion*, ed. Joseph Campbell (New York: E.P. Dutton, 1970), pp. 177-180.

which he is, until his last shining moment, a pawn.[7]

Dreams are also an important element in *The Devil is Dead*, and there is a strong suggestion at the beginning of the novel that the whole voyage is a dream (DD, p. 28). The ocean is indeed the world of the dream, and Finnegan has quite a few, quite odd introspective ocean dreams. In one of them, for example, he learns the archetypal truth about Marie Courtois, the Golden Ogress, who is allied with Seaworthy, in which Marie says "that she was Demeter, and that she was also her own daughter Persephone, that she lived in Hell in her one person, but that she returned to Earth every year in her own reincarnation" (DD, p. 74). Similarly, he dreams of the mermaid Anastasia and of her sisters, the Oreads, in a dream that manifests under the influence of the Greek moon shining full on the ocean far below the mountainside where Finnegan and Anastasia lie. Lafferty speaks of the reality of ocean and space dreams in a chapter heading: "We speak now of the physical areas of dreams, particularly of sea-dreams . . . . Dreams do have a strange topography. Men do dream the same dreams when they go through the same sectors. How will it be when they go through the sectors of space?" (DD, p. 65).[8]

Though the old and new recensions are eternally at war with each other, they share a common element—a promise of a "Transcendent Something" that will last beyond the end of the world. In the Western esoteric tradition, spiritual unity is the creative force. This force, the Transcendent Something, sends forth emanations from itself of which the physical incarnation of the universe is the ultimate result. These emanations are

---

[7] The passage dreams in *Past Master* are to be found on pp. 23, 24, 25, 35, 38, 53, 57, 59, and 62.

[8] Lafferty's chapter headings are perfect examples either of a tremendous imagination and store of knowledge, or a frustrating habit of leading his reader down an intellectual garden path, depending on the reader's viewpoint. Some of his chapter headings, such as the one from Galen, chapter eleven, are genuine; some are plainly Laffertian inventions; some are, I suspect, both. Again, it is their function rather than their analysis that is important, and the reader is cautioned against sleepless nights deliberating on Lafferty's sources.

both positive and negative, light and dark, and their eternal struggle is necessary to ensure the flow upwards and back from the Transcendent. Thus, in *Past Master*, there is a scene of the killing of the Devil which is an essential part of the Promise. As the Scrivener, a half-human, half-mechanical member of Thomas More's party on his journey into the feral wilds, says, the materialist Dream of Astrobe is not perfect: "It is only half the thing. It must be conjoined to some other things that I do not understand yet. Perhaps after all we must kill the Devil afresh every day" (PM, p. 109). We must, in other words, create the Paradise within ourselves, and it is an unending battle, a condition of life. The Golden Astrobe Dream offers physical paradise, but removes the struggle that leads to the realization of the spiritual paradise. Father Oddopter, who as a priest is the spiritual fisher-king of the feral wilds as Thomas is of civilized Astrobe, uses himself as bait to catch a small devil. He then uses it to help kill the true hydra-Devil, a monstrous serpentlike creature, just as Apopis, the serpent of darkness in Egyptian myth who is the perennial antagonist representing collective evil, is slain each dawn by Horus, the hawk-headed god.[9] Meanwhile, Evita waits to feast on its brains. Evita is not only Eve, she is also Lilith, the one who came before Eve, i.e., the old recension. Evita's nature corresponds very closely to a much older Eve than the one of the Bible. There is a Sumerian vase of approximately 2000 B.C., described by Joseph Campbell in an essay entitled "Mythological Themes in Creative Literature and Art" as:

> the female power [of the creative Self] in human form, and the male serpent behind her, the Tree of Life before, and beyond that, a male personage wearing the horned headdress of a god who has evidently come to partake of the wondrous tree. A number of scholars have recognized in this scene something analogous to the episode in Eden, a full thousand years before Yahweh's day however, and when the figure rendered in the Bible as a mere creature, Eve, would have been

---

[9] Dorothy Norman, *The Hero: Myth/Image/Symbol* (New York and Cleveland: World Publishing Co., 1969), p. 48.

recognized as a goddess, the great mother goddess Earth, with the primal, self-renewing serpent, symbolic of the informing energy of creation and created things, her spouse.[10]

The old recension, represented by Lilith and the fisher-king, is this same informing energy of Creation that contains both the golden age of primordial times and the Promise that, in killing the darkness inside ourselves, we approach again the Something Beyond. The cyclic conclusion of *The Devil is Dead* demonstrates to an even greater extent the essential dualism of the forces of light and dark. Though the battle will be fought, and Doll Delancey, the only new recension human involved, will be left alive to reap the benefits and continue her business of salvaging the world, that is, reaching for the spiritual World, "there can be no victory. The victory of either of us kills all of us. We become the broken bow. Our limbs, our lives, our world become unstrung, and we die" (DD, p. 215). The projection of myth into the future, then, does not balance the dualism but continues it, and the implication for Lafferty is that we neither can nor should try to end it.

On Astrobe, something has been artificially imposed on this natural order—the Programmed Persons. At the beginning of chapter twelve in *The Devil is Dead*, Lafferty says through the mouth of Wimbish A. McDeannott, a character invented for the sole purpose of lending his name to this chapter heading:

> There are but two sciences, the Science of God, and the Science of Man. Perhaps the soundest scientist who ever studied and produced among us was John de Yepes (St. John of the Cross). He studied the highest subject (Divinity) by the direct experimental method applicable (mysticism). Yet there are those who say that mysticism is the opposite of the scientific method. Latterly there are those who thrust back as 'soft sciences' these two basic sciences, and who bring

---

[10] Joseph Campbell, "Mythological Themes in Creative Literature and Art," in *Myths, Dreams, and Religion*, p. 155.

forward as 'hard science' a distant derivative with no sound claim to reality—the Science of Things. (DD, p. 135)

Slider, another member of Thomas More's party in *Past Master*, says that Astrobe is not the World, and that no promise was ever given to those of the Golden Utopia of Astrobe. They cannot even assume that they are strictly human, for no one of them knows how much of programmed descent is in those who regard themselves as old-line humans. The dying Metropolitan of Astrobe, however, the last representative of the Catholic Church on the planet, insists that Astrobe surely has the Promise. Slider realizes, moreover, that he feels he is coming near some truth when the Programmed Killers, the product of the Science of Things whose function it is to kill any who are false to the vision of Astrobe, pursue him. But when they let him alone, he knows that he is dealing in trivialities (PM, p. 75).

This Promise is the thing for which the historical Thomas More died the first time and for which he dies on Astrobe, thereby kindling the flame that rises to destroy the old world and effect the birth of the new. When the Programmed Persons attempt to "murder the thing [i.e., the Promise] on its death bed," Thomas revolts: "Whether there be Things Beyond I do not know. Ye'd forbid the mind to consider them. I forbid the forbidding" (PM, p. 164).

Where does the Promise lie on Golden Astrobe? Astrobe is described for Thomas by a précis machine, an encyclopedic commentator and guide given him for his use, as the perfect materialistic utopia:

> "There is every luxury and every interest available to everyone. There is almost perfect justice . . . . New dimensions of pleasure are achieved daily and almost hourly," the precis machine played. "All live in constant ecstasy. We are all one, all one being, the whole world of us, and we reach the heights of intense intercommunion. We come to have a single mind and a single spirit. We are everything. We are the living cosmos. The people of Astrobe do not dream at night,

for a dream is a maladjustment. We do not have an unconscious, as the ancient people had, for an unconscious is the dark side, and we are all light. For us there is no future. The future is now. There is no Heaven as the ancients believed; for many years we have been in the only after-life there is" (PM, P. 65).

In the development of this passage, the perfect fruit is revealed to contain a deadly worm. The perfect materialism of the original Thomas More *Utopia* is used by Lafferty as a springboard for his dystopia. In *Past Master*, More says that he wrote his Utopia as a bitter joke, and Lafferty makes us very aware of the irony inherent in the living presence of a creator whose invention now rebounds on him. This utopia denies the promise of anything Beyond—denying humanity the elements of the dark, the negative, the unconscious—and believing itself to contain its own perfection. It seems that imperfect man has at last created something more perfect than himself, and it threatens to destroy him. When Evita, as a child, decided to go to Hell, she at first committed all the old-fashioned abominations in her search. But, like the boy who had to travel around his planet to recognize his own house for the first time, Evita found Hell in Golden Astrobe of the Dream.

In describing this Golden Dream, the précis machine refuses to consider Cathead, calling it a cancer and dismissing it as something that will be dealt with by the Programmed Killers. Thomas is puzzled about the existence of this horrendous cancer. He has been caught up in the Astrobian dream, not recognizing his own joke, and cannot understand why more and more people every day leave the world of perfection to join the incredible misery of Cathead and Barrio. It is not until he is shown the back side of the tapestry of Golden Astrobe by the Nine Unknown programmed snakes who secretly manipulate Astrobe that Thomas at last has the answer for the existence of Cathead. The people who set it up, he says,

wanted life itself, however mean. They set up their own complex with every sanction against them. They built extreme suffering into it, as a man will smash his hand against a post in pain to prove that he is awake. They undercut and undersold the machine-mind men with their own lung's blood. Worse than any death is never having lived in life. I'd rather be a soul in Hell than nothing at all (PM, p. 151).

Besides the people of Cathead and Barrio, there is another group on Astrobe that maintains the dualism and the Promise that the Programmed Persons are trying to kill—the ansels, the oceanic men. Few symbols of the unconscious are as widespread as the ocean, and the mythological creatures associated with it are the often misunderstood and wrongly vilified projections of the "ghostliness" within us. There were no ansels on Astrobe when Earthmen came (none, at least, that were creatures of intellect and therefore human). Their beginnings have been garbled as legend, according to Rimrock, as our own beginnings have been, but their legend is that they are the people who climbed all the way to the sky, broke holes in it, and climbed out into a strange world that is above the sky, becoming different creatures with minds formed again. This vision is directly analogous to the search for higher consciousness that the men of Astrobe, like ourselves, should be making but are not. Instead, Rimrock says, "Regular people have sealed off the interior ocean that used to be in every man. They closed the ocean and ground up its monsters for fertilizer. That is why we so often enter into people's dreams. We take the place of the monsters they have lost" (PM. p. 73).

The real enemy of the Promise is thus not the old recension, though its people are often the monster children of Ahriman, as they are called in *The Devil is Dead*. Instead, the real enemy is to be found in what Kenneth Grant calls the Nightside of Eden. Grant is a *magickal*[11] initiate who has been

---

[11] Grant was one of the students of Aleister Crowley and adopted and spread his orthography of the word "magic." Crowley was concerned that the word had become associated with stage trickery and illusion, and he revived the old spelling, "Magick," to distinguish the Science of the Magi from all its counterfeits. The spelling has now become current in the occult sciences. See Kenneth

one of the major proponents of the *magickal* Renaissance, and in his book entitled Nightside of Eden he develops the thesis that

> the early mythologies, unable properly to comprehend the forces of Non-Being, cast them in a false mold from which they emerged as powers of 'evil.' In consequence, myth and legend are alive with demons, monsters, vampires, incubi, succubi, and a host of malignant entities all of which arc symbols that conceal unnamable, appalling gulfs and—to primordial man—unknowable concepts of Nothingness, Inner Space, Anti-Matter, and the ultimate horror of Absolute Absence. This 'other universe' that we cannot know—for we are it, in a sense too intimate to fathom—has been hinted at by Qabalists and Gnostics. Some of their strange doctrines are re-emerging today wearing new masks curiously similar to their ancient ones, yet with an altered facial cast suggesting affinities with even stranger speculations. In some way as yet inadequately understood, Da'ath would seem to be a 'black hole' or gateway to the parallel universe represented by the other side of the Tree of Life.[12]

The Tree of Life is a Cabalistic glyph that forms the basis of the Western mystical and occult tradition. It is a map of the consciousness of the universe and is an essential symbol in Western literature from Genesis through Blake to Joyce. There are two sides to the Tree: the right is the Pillar of Mercy, the left the Pillar of Severity; and the antithetical emanations that flow both vertically and horizontally are reconciled in a central pillar that leads from man up to the Limitless Light. In addition to the Tree of Life, we also see the Tree of Death, the back side of the tapestry, in both *Past*

Grant, *The Magical Revival* (New York: Samuel Weiser, 1973); and Aleister Crowley, *Book 4* (Dallas: Sangreal Foundation, 1972).

[12] Kenneth Grant, *Nightside of Eden* (London: Frederick Muller, 1977), p. 142.

Master and *The Devil is Dead*. In *Past Master*, the appalling gulf of Nothingness is presented directly as the Ouden, while in *The Devil is Dead*, we see it wearing those new masks so curiously similar to the ancient ones.

The true nature of the High Vision, the Astrobe Dream, is revealed to Thomas More by Pottscamp, member of both Inner Circles of Masters: "The Vision is the Golden Premise of Nothing Beyond; and the Conclusion is Holy Ouden, Nothing Here Either, Nothing Ever" (PM, p. 152). Having seen the Promise of Something Beyond, we now see the Promise of Nothing Beyond. The figure—if Nothingness may be so called—of the Ouden runs through the entire novel and is first introduced in one of the passage dreams, one that was "somehow left over" from the passage to Astrobe. The Paul-Thomas host that carries on the conversation with the shriveling presence of Ouden in the dream asks it which came first, the Ouden or the belief in it. Ouden replies "I was always, and the belief in me comes and goes. Ask the ansel [Rimrock]: was I not of the Ocean from the beginning?" According to Thales, everything came of water, and Homer speaks of Oceanus as both the "source of the gods" and as the "source of all things." Ouden therefore belongs to this primordial reality and insists that its nature has always been misunderstood: "All who encounter me make the mistake of misunderstanding my nothingness. It is a vortex. There is no quiet or static aspect to it. Consider me topologically. Do I not envelop all the universes? Consider them as turned inside out. Now everything is on the inside of my nothingness" (PM, p. 44).

The Ouden gained its foothold on utopian Astrobe through the Programmed Persons. Scrivener, who is partly a Programmed Person, and who ends his life an alien to both his recensions, tells a story told him by one of his grandmothers, the one from whom he has his mechanical descent. The Programmed Persons in their early days wished to have a mythos like the one humans had before they gave up hero tales altogether. A people cannot form themselves without a mythos such as the one of "a sleeping king who would one day awaken and rule again in a new golden age," and every Old Earth nation had one. So the early mechanical men searched the histories of Astrobe and of Old Earth trying to find a sleeping king "for their own solidarity":

> They settled on an old small broken gear train that had been taken from an Egyptian tomb. . . . Then Ouden came, the Celestial Nothingness. "Put away such toys as that," Ouden said, "I am your god and your king." And so he has been god and king for all Programmed Persons from that day till this. And quite soon he will be god and king of all beings of every sort. But we were his first people, we the mechanicals. He grows and grows and all the other kings die (PM, p. 111).

The Tree of Life in Cabala consists of ten spheres, three each on the two pillars and four in the center, of which Malkuth, or the kingdom in which we live, is the lowest, and the glorious creative light of the top sphere, Kether, or Crown, filters down through the nine higher spheres. Analogies to this structure are of course to be found elsewhere, as in the nine-member Ennead of the Egyptians or the nine Roman gods. On the Tree of Life there is sometimes represented an eleventh sphere, Da'ath, which is the gateway mentioned by Grant, among many others, to the back side of the Tree. In *Past Master*, Thomas escapes the pursuit of the Programmed Killers through a gateway that suddenly appears before him, and he finds himself in total darkness:

> There were nine of the Things there. Thomas had learned to think of them as Things in his last defiant surge back to reason. What were they? What was their form?
> Men. Men seen from the other side. From the back side? Yes, in the sense, that a tapestry may be seen from its back side, the same picture but rough and deformed. These things were the deformation of mankind (PM. p. 143).

These nine snakes are the nine lower spheres of the reverse Tree, and an empty chair has been left to represent their Crown, Ouden. They have the appearance of

Programmed Persons, and they foster this belief in Thomas. In beginning a completely false story of the origins and nature of their people, however, Pottscamp says:

> "We turn aside for a moment in the explanation, Thomas. Hear one thing and then forget it:
>
> "You 'believe' a little bit at times, Thomas; and with your tatters of faith you guess a little who we are. According to your ancient belief we are Devils. What we call ourselves is another thing, but we are older than our own manufacture and older than our programming. These are houses, and well-made ones, that we found swept and garnished; and we moved into them. This particular bit of information, Thomas, is that part which you will forget most quickly and most thoroughly. See, you have forgotten it already."
>
> Pottscamp had seemed to stutter in the inside-the-maw-no-light that illumined all things there, and he went on. . . . (PM, p. 147)

In *The Devil is Dead*, a chosen assortment of old recension humans and the group of nonhuman figures from the dark side of the tapestry, led by Seaworthy and the Devil, form the passengers and crew of the Brunhilde. There is not a single new recension human on board, and indeed, only one—Doll Delancey—in the novel. The forces of the dark Tree are literally devils, and the stowaway Manuel says that "there is a source, but we do not know what country it is in or where it gets its particular venom" (DD, pp. 45-47). Although the source is not on board the *Brunhilde*—we learn in the second part of the book that Seaworthy's group is relegated to the fringes of the conspiracy after Papadiabolous dies—the ship is certainly a focal point. The nature of this group, which consists of Seaworthy and the Devil, William Gerecke, Peter Wirt, and the captain, Orestes Gonof, is shown in a passage from Galen that Lafferty quotes at the head of chapter eleven:

> Some believe that the Tityroi are not of our world, that they are of another world beyond the moon. Yet I believe that they are born of women of this world.

Daemons, who may be of worlds beyond the moon, beget Tityroi or Satyroi on world women. Their children are hardly to be told from mankind, though they have ravening passions for the destruction of mankind and have always a seeming of ape or goat or wolf or panther or other animal. They are the Satyrs. Those of the first generation, those begotten by the Daemons directly, are fertile and generate offspring. But those of the second generation, the offspring of Tityroi on Earth women, are not fertile, do not generate offspring, though they are in appearance and passion similar to the first generation. For this reason, the race must be renewed, and in every century the Daemons must come back to women of the world. In our own time, a Daemon begot children on thirteen women in Calchedon in Bithynoi in a single night.

—*GALEN,* Techne Iatrike

And remember, passerby, that Galen himself studied medicine under a man named Satyrus. Whence had the teacher his name? Whence had Galen his information? (DD, p. 123)

The original Papadiabolous (or Papa Devil), and the twin who takes his place in the *Brunhilde* unbeknownst to Seaworthy, are the sons of the son of the devil, Ifreann Noonan Columkill Gregorovitch Papadiabolous Chortovitch, whose history is given in this book (and a story of his life in another Lafferty novel, *The Flame is Green*).The substituting twin Papa Devil has the appearance of a curious goat, and the original Papa Devil was a working revolutionary, as his father was. He was one of a group of nine "men" that worked under the direction of the old man Ifreann (which means "Hell" in Irish). Again, this is analogous to the Tree of Death. When Finnegan in his gargoyle or cat aspect climbs up the side of a building to spy on: the enemy, he looks inside at a "coven or meeting of gargoyles . . . . Eleven of them, all of them men or whatever of some age and authority" (DD, p. 125). Eleven is the number used in all Western magical rituals of a kliphothic, that is, unbalanced, nature.

Both elements of darkness, Devils and Elder Race, are

destroyed in the end, however, and it is left to Doll Delancey to pick up the threads of the fight. She is the representative of the conscious, temporal recension that is not content to let the battle rage through the aeons, who wants a climax to the story and a salvation of the world. Man cannot feel satisfied that the eternal conflict rages, since man is not eternal. In man's unconscious, however, there is no time, and the golden age that was is identical to the golden age that is to come. Creation is as much a future event as a past occurrence. As Mircea Eliade says:

> For something genuinely new to begin, the vestiges and ruins of the old cycle must be completely destroyed . . . . To be sure, all these nostalgias and beliefs are already present in the mythico-ritual scenarios of the annual renewal of the World. But from the protoagricultural stage of culture on, there was a growing acceptance of the idea that there are also real (not merely ritual) destructions and re-creations of the World, that there is a "return to the origin" in the literal sense, that is, a relapse of the Cosmos to the amorphous, chaotic state, followed by a new cosmogony.[13]

Thus, *The Devil is Dead*, like *Finnegans Wake*, is a circular book. It begins with Finnegan sitting on a sidewalk talking to Saxon Seaworthy as the sun comes up. "That may have been the beginning of the world." Finnegan says subsequently to Anastasia, "but I can't prove it" (DD, p. 14), and Doll's concluding poem represents both the creation that day of a new world and a return to the world of the beginning.

In bringing about the creation of the new world and resolution of conflict in Lafferty's works, complete reduction forces a decisive action on the part of the protagonist. Since man has the responsibility of free will, he must plant the seeds of the new world himself, and action is thus the necessary response to conflict. Thus, in *Past Master*, the hawklike Fabian

---

[13] Mircea Eliade, *Myth and Reality*, trans. Willard R. Trask (New York and Evanston: Harper & Row, 1963), pp. 51-52.

Foreman of the human Inner Circle has engineered the ethical crisis that will force Thomas More into his moment of complete honesty, and as Thomas sits in his cell waiting for rescue or for death, Foreman explains that he has done this to him because "it is no metaphor about the worlds ending today. ...Or not entirely metaphor. The worlds do die periodically..." (PM, p. 178). Foreman has noticed that the cycles between Worlds were once very long, but that they shorten and shorten, and now a World runs its course every five hundred years. He refers to the birth of Christ and the coincident birth of the Late Empire. Five hundred years later, the Empire died and was followed by the Lower Middle Ages. The High Middle Ages succeeded, and the death of Thomas More signaled the beginning of the Industrial Age of Old Earth. The first settlement of Astrobe became the New World, and Old Earth lost importance and meekly followed Astrobe's leadership. Now the time has come again, and Foreman knows that this birth will be extremely difficult, perhaps impossible. So he has planted the mustard seed: "The previous yeastings were all such simple things, but they were necessary. *There really is this necessity* that a small quantity of the immaterial (however it is named in the equation) be added to the mass every five hundred years or so. . . . Your death and the reaction to it will be the trigger, the mustard seed. We plant it now" (PM, p. 183; emphasis in original). Finnegan , in *The Devil is Dead*, is in the same situation—his death, engineered by a spy named X, who commands the forces of the Elder Race in the final battle, is the "yeast of the immaterial" necessary to enable Doll to continue the battle for man's spiritual rise. Though it means becoming a traitor to his recension, a renegade, Finnegan chooses to act.

The function of the archetypes of humanity and the purpose of their inter-play in Lafferty's works is to ensure the addition of the yeast of the immaterial, of the transcendent yet immanent Promise of Something Beyond, to the World of human experience. Lafferty's mythos, based on the mysticism of the early and medieval Church, permeates his imaginary worlds and lays a foundation of primordial reality that resolves into an expression of the continuing ambiguity of the human condition. As I mentioned, however, although

Lafferty's knowledge of his subject is extensive, his attempts to meld the deeper concerns of myth with the lightness of a folktale style often result, particularly in *The Devil is Dead*, in an unfortunate, sometimes frustrating, obscurity. He has been accused by the *New York Times* of "obfuscation," and the criticism, though somewhat obfuscatory itself, is not without justification.[14] His mythos, however, is well worth the effort of the reader who is willing to delve into it, and Lafferty's vision exerts an ever-increasing influence in science fiction's explorations of man's mythic traditions.

This work © 2015 Dena C. Bain Taylor.

Dena C. Bain Taylor is the Director of the Health Sciences Writing Centre at the University of Toronto. She earned a BA (Hon) from the University of Toronto, an MA at University of Waterloo, and a PhD from the University of Toronto, as well as an ARCT diploma from the Royal Conservatory of Music of Toronto. Her most recent publication is Writing Skills for Nursing and Midwifery Students (London: Sage Publications, 2012). Among her professional associations are the Canadian Association for the Study of Discourse and Writing and the Canadian Society for the Study of Language and Learning. Her faculty page is at: http://physical.utoronto.ca/FacultyAndResearch/Meet_the_Faculty/Taylor.aspx.

[This essay was originally published in Extrapolation 23:2 (1982), pp. 159–174. It appears here by courtesy of the author Dena C. Bain Taylor and the publishers of Extrapolation: http://online.liverpooluniversitypress.co.uk/loi/extr]

---

[14] "R.A. Lafferty: An Interview," p. 3.

"I didn't mean to lie, I forgot about that thing,"
Clarence Little-Saddle said.
R. A. Lafferty, "Narrow Valley"

Illustration "War Bonnet" © 2015 Anthony Ryan Rhodes

Thus We Frustrate Charlemagne
by Paul Kincaid

This is another of my "In Short" columns. It originally appeared in *Vector* 275, Spring 2014.

I am not now, nor have ever been, a Catholic. I accept, therefore, that there might be niceties of theology that may pass me by in some fictions by Catholic writers. Nevertheless, one thing I do not expect to come across in Catholic fiction is existential despair. The mercy of God, the hope of heaven, offer the chance of salvation no matter how bad things may get. There is always a way out. One of the two great Catholic science fiction writers of the late 20th century (by which I mean that their Catholicism was integral to their science fiction) was Gene Wolfe, and in his work there is always a new sun. But in many of the stories by the second great Catholic science fiction writer, R.A. Lafferty, there was no new sun. Time and again his stories trap us in endless repetition in which we can go back to the beginning and start all over again, but we cannot escape. There is no exit from stories like "All Pieces of a River Shore" or "The World as Will and Wallpaper" or, one of his finest stories, "Thus We Frustrate Charlemagne." And the fact that these stories are cast as comedies only makes the inability to get out of the world, to find heaven, that much more suffocating.

"Thus We Frustrate Charlemagne" was first published in *Galaxy* in 1967. Much of Lafferty's best work appeared in *Galaxy* and in Damon Knight's *Orbit*, because these were the edgier, less conventional markets for science fiction in America at the time, and writers don't come much edgier or less conventional than R.A. Lafferty. His usual technique was to present some extravagantly impossible situation—the actual banks of the Mississippi reproduced as a sideshow diorama, a narrow valley which warped space—and then have its consequences explored, often by members of a recurring cast who were more caricatures than characters. The grand idiocy of his invention and the silliness of his characters made the stories seem as if they were a joke on the genre. I suspect that is how many at the time would have read "Thus We Frustrate Charlemagne," a comic exaggeration of a familiar time travel paradox. But I don't think that was ever how Lafferty saw them. There was always something darker and more serious under the comedy. Which may be why, as a writer, he is so hard to pigeonhole.[1]

The familiar names are all here: Gregory Smirnov, Willy McGilly, Audifax O'Hanlon, Diogenes Pontifex, Aloysius Shiplap. I used to wonder whether there was some significance in the fact that Raphael Aloysius Lafferty used part of his own name for a member of this repertory company of caricatures. Did he, perhaps, stand as in some way representative of the author? But in fact Shiplap is no less roughly delineated, no less silly in action or pronouncement, than any of his fellows. Lafferty was simply using his own name for comic effect. They are joined by Epiktistes the Ktistec machine, Lafferty's baroque and at times rather incoherent version of an AI, that would feature in a number of stories and the novel *Arrive at Easterwine* (1971). Indeed, as this story makes explicit, Epikt (as the name was often abbreviated) was as much a fetish object as it was a piece of technology; but then, technology in Lafferty's work was rarely separated from superstition. But even this hugely complex, hugely powerful device is made out to be comic: "Epikt had also given himself human speech of a sort, a blend of Irish and Jewish and Dutch comedian patter from ancient vaudeville. Epikt was a comic to his last para-DNA relay" (171). Although Lafferty is, as always, at pains to point out that the assembly represented "the finest minds and judgements in the world" (172), everything from their names to their petty behaviour undermines any confidence we may have in them. In Lafferty's world, intelligence or genius is not necessarily something to be applauded.

---

[1] All subsequent quotations are taken from "Thus We Frustrate Charlemagne" by R.A. Lafferty, in *Nine Hundred Grandmothers* (New York: Ace, 1970), pp. 171-184.

Their plan is to change history: "We are going to tamper with one small detail in past history and note its effect" (172). Specifically, Epiktistes will send an avatar back in time to kill the man who betrayed Charlemagne at Roncevalles in 778, and who thus effectively caused Christian Europe to be cut off from Islamic and Jewish scholarship. It is interesting to note that Lafferty is careless about the technology of his story. He has no interest in telling us anything about how time travel might be possible, not even using the sort of gobbledegook that Willy McGilly and Audifax O'Hanlon and their fellows commonly employ. It is, rather, a form of wish fulfilment. All it takes is for someone to say "Push the button" and "From his depths, Epiktistes the Ktistec machine sent out an Avatar, partly of mechanical and partly of ghostly construction" (175). And that is the extent of the scientific explanation that Lafferty offers. In contrast, he spends a good part of three pages detailing the delicate web of alliances that held across France and Spain prior to the battle of Roncevalles, and how the consequences of that battle changed the access to learning across medieval Europe.

As they are preparing for the experiment, Willy McGilly reveals that, when he was a boy, he went back in time and, with a dart made of slippery elm wood, killed: "King Wu of the Manchu, Pope Adrian VII, President Hardy of our own country, King Marcel of Auvergne, the philosopher Gabriel Toeplitz. It's a good thing we got them. They were a bad lot" (174). When the others protest that they have never heard of any of these people, Epiktistes backs him up: "Where do you think I got the idea?" (174). In this exchange, it seems that we have the whole plot of this story laid out in advance. Someone changes history, and no-one can remember how things were before the change. Except that it isn't quite like that: because obviously Willy McGilly remembers both histories or he wouldn't have been able to recall his exploits; and Epiktistes, who played no part in the events, remembers it also.

There follows a quick survey of the state of things before the change. There are eight humans plus Epiktistes; they are in a "middle-sized town with half a dozen towers of pastel-colored brick" (174-5); there are two shows in town that Valery hasn't seen; and the arts have never been in meaner shape. This means that, as soon as the change has happened, we can see the difference. There are, immediately, ten humans and three machines; they are in "a fine large town with two dozen imposing towers of varicolored limestone and midland marble" (176); there are now two dozen shows that Valery hasn't seen; and the arts have never been in finer shape. In other words, as we can see from outside the time of the story, the world has apparently been changed for the better. But our slightly revised cast of central characters are not aware of any change, even Epiktistes "can't see any change in anything either" (175). As Willy McGilly, so often Lafferty's mouthpiece, sums it up: "The very bulk of achievement is stupefying ... The experiment, of course, was a failure, and I'm glad. I like a full world" (178, my ellipsis).

And yet, despite their evident satisfaction with the world as it (now) is, they decide to continue with the experiment. Abruptly, the moral underpinning of the story is transformed. Willy McGilly's initial efforts to change history removed from the record characters who were "a bad lot". The group's first experiment was designed to improve the world by facilitating the spread of human knowledge and thus eliminating the Dark Ages. Even their target for assassination, a traitor whose actions brought about a massacre, was no innocent and so might be considered worthy of his fate. So far, what has been done can be presented as morally worthy. But the decision to continue with the experiment is not made for the betterment of humankind, but out of the sin of pride, and hang the consequences: "And if there is a present left to us after that, we will make a third attempt the following day" (178). Even their new choice of target illustrates this moral compromise. John Lutterell is no traitor, no facilitator of mass slaughter, but rather the sickly former chancellor of Oxford University who, in this history, bested William of Ockham and changed the intellectual underpinning of European thought in the Middle Ages. It is clear that this choice is not only morally dubious, it is recklessly dangerous: "we would have liked Ockham. He was charming, and he was wrong, and perhaps we will destroy the world yet" (179).

Interestingly, it is as they decide to reinstate William of Ockham's thought within the philosophy of medieval Europe that we get the first hint of a bleed-through from the different timelines. As Gregory Smirnov says: "There is something amiss here, though. It is as though I remembered when things were not so stark with Ockham, as though, in some variant, Ockham's Terminalism did not mean what we know that it did mean" (178). Lafferty's convoluted syntax here representing the convoluted temporal structure of the story. Naturally, this sense of dis-ease doesn't stop anyone, and the presentiments of doom that have undercut this last section of course come to fruition.

Suddenly the group is reduced to four: "the three humans and the ghost Epikt, who was a kachenko mask with a speaking tube" (181), and they are reduced to stone age conditions, "nude in the crude" (181) as Lafferty puts it, such overt rhymes and rhythms being a characteristic feature of his prose. Again Lafferty both extols and undermines the intelligence of his characters, the three humans are the "finest minds in the world ... (the *only* humans in the world unless you count those in the other valleys)" (181, my ellipsis). While Epiktistes the AI is here reframed as a cult object: "We made his frame out of the best sticks, and we plaited his face out of the finest weeds and grasses. We chanted him full of magic and placed all our special treasures in his cheek pouches" (181). Even at its most technologically advanced, Epiktistes is as much magical as scientific, so this new version seems to belong with the two versions of Epiktistes we've already encountered. Science, in Lafferty's stories, is never differentiated from magic, and the work of the characters he apostrophizes as "the finest minds" is as much ritual observance as it is any sort of scientific endeavour. Lafferty was probably the most anti-scientific science fiction writer of the latter part of the twentieth century, but then, his work is only classed as science fiction because it does not really fit anywhere else.

The scene that follows in this third version of reality, therefore, is in many ways an encapsulation of all that has gone before. The humans are reduced to basics, eating hickory nuts and "rump of skunk" (181), helpless despite, or perhaps because of, their intelligence. They are unable to see their world, unable fully to function within it, because of their desire to change it. And the endless regressive trap has been sprung by the fetish Epiktistes, the object of their own manufacture in which is invested all their scientific belief and endeavour (here recast as superstition), and which can address them only when they provide the voice. They are the architects of their own despair. It is, in John Clute's term, a godgame, but a game in which god is absent, replaced by the false god Epiktistes. And because god is absent, unlike, for instance, in the godgames of Gene Wolfe, there is no way out of the trap. It is a totally enclosed world, a world that can only represent existential despair.

In this stone age reality, the three humans recall the legend of the folk hero Willy McGilly who used a dart of slippery elm wood, and with this model in mind send the ghost Epikt back in time to kill the original Avatar of the original Epiktistes. And suddenly everything is restored to what seems to be how things were when the story began. As before, there is an ill-formed sense of how things had been otherwise: "'Is it done?' Charles Cogsworth asked in excitement. 'It must have. I'm here. I wasn't in the last one.'" (183). Yet this suggestion of slippage between realities is immediately contradicted by the fact that, as ever, they have no awareness that anything has changed. They do not even know if they tried to change history.

> "Push the button, Epikt!" Diogenes barked. "I think I missed part of it. Let's try again."
> "Oh, no, no!" Valery forbade. "Not again. That way is rump of skunk and madness." (184)

But is it? If no-one knows whether they have changed history, no-one can know that they shouldn't do it. The godgame can only be repeated.

This work is © 2015 by Paul Kincaid

Paul Kincaid is the author of What It Is We Do When We Read Science Fiction *and* Call and Response. *He has received the Thomas Clareson Award from the SFRA and the Best Non-Fiction Award from the BSFA.*

"Oh, no, no!" Valery forbade. "Not again. That way is rump of skunk and madness."

R. A. Lafferty, "Thus We Frustrate Charlemagne"

Illustration © 2015 Anthony Ryan Rhodes

R.A. Lafferty, Sir Thomas More, and the Problems of Utopia

by Robert Bee

R.A. Lafferty is one of the great eccentric geniuses of science fiction whose work remains woefully neglected. Lafferty was a devout Catholic who started writing in his 40s, itself unusual in a genre filled with young fans and writers who tend to publish in their teens or early 20s. Despite his late start, Lafferty wrote thirty-two novels and over two hundred short stories, a great deal of which have only been published in small press chapbooks by enthusiastic fans and editors. No one knows exactly how much Lafferty wrote because much of his writing is too unusual for the commercial presses and remains in manuscript.

To obtain Lafferty's work, readers have to prowl used book sites and stores for battered paperbacks. The Wildside Press has done a service by reprinting several of his books, including the Hugo and Nebula award nominated novel Past Master, which is now available in a sturdy and large trade paperback edition. A careful examination of *Past Master* provides an opportunity to reassess Lafferty's writing.

Past Master has been neglected by fans but highly praised by writers and critics. Judith Merrill said of the novel:

> It is a minor miracle that a serious philosophical and speculative work should be written so colorfully and so lyrically. There is, happily, no way to categorize the book: it has elements of science fiction, of pure fantasy, of poetry, of historical fiction; it is sharply critical and marvelously gentle.

Samuel R. Delany commented:

> The Lafferty madness is peppered with nightmare: witches, lazarus-lions, hydras, porsches's-panthers,

programmed killers that never fail, and a burlesqued black mass. One hears of black comedy? There are places in Past Master where humor goes positively ultraviolet.

The novel, a serious exploration of the Utopian genre and the collapse of values in the modern world, deserves the praise. Lafferty creates his own genre by combining science fiction, fantasy, tall tales, and even medieval allegory. Lafferty let his writing go wherever his wit and fancy led him, with little regard for narrative convention. Many readers—even experienced SF fans—find his work obscure and difficult as Lafferty ignores genre conventions and refuses to suspend disbelief or world-build. Lafferty's work—which is rarely realistic and relies on unusual narrative structures and events—should be approached like surrealism, with the expectation that anything can happen.

In *Past Master*, the desperate, perplexed committee that rules Astrobe, a futuristic attempt to create a Utopia, is overwhelmed by the planet's problems. The committee uses a time machine to bring Sir Thomas More from the past and make him world president because Astrobe needs an honest man and a symbol.

According to the committee, Sir Thomas More is a man who had a completely honest moment: when Henry VIII asked Thomas to support his divorce and the king's supremacy over the English church, Thomas refused to support it, even though it cost him his life. Thomas was made a saint by the Catholic Church because of his martyrdom.[1]

---

[1] Sir Thomas More's honesty is an important part of his historical reputation. Sir William Roper—who was married to More's beloved daughter Margaret—wrote the Life of More, a lively biography that emphasized More's religious devotion and tends towards hagiography (so some of its claims should be taken with a grain of salt). According to Roper, More was one of the few great men of his time who did not enrich himself through bribes. He told one of his sons-in-law, "if the parties [of a legal case] will at my hand call for justice, then were it my father stood on one side and the devil on the other side (if his cause were good), the devil should have right" (237 Life of More). In at least one legal case, More ruled against another of his sons-in-law when he was in the wrong, and

More was also the author of Utopia, the book that created the genre of imagining perfect worlds. Over the course of Past Master, he discovers that the strengths and weaknesses of Astrobe resemble his own imaginary world.

On Astrobe there is no sickness, poverty, misery, guilt, repression, or superstition. Justice is nearly perfect, requiring few courts since crime is rare. Humans enjoy freedom and every luxury. Citizens can pursue their interests in any of the arts and sciences. Travel over the planet is instantaneous. Even the weather is controlled.

When Thomas first sees Astrobe, he is astounded:

> The riches of civilized Astrobe were almost beyond comprehending. Thomas had a quick eye and a rapid mind, but he was dazzled by the wonders. Here were the homes and buildings of many millions of people, grand city after grand city, all in luxury and beauty and ease. Nor was it only the buildings and perfected land and parks. It was the people. They were elegant and large and incredibly urbane, full of tolerant amusement for the rolling spectacle, of a superior mien, of a shattering superiority. They were the true Kings of Astrobe. Every man was a king, every woman was at least queenly (55).

Overwhelmed by the beauty and splendor of Astrobe, Thomas comments: "For good or bad, this is what all folks have wanted from the beginning" (55).

Strangely though, Thomas discovers that the people of Astrobe are discontented. Millions of citizens migrate to Cathead, the Barrio, and the feral regions, unregulated areas outside golden Astrobe where life is nasty, brutish, and short. Cathead has become the planet's largest city as people abandon the most pleasant life ever devised for an existence of misery. No one is forced to enter the poverty of Cathead:

> The people had entered the Cathead thing by free choice, and they could give it up any instant they

---

this occurred at a time when justice was generally dispensed by family connections and bribes.

wished. The people who coughed up their lungs at the terrible labor there were low poor people who could be high rich people by sundown tonight if they wished. They were hard surly folks who had entered the slavery deliberately, and more were entering it all the time. They went out in the sea-harvest boats that made old-fashioned garbage scows seem like dream ships. They worked twenty hours a day on the noisome sea, and three years of such work would kill the strongest (155-156).

Thomas's initial reaction to Astrobe is perplexity: how can the people of Cathead reject happiness when they have been offered it on a platter? Why choose misery over a golden life? The people of the slums inform Thomas that a miserable life is better than no life at all. As he asks questions and explores this brave new world, Thomas discovers that the best people on the planet, those of finest intellect and judgment, have migrated to Cathead.

Thomas falls in love with the golden dream and is contemptuous of those who reject it. He promises to pull Cathead down brick by brick and remove the cancer. He "spent entire days marveling at the wonderful ways of Astrobe. And yet he wanted to look more deeply into the workings of the thing, to examine its more distant roots and sources" (85-86). Although Thomas is enthralled, he's an independent-enough thinker to examine it root and branch, and finds himself wondering if is it possible the dissenters have a point that he just cannot see.

According to an educational computer, the précis machine, everyone in Astrobe lives

> ...in constant ecstasy. We come to have a single mind and a single spirit. The people of Astrobe do not dream at night, for a dream is a maladjustment. We do not have an unconscious, as the ancient people had, for an unconscious is the dark side, and we are all light. For us there is no future. The future is now (80).

In its reiteration of Astrobe's perfections, the educational computer has alerted us to its flaws. Humans do not want to live in a world without dreams, or without an unconscious, or even without a dark side. The future should never be now, because then there is no opportunity for change, creation, or achievement. Astrobe maintains its perfect, unchanging world by crushing individuality and molding everyone into a single mind. Telepathic, programmed killers patrol the planet and kill anyone whose thoughts run against the Astrobe dream, thus creating a world where even thought is not free. Lafferty demonstrates one of the problems of the Utopian genre: maintaining a perfect world often requires totalitarian measures that destroy the perfection.

On Astrobe: "There were no individuals with sharp edges, there were no dissenting or pernicious elements, there was the high flat plane of excellence in all things. What can you say against a world that has gained every goal ever set? And there was pleasant termination available as soon as a touch of weariness set in" (82). Strangely though, Thomas had "to hold onto [himself] with both hands every time [he] pass[ed] a termination booth" (82).

Why does Astrobe weary its citizens until they flee to slums or clamber into termination booths? As Thomas attempts to unravel these mysteries, he discovers that politics on Astrobe have degenerated into a sorry joke, and spectacle: the recent World Presidents include Mr. X, the Masked Marvel, the Asteroid Midas, and the Hawk-Man from Helios, names reminiscent of Roman gladiators or "medieval" American wrestlers. The committee that brought him to Astrobe plans to use him as a front. Thomas is introduced to the people as the "Past Master," another short-lived entertainment for a sodden mass that has few interests other than meaningless pleasures. Yet Thomas insists that *he* will not be a puppet for powerful men, or the planet's machines; he will *preside.*

As the novel progresses, Sir Thomas More develops into the most complex and well-rounded character in Lafferty's corpus. Lafferty tends to create characters that are symbols more than people, but Thomas comes through as an interesting person: a rational Renaissance humanist with an agile, open mind, and an earthy sense of humor.[2] More also is an ethical and honest man who would rather die than support something that goes against his conscience.

Lafferty's More bears an interesting relation to the historical figure, who has fascinated a number of writers, including Robert Bolt in *A Man for All Seasons* (which was also made into an excellent movie). More is remembered as a writer because of Utopia, a book that is partly a traveler's tale and partly a philosophical dialogue between More, his friend Peter Gilles, and an imaginary traveler Raphael Hythloday. Raphael describes Utopia: an island he visited in the New World where the people have created a rationally planned state where religious tolerance is practiced, divorce because of mutual incompatibility is accepted, a communist economic system is enacted, and the aristocracy is abolished. Everyone works six hours a day, and the material benefits are spread equally throughout the population. More coined the word "Utopia" by punning on two Greek phrases, "no place" and "good place," making it difficult to discern whether More meant his Utopia to be an ideal world, or an entertainment describing an impossible world.

At the end of the book, More disputes many of Raphael's points, claiming that without private property people will not work hard, and without an aristocracy a society cannot achieve greatness. More left his Utopia deliberately ambiguous—in sixteenth century England, someone expressing radical ideas could be hung, drawn, and quartered, so even if More agreed with Raphael's points it would be politically injudicious to admit it. Putting the description of Utopia into the mouth of an imaginary traveler and then denying its more controversial features gave More plausible deniability.

Interpreting More's Utopia is complicated by the fact

---

[2] An aspect of More's personality that Lafferty portrays well is his renowned sense of humor. When he was a youth, he would amuse the court of Cardinal Wolsey by walking on stage during plays and creating impromptu parts for himself. He was immensely fond of court jesters or fools, which were certainly an example of the coarse, earthy humor of the day. Thomas's comments and jests in the novel illustrate this side of his character.

that his behavior as a public figure contradicted the ideals of his book. He was a heresy-hunter rather than a religiously tolerant man. He supported the aristocracy and worked for the king most of his life. He eventually lost his head because he refused to support a divorce that most of the political and religious authorities of his day endorsed.

The ambiguities of Utopia and More's life have fascinated commentators for centuries. Socialists have often read Utopia as a "good place," a blueprint for a communist society, whereas Catholics tend to view it as "no place," an impossible world that satirizes the evils of its time.

Lafferty's novel—partly a response to More's book, and partly an examination of utopias in general—attacks the socialist reading of More's novel. In Past Master, More claims that he "wrote in bitter and laughing irony of that sickest of all possible worlds"(33), and is surprised that his book has been misunderstood. When the précis machine tells More of the material plenty and the socialist egalitarianism of Astrobe, More responds, "I invented [Utopia]. It was a bitter joke. It was how not to build a world" (81).

As Thomas finds out more about Astrobe, he feels like a science fiction writer who lives in his own sour joke of a world. The flaws of Utopia and Astrobe are similar in that they both destroy individuality and privacy.

In Utopia everyone shares the work, eats in communal dining halls, and lives in identical houses and cities. All houses are open to the public and devoid of privacy. In More's Utopia, despite the apparent justice and equality, inhabitants suffer from a complete lack of personal freedom: they cannot travel without permission, and everyone watches everyone else. Many of the minor, frivolous pleasures of life are banished; for example, clothing is uniform and devoid of ostentation.[3]

---

[3] More was attracted to the Utopian scorn for luxury because of his religious upbringing. He spent part of his youth in a monastery and developed great respect for the monks' devotion. More considered joining the religious orders until his father pushed him into the law, and wore a hairshirt most of his life, even as his successful career brought him much wealth. When More's favorite daughter Margaret visited him in the Tower during his

On Astrobe the lack of privacy and individuality is even more pronounced: computers read your thoughts and kill you if you deviate from the Astrobe ideal. The Open Mind Act is a law that gives anyone on Astrobe the right to use a telepathy machine and "dial up" another citizen and read his or her mind so that even one's thoughts are not one's own. Maintaining the egalitarian, unchanging worlds of Astrobe and Utopia requires constant spying and regulation of the citizen's movements, actions, words, and even thoughts.

Thomas announces early in the novel that he will study Astrobe until he finds the real king, the puppeteer pulling everyone's string. He discovers—as is common in Lafferty's work—conspiracies within conspiracies. At the beginning of the novel, a small committee of powerful men appears to control the planet, but Thomas peels away layers of deceit to discover that the mechanical, programmed men really run the world, and that most humans have become as programmed and mechanical as their masters.

The machines horrify Thomas by informing him that neither they nor people have consciousness. Thomas feels that without consciousness human existence has no meaning or value, whereas to the machines humans are nothing but cogs in a mechanical universe. The great theme of Lafferty's writing is the collapse of values in the modern world, and in this novel he portrays a machine-dominated world drowning in nihilism. The pervading sense of meaninglessness drives millions to abandon the material plenty of Astrobe for Cathead, where they feel their existence can have some purpose, despite the poverty.

Astrobe's rational machines cannot understand many

---

imprisonment, he told her: "I believe, Meg, that they that have put me here think they have done me a high displeasure. But I assure you on my faith, mine own dear daughter, if it had not been for my wife and you that are my children, whom I count the chief part of my charge, I would not have failed, long ere this, to have closed myself in so narrow a room and narrower too [he meant a monk's cell]" (Roper, *Life of More*, 261). More's Utopians were as austere as he was. The Utopians were contemptuous of gold and jewelry. Children were given gold as baubles, but they were expected to outgrow them. Criminals and slaves were weighed down by gold because wearing gold or jewelry was considered a sign of immaturity and infamy.

facets of human consciousness; creativity and faith have largely been banned from Astrobe. For all its material progress, Astrobe only offers half a life, with no room for creativity, dreaming, or art. The wellspring of human consciousness, the unconscious, is banished by the rational machines as an aberration. Lafferty does a remarkably good job portraying a society in which humans are given every luxury and pleasure, but find their existence miserable.

Science Fiction is always as much about the author's own time as about the future, and Lafferty's future "Utopia" is a critique of the modern world as a time of material plenty and spiritual impoverishment, in which politics and values are degraded into spectacle.

Lafferty's concern with nihilism undoubtedly derives from his Catholicism. One of the problems of Astrobe is the death of religion. No one on Astrobe attends Mass; it is out of place on a world so rational. Even before the Church died it degenerated into a joke and a spectacle. The only believers in the Mass abandoned Astrobe for the miseries of Cathead and the Barrio. However, Lafferty's opposition to nihilism is based on a broader set of concerns than religion. He feels that the modern world has caused a deterioration in all values, producing people who don't believe in anything.

Lafferty's More replicates his historical end by dying a martyr. The novel telegraphs that ending through obvious foreshadowing; suspense was never Lafferty's strong point, and he's much more interested in his theories and ideas than in the plot. More opposes a law the Programmed People create banning any belief in a beyond, either God or an afterlife. Since Astrobe is perfect, the Programmed People argue there is no need to desire anything beyond, that belief is regressive much like the unconscious or dreams. More prefers to die rather than sign that law, which has as its real purpose to crush the small remnants of the human spirit.

Thomas's martyrdom results in the people rioting against Astrobe, and overthrowing the rule of the programmed persons. More's sacrifice shows the people of the future that dying for a set of values is better than a pointless life, even if that life has every material satisfaction. There was a tradition among Renaissance humanists that the value of a person's life is determined by how he or she faces death. A man willing to face death and meet his/her maker has lived a just life. Michel Montaigne's essay, "To Philosophize is to Learn to Die," is an excellent analysis of that tradition. By bringing that Renaissance tradition into his future world, Lafferty contrasts the hollow, pleasure-filled lives of the Utopians to a devout person willing to die for a set of values. More's death helps humanity survive a dire period and offers the possibility for humans to create new meaning and new societies in the future.

Past Master is a novel laden with ideas, theories, and a colorful robust future. It offers innovative narrative techniques, and criticizes the genre of Utopianism for obsessing over material progress at the expense of inner development. Overall, Past Master is a novel so dense with ideas that it rewards both careful reading and rereading.

Works Referenced

Lafferty, R.A. *Past Master*. Wildside Press: Berkeley Heights, N.J., 1999.

More, Sir Thomas. *The Utopia of Sir Thomas More including Roper's Life of More and Letters of More and His Daughter Margaret*. Modernized Texts, with Notes and Introduction by Mildred Campbell. Classics Club: Roslyn, N.Y., 1947.

Robert Bee is a freelance writer living in New Jersey. For his day job he manages a library in Trenton. He has published over 30 short stories and a dozen book reviews in magazines, e-zines and anthologies such as Outer Darkness, Parchment Symbols, Letter Magazine, Blue Murder, Parageography, Alienskin, Glyph, Cabal Asylum, Welcome to Nod, Nocturnal Ooze, Dark Krypt, Kings of the Night.

Introduction to R.A. Lafferty's *The Fall of Rome*

by Darrell Schweitzer

I've travelled quite a ways with this book, and maybe after many years I'm beginning to understand it.

What precisely is R. A. Lafferty's *The Fall of Rome* anyway?

It is of course the rarest of the books by Raphael Aloysius Lafferty. It was published by Doubleday in 1971. The first edition can easily command in excess of $100 on the used-book market.

Which tells us nothing, for our purposes here.

Lafferty was a unique voice in science fiction and fantasy from the 1960s into the 1980s. Born in 1914, a World War II veteran, he came to writing rather late, after he retired from the electrical supply business around 1960. At that point, as he described it in an interview I did with him in the 1980s (which may be found in the United Mythologies Press booklet, *Cranky Old Man from Tulsa*), he decided he might want to try something else and so wrote a *Saturday Evening Post* story, a *Collier's* story, a western, a mystery, a science fiction story ... and the science fiction story sold where the others didn't, and so the rest is history.

Which for our purposes tells us almost nothing.

Lafferty subsequently had a whirlwind career. He gained a strong cult following (particularly strong among fellow writers), some awards, and a long list of publication credits. Toward the end, as the corporate homogenization of American publishing accelerated, Lafferty became primarily an "underground" author, one who was too quirky, too unclassifiable to be published conventionally. A book like

Sindbad: The 13th Voyage, if published in the late '60s, would have been an Ace Special and probably a Hugo finalist. By the late '80s it was only viable in the small press. Happily, Wildside Press has that one, and many other Lafferty titles, back in print.

It isn't so much that Lafferty is a square peg who doesn't fit into a round hole; he is a Protean, ever amorphous peg who will never fit anywhere, at least not precisely. One can well imagine that if his experimental detective or western stories had sold in 1960, and his career had taken off in that direction, he would have been one of the strangest detective or western writers ever to come down the mean streets or dusty trail ... and I think the results would have worked out about the same. Lafferty is one of those utterly unique writers who puts his own unique stamp on everything he does. His work contains mysteries (in the non-detective, more theological sense) which are not easily fathomed. He is like a Zen master, who keeps us entertained and befuddled at the same time, in hope that the befuddlement may someday lead to enlightenment. (Though one of the keys to understanding Lafferty is that he is not a Zen master, but a Catholic, very learned in theology and philosophy, history, and literature.)

All that being said, you would think, particularly if you had a copy of the first edition in your hands, that *The Fall of Rome* is pretty straightforward. It looks like, and was published as, a work of popular history, describing the events leading up to the sacking of Rome by the Visigoths in A.D. 410. The Publishers Weekly blurb reads, "Rousing ... popular history, with enough cliff-hanging episodes to fill a dozen novels."

Which tells us, again, very little, but something.

In my callow and naive youth (which must have been more callow than actually youthful, as I was about thirty at the time), I believed I could appropriate some of those above-mentioned cliffhanging episodes and write one of the dozen novels to be mined out of *The Fall of Rome*. I was intrigued by Lafferty's characterization of the "goblin child," Galla Placidia, whom Lafferty describes at the end of Chapter 17 as both saint and devil. I thought I would use the firm basis of Lafferty's history and spin off a strange and imaginative tale of my own. What if Galla Placidia were actually, in her youth, a witch ... ?

As frequently happens to vast edifices built by junior writers going off half-cocked (if I may mix metaphors as such a writer would), this one soon proved to have a foundation of quicksand. The first step to enlightenment is understanding that *The Fall of Rome* is not history in the modern sense but history in the ancient sense. It does not fit into any conventional publishing category, which is why we should be grateful to the folks at Doubleday who faked out the system in 1971 and caused the book to be published at all.

Presently, we think of history as a kind of scholarly journalism, a matter of research and presenting the facts, and of careful analysis. It is difficult (or just plain confusing) to speak of aesthetics in this context, of history being beautiful in the sense that a poem is beautiful. That is not the Twenty-First Century idea of history.

But it is the late fourth-century idea. In the old days, the period Lafferty is writing about history was one of the modes of literary discourse along with dialogue, epic poem, the letter, the satire, and, rather at the bottom of the literary heap, the novel, which by late Classical times tended to be trashy romances written in low-class Greek. (The great Latin novelists, Petronius and Apuleius, were already well in the past.) The difference between fiction and nonfiction was not as distinct as it is today. Reaching back well before the Fourth Century, we see that Homer was "true" but not necessarily factual. (Though there were Homeric fundamentalists, who insisted that if Homer says the Indian Ocean is landlocked, then, by Zeus, it is landlocked!) Plutarch wrote to be entertaining, moral, and, oh by the way, if it wasn't too much of a bother, factual. Tacitus wrote in a great thundering symphony of moral outrage.

History was art in those days, not science, and the distinction between art and science hadn't necessarily been made anyway.

If you start to research into the sources of *The Fall of Rome* you are soon on very shifty ground indeed. We have no major, first-rate historian for the period. The best is Zosimus, a pagan with an axe to grind, who wrote at least fifty years later. His work is fragmentary and stops suddenly with a sneak attack of the Gothic renegade Sarus upon Alaric, which messed up negotiations in mid-crisis, and sent Alaric irrevocably on his collision-course with Destiny. From the poetry of Claudius Claudianus, who was at least a contemporary (and Stilicho's spin-doctor) we learn much about the characters in the story, though anyone who has read "Against Eutropius" cannot possibly believe that Claudianus was even trying to be fair. No, he was a propagandist, a hatchet-man. The letters of St. Jerome convey to us some of the shock felt throughout the world by Alaric's desecration of the Eternal City. *The City of God* by St. Augustine was written in response to the event to remind us that the city of brick and marble, the City of Man, is not eternal after all. (Lafferty seems to be firmly in the Augustinian camp; note his characterization of the saint as the person "who understood why the world must end, and when.") From ancient sources, it becomes a matter of reconstruction of events from Byzantine chroniclers and occasional bits of backfill provided by the sixth-century Procopius in his *The Gothic War*, from incidental references in the lives of the saints, from church history stray paragraphs of otherwise lost writers such as Olympiodorus of Thebes, and so forth. The sixth-century Gothic writer, Jordanes, can also be used with caution, as he is both extremely partisan and often confusing.

The modern sources are more obvious: Gibbon, Bury, the *Cambridge Medieval History*. My interest in Galla Placidia led me directly to Stewart Irvin Oost's *Galla Placidia Augusta* (University of Chicago Press, 1968), which, while book-length, is called "a biographical essay," not a biography, because the sources of information are so sketchy.

In all of these sources, you will find the broad outline of the events narrated by Lafferty, but precious few of the incidental details. You certainly will find nothing of Alaric's interview with a ghostly ancestor on the Island of the Dead in the Danube as related in Chapter 7. It fits perfectly into the story that the ghost describes the only possible union of Goth and Roman as being like the union of fox and hare after the fox has eaten the hare. That sums up the political situation neatly, from the conservative-tribal Gothic point of view, but I at least cannot discover the ghost's words written down anywhere.

Mr. Oost has nothing to say about the adventures of Galla Placidia as described by Lafferty, much less about the ghost.

The one clearly counter-factual statement I can take Lafferty to task for is the odd one at the end of Chapter 5 that the pro-pagan western pretender Eugenius (A.D. 392-94) placed on his coins and medallions the face of Jesus Christ. No, the coins of Eugenius show a conventional late-Roman emperor's profile. It is not an individual's portrait at all, save that this one is bearded, whereas the contemporaneous, legitimate emperors are depicted as clean-shaven. But Julian the Apostate had made a political point of his beard too, back in the 360s, when he converted from Christianity to paganism and tried to return to the days of Hadrian and Marcus Aurelius (both of whom were memorably bearded). Most likely the partisans of Eugenius wanted to present their man as another Julian.

Yet this too is interpretation. It is easy to imagine a contemporary Christian viewing the image of Eugenius as a mocking caricature of the Savior, even though late fourth-century Christs are usually shown face-on and not necessarily bearded.

What about the description of Alaric praying by his saddle and what Singerich thinks finding him thus? This is not the sort of thing you get out of a history-book in the modern sense. It comes out of a novel or out of epic poetry.

Indeed, the ancients thought of history as a form of prose epic. It was perfectly acceptable to insert set-piece speeches into the mouths of the characters, if that was what that person might have said, or even should have said. The idea of ancient historiography, as I understand it nearly two thousand years later, was to shape and reconstruct the meaning of what happened. It is not mere reportage, but something closer to the codification of myth.

And that's what *The Fall of Rome* is. It is an imaginative reconstruction of some of the most terrible and exciting times the world has ever known. The age of Alaric and Stilicho and

Honorius was not one of simple decay of a dry-rotted edifice given the final shove which made it collapse into a cloud of dust. It was a time of enormous ferment, in which, indeed, everything which had been taken for granted since the beginning of human memory (such as, for instance, Homeric fundamentalism) was being picked up, reexamined, and either cast into the flames or put back on the shelf to be reclassified. It was the age of the Church Fathers, the beginning of the Middle Ages (though of course no one knew it at the time, not seeing themselves in the "middle" of anything), the time in which the political actuality of the Roman Empire was transmogrified into an enormously powerful myth, which is the most enduring of all Roman creations.

Lafferty's *The Fall of Rome* is a history of this time, but a history as Thucydides or Tacitus or Ammianus Marcellinus or even grumbly old Zosimus would have understood the term: a beautifully imagined, epic prose narrative of a time in which the meaning of everything changed. It is also, incidentally, much of the time, factually verifiable.

This work is © 2015 Darrell Schweitzer.

Darrell Schweitzer is the author of 3 novels and about 300 published stories, a former editor of Weird Tales, and a prolific essayist, critic, and interviewer. His work appears in The New York Review of SF regularly.

Introduction to The Devil Is Dead
by Charles Platt

[This is an introduction especially written for the Gregg Press hardcover edition of *The Devil Is Dead* published as part of The Gregg Press Science Fiction series in June, 1977. It is the first time that it has been reprinted since its initial appearance in that now long out-of-print book, and is presented here by the kind permission of the author.]

The Devil Is Dead was first published as a paperback original by Avon Books in 1971. It is an idiosyncratic, playful book that defies categorization and evades analysis. It takes liberties with plausibility, plays games with reason, and draws on a grab-bag of mythic and Catholic source materials to stage its unserious entertainments. Those who expect something comparable to other science fiction and fantasy will not find it here. Those who expect rational explanations for paradoxical events will not be well pleased either (they will be thrown only an occasional scrap of pseudologic to ease their hunger for something that makes sense).

But those who enjoy individualism in a writer, lack of artistic compromise, and (on a simpler level) tall tales told tor their own sake, will find *The Devil Is Dead* pleasing, entertaining, and in every way delightfully unusual.

Lafferty is an unusual writer. Born in 1914 in Iowa, he settled with his family in Tulsa, Oklahoma—his "favorite city in the world"[1]—where he spent most of his life working in the electrical wholesaling business. He joined the army when he was 27 and saw Australia, New Guinea, Indonesia, and the Philippines; after five years he returned to his electrical business, though he had clearly developed an interest in travel.

---

[1] All quotes by R. A. Lafferty in this Introduction are taken from an interview with Lafferty in a small-press magazine, *The Hunting of the Snark* No. 10 (1976), edited and published by Robert J. R. Whitaker—except where otherwise noted.

He did not start writing until he was 45 years old (circa 1959), and took it up "to try to find a hobby that would make a little money instead of costing a lot, and also to fill a gap caused by cutting down on my drinking and fooling around." He sold his first short story in 1959 and his first novel in 1967. He retired from the electrical business in 1971, and has been writing ever since. In 1973 he won a Hugo Award for "Eurema's Dam," a short story, and he has achieved wide recognition for the quality of his work in the science fiction/fantasy field.

He says he has been influenced by Robert Louis Stevenson, Mark Twain, Bret Harte, Herman Melville, Hilaire Belloc, G. K. Chesterton, Dickens and Balzac, among others (he mentions no science fiction authors as influences). In addition he says: "there's a lot of the American tall tale in my background... The three best tall-story tellers I ever knew, Hugh Lafferty, my father; Ed Burke, the brother of my mother-to-be; and Frank Burke, her cousin, homesteader near Snyder, Oklahoma, in the 1890s." And it is their influence that is probably most noticeable in *The Devil Is Dead*.

The telling of tall tales is not a modern art. It harks back to a period when there was time to kill, as opposed to the contemporary feeling that there is never enough time to spare. The tall tale, surely, is best suited to a family sitting around a fireplace in the evening, needing some kind of diversion; or some old friends hanging out in a bar together, looking for a conversational topic beyond their own true lives. The tall tale has elements of ritual, game, and myth; like any good mythic form, it contains its share of wonder (amazing incidents, far-flung travels, larger-than-life events), but unlike most myths, it never takes itself entirely seriously.

Lafferty's unusual mixing of classic American tall tale methods with archetypes drawn from more conventional mythic sources, plus a few elements of conventional science fiction and fantasy, gives his work its unique flavor. It is hard to compare him to any other writer whose work is being published today under the usual genre labels. In some ways, there are similarities to Lewis Carroll (whose fantasies showed the same enjoyment of paradox, illogicality, semantic games, and surreal events occurring in the course of a quest). But where Lewis Carroll is distinctively British and wrote about, and for, children, Lafferty is distinctively American, and his recurring themes tend to involve booze and barmaids (in that order) in an unconventional Catholic America, rather than conventional children's story fare.

The difficulty in classifying, categorizing, or comparing Lafferty's work is associated with some difficulty that he has had in seeing his work published. The practical end of literature—getting books into print and keeping them in print—is an aspect commonly ignored in introductions such as this one, but it seems to me that these practicalities are very relevant here. At the time of this writing, R. A. Lafferty has no fewer than *nine* complete novels in manuscript form, unsold, looking for a publisher; two novels that have been accepted for publication; and ten that have actually been published. But of these ten, how many are still in print? And of the unsold nine, how many will *ever* see print? To deal with these depressing and distressing questions it is necessary to digress for a moment into some sordid facts of genre fiction publishing.

In his history of science fiction, *Billion Year Spree* (1973), Brian W. Aldiss writes: "It is easy to argue that Hugo Gernsback... was one of the worst disasters ever to hit the science fiction field. Not only did the segregation of science fiction into magazines designed especially for it, ghetto-fashion, guarantee that various orthodoxies would be established inimical to a thriving literature, but Gernsback himself was utterly without literary understanding. He created dangerous precedents which many later editors in the field followed."[2]

The suggestion that Gernsback retarded development of the science fiction field can be debated endlessly and is not the focus of our concern here. What seems to me important (and beyond any debate at all) is Aldiss' inference that Gernsback, in 1926, was solely responsible for identifying and creating a new genre: scientifiction or science fiction (the exact term is irrelevant). What mattered was that, once labeled, the majority of imaginative fiction could never again be lost in

---

[2] *Billion Year Spree: The True History of Science Fiction,* paperback edition (New York: Schocken Books, 1974), p. 209.

the amorphous body of contemporary literature. Thenceforth, it was to be segregated.

In Gernsback's time, the pulp magazine field was of course already subdivided into other categories (westerns, mysteries, etc.). Creating a new category for science fiction made reasonable magazine publishing sense, especially since most of the fiction then to be published under that label was really much the same in character, and was no better than the pulp image that came to be associated with the label.

But when science fiction started developing in the 1950s, and some writers sought to transcend the pulp image of the genre, they found it was too late. The "Flash Gordon/Buck Rogers" image was established. The new paperback-book publishing industry of the 1950s was employing the same categories as magazine publishing of the 1930s. Editors considered science fiction a juvenile market where higher literary values might be more of a burden than an asset. And the general reading public did not of course take science fiction seriously at all.

Before the creation of the discriminatory science fiction label, under which the small amount of good writing ended up packaged identically to the bad, this problem did not exist. Victorian and Edwardian "scientific romances" were part of the main body of literature; H. G. Wells and Jules Verne were not segregated on a separate shelf, under a separate label, at the backs of bookstores.

But by the 1960s, an author such as Kurt Vonnegut, Jr. was treated differently. *He* ended up waiting more than ten years for recognition (that came via *Slaughterhouse Five* in 1969) before his earlier books were brought back into print, decategorized, and moved out of the science fiction section into the public eye. And there are other good writers for whom it still has not happened. They remain victims of the category system invented by the "father of modern science fiction."

To be fair, even if Gernsback had never created a category for science fiction, some other editor or publisher would probably have done it. Modern publishing is wedded to the concept of categories in general. Modern sales practice requires it. Booksellers expect it. Readers, too, are supposedly programmed to respond to categories: show a bunch of book buyers a novel without a label (the theory goes) and they will not know what to make of it, but show them a "mystery" or a "historical romance" or a "bestseller" (often printed on the cover of this category, reflecting expectations, not actuality) and they will know right away what they can expect and whether they will enjoy it or not.

Categories eliminate some of the uncertainties and indefinables of publishing. Sales become more predictable, because books are packaged like each other within each category. More and more, you *can* judge books by their covers. Ideally, literature will one day become as easily marketed as products on supermarket shelves—the contents of gothics, detective novels, and westerns will be as programmed and predictable as the contents of boxes of breakfast cereal, laundry detergent, and cake mix. Publishers and distributors and sales representatives and bookstore owners will then sigh with relief, having drastically reduced the risks of their business.

We have not yet reached that utopia, but we are more than halfway there. As a result, it is getting harder for the unconventional, non-category novel to see publication.

An editor who is faced with such a non-category novel has three choices. His first choice is to publish the book without categorizing it, in a package that truly reflects the subtleties of what the book is really about; in which case the sales department will complain that its appeal is impossible to evaluate, and the editor's own associates may give him a hard time in that week's editorial conference. His second choice is to put the book under one of the existing category labels, and package it like all the others in that category, even though this is not really appropriate. His third choice is to reject the book on the grounds that it has no defined audience or market, does not conform to the parameters of what is generally being published, and therefore will probably not sell. (Interestingly, according to this argument, a book like Jonathan Livingston Seagull should not have sold 7 million copies; it should have been a disaster.)

George Ernsberger, the editor who bought *The Devil Is Dead,* chose the second choice of the three I have listed above.

The first edition of Lafferty's novel is clearly labeled "Avon science fiction original" and was distributed to the science fiction racks in bookstores and newsstands.[3]

On the other hand, in keeping with the real nature of the book, it was "tastefully packaged"—which is to say, it did not have a garish cover showing pictures of monsters or spaceships or naked women. It had a gentle, whimsical, artistic cover; this was a nod in the direction of choice number one.

The marketing strategy was well-intentioned but unsuccessful. Probably the diehard science fiction fans who saw the book found that its cover art and back-cover blurb did not fit their preconceptions about what science fiction should look like. It was unfamiliar. It did not feel right. Conversely, the buyers of "'general fiction" who might have wanted to read the book, had they known it existed, never saw it, because its tasteful cover was buried among all that garish, juvenile science fiction at the back of the store.

So this enchanting, amusing, eloquent, original, clever novel never reached its potential audience and was allowed to go out of print,[4] because publishing is a business of categories, and also because readers have come to think in those categories just as much as the publishers themselves (though the thinking may not be on such a conscious level).

Authors, too, are now motivated to think and work in category terms; and this is surely the most depressing aspect of all. For every author who sits down and thinks, "What do I want to write?" there must now be at least 20 who sit down and think, "What can I sell?" Correspondence courses that teach people how to write have a term for this kind of thinking. It is called market study. It means that you write to suit the categories and preconceptions of the media, rather than to express your own individuality.

It is because *The Devil Is Dead* is such an exception to this

---

[3] *Editor's Note:* Shortly after the publication of *The Devil Is Dead,* Charles Platt succeeded George Ernsberger as SF category editor at Avon Books.

[4] It was nominated for the Nebula Award of the Science Fiction Writers of America as Best Novel, but lost on the final ballot to Robert Silverberg's *A Time of Changes.*

pattern—such an individual, idiosyncratic book—that I am so pleased to see it made part of the Gregg Press series, where it will achieve far more permanence than in any paperback edition. And for the same reasons, I feel especially pleased to write this introduction, emphasizing what a rarity it is. R. A. Lafferty is that one writer in 20 who does not seem to have heard of market study, and seems never to think "What can I sell?" when he begins work. (If he did think it, he might have fewer than nine completed-but-unsold novels looking for publication.)

Lafferty himself comments: "I don't compromise very much on what I write. That's partly because of stubbornness and partly due to principle, and partly to circumstances. I didn't begin to write till I was forty-five years old, and I never depended on writing for a living. That does make a difference. One or two of my unsold novels might have been sold if I had compromised a little bit, but for most of them it's just that they are a bunch of misfits that do not fit into any category. . . "[5]

As for the editors who work within the science-fiction category, Lafferty remarks, "Science fiction editors are as uncomprehending of anything outside the field as are mainline editors of science fiction." And his own regard for the bulk of science fiction is quite critical. He feels there are periods in science fiction when "almost all the stories that are published are rotten, but there are a few good ones to be found;" and other periods when "all the stories are rotten and there are not *any* good ones to be found." As of 1975, in his view, "We are presently in a Type 2 period."

He is no less critical of his own work. For example, he believes that his story "Eurema's Dam," which won the Hugo Award, was not necessarily worthy of it. He felt "considerable exasperation at the two worst short stories [on the ballot] . . . tying for the award, and one of them being mine. This isn't a put-on. I had come in second the year before with the best short story in the group. . . . And in the fateful year [when he did win the award] I had at least five short stories published

---

[5] Quoted from personal correspondence written by Mr. Lafferty to the author of this Introduction.

that were much better than "Eurema's Dam."

If these statements and anecdotes add up to an image of R. A. Lafferty as a science fiction writer who is an individualist and a little alienated from his contemporaries, the image could be accurate. He certainly seems as unbothered by appearing a "misfit" as he seems unbothered by his unsold novels being "a bunch of misfits." In fact, in his work, he seems to delight in playing up the idiosyncrasies and evasiveness that make his writing hard to classify and difficult for some readers to accept. By "evasiveness" I mean his tendency not to play entirely fairly with the reader; it is always hard to tell what to believe and what not to believe in Lafferty's work. In his "promantia" in *The Devil Is Dead*, he promises the specific location of the "Terrestrial Paradise"... and delivers on his promise, but in such a way as to disappoint rather than reveal. He pretends willingness to expose his influences and sources, in italicized quotations at the head of each chapter; but it turns out that many of the quotations are credited to names of characters whom Lafferty has created himself, in his other novels. ("After all," he says, "if you have characters who are more erudite than yourself, you might as well cite them. Several of the quotations are genuine: Asimov, Aquinas, Numbers, Genesis. Most of them are made up.")[6] Even the title of the book, and the "name on the tombstone where the Devil is buried," are come-ons in a sense, ultimately deflating the reader's initial expectations.

In a way the whole art of telling tall stories entails maintaining a distance between the reader and the narrator. The tall-tale teller must keep the truth about himself as mysterious as the pseudo-truth of his tales; the audience must be tempted with apparent facts (which can never quite be proven or disproven) and encouraged with apparent sincerity, while the narrator keeps himself and the real truth of the matter just out of reach. In this way, the reader is tantalized, just as the audience at a magic show is tantalized by not knowing exactly where the sleight of hand is employed. But, after all, it can be enjoyable to be tantalized (and magic tricks are never much fun when you know how they're done). That

---

[6] Quoted from personal correspondence with Mr. Lafferty.

is the whole appeal of the game.

Appropriately enough, this book that is something of a misfit, written by a man who projects an image of being something of a misfit himself, is a story *about* misfits. Some of them are good-natured misfits; some of them are evil ones who like to infect other people with their evilness, causing riots, insurrection, and mayhem as a result. At one point the character named X explains: "The whole clique is a catastrophe looking for a world to happen to." Another character, Don Lewis, suggests elsewhere in the novel that the evil-doers are motivated out of jealousy toward the rest of humanity, who are not evil (but who *are* wholly human).

This touches on that most familiar science fiction theme, alienation—a condition where loneliness and withdrawal are balanced by camaraderie with others who are alienated, and a notion that the alienated minority could really be *superior* to the rest of the world. The evildoers and the "halfbloods" in Lafferty's story, mixed up together on their global cruise, are all social rejects with ambivalent feelings toward the world at large. They have a divine discontent that leads them to forsake even the island of paradise, after a while. They feel most at home, it seems, in the social microcosm of a bar room, in the exclusive company of bottles of booze and the occasional friendly barmaid.

The Devil Is Dead tempts much more analysis—in mythic rather than psychological terms—but the temptation is dangerous, because any would-be literary analyst, confronted with such a mess of tall tales, cannot hope to be sure where the author has involved his own psyche, where he has drawn from outside sources, where he has played a game, and where he has exposed his true feelings about how the world works. There are tricks and traps, from the false quotations to the tantalizing little poem at the end of the book, with its last line hinting at a kind of circularity. What is to be taken seriously? What is to be believed?

My own feeling is that it is not really important whether (for instance) the voyage of Saxon X. Seaworthy is really symbolically equivalent to the Voyage of Sindbad. Nor does it matter whether this book is really trying to be profound about questions of reality and identity (but perhaps a frighteningly analytical graduate thesis could be written comparing Lafferty's thoughts on the subject to Carlos Castaneda's dialogues on the same topic; the mind boggles). I think it would be equally irrelevant to start a discursive study of the obsession with death in Lafferty's story (in which many of the anecdotes and premonitions are concerned with dying, and more than half of the characters do die, in more ways than one). Nor do I have the initiative to begin a point-by-point comparison of Lafferty's deceptively simple prose style, false trails in the plot, and sense of humor, to similar traits in the earlier work of Kurt Vonnegut Jr. (such as *The Sirens of Titan*, 1959). And I would certainly refuse to start asking nasty questions about the role of women in *The Devil Is Dead* (they are accessories to the men, every one of them; loveable but no more highly motivated than barmaids—two of them *are* barmaids). The feminist reader might note that these adorable creatures are strangely attracted to our hero, Finnegan, a derelict type with an unprepossessing physical appearance who hangs around getting drunk and sleeping on the beach. The feminist might ask what this tells us about the state of Mr. Lafferty's consciousness.

But I think such questions are best left unasked, and definitely unanswered (I mention them at all only to fulfill the expectations of those who like taking or teaching college literature courses in science fiction). *The Devil Is Dead* really isn't suited to that kind of literary analysis. Some of its source material is surely drawn from identifiable myths and legends, and some of its concerns go well beyond simple entertainment. But its essence is in its mood, its characters, its outlook on life, and its language, and all of this is laid out plainly and accessibly enough to he appreciated by anyone, without need for a guidebook. The playful mood has already been described here. As for the characters, they are whimsical, moved by an intuitive sense of "rightness" that transcends rationality, just as a fairytale scoffs at the pedestrian habits of logic and boring real-world necessities. The outlook on life displayed in this book shows equanimity and a simple enjoyment of what is there, outweighing the spirit of alienation and discontent referred to previously. Lastly, the language of the book is immensely refreshing (especially compared to the usual "fantasy novel" written in pseudo-British idiom with no trace of sensitivity to the real magic of words). Lafferty's vocabulary and semantics are just as full of jokes and entertainments as his anecdotes, reflecting the author's fascination with patterns of languages both English and foreign.

Of his stories, Lafferty has said, "...almost all of them are indirect results of dreams. The unconscious... is a soil out of which all actions and ideas grow."

In that spirit of myth and mystery, this book was written. In that spirit it should be enjoyed.

Charles Platt
New York

This work is © 2015 Charles Platt

Charles Platt is an author, journalist and computer programmer. During the 1960s, Platt joined Michael Moorcock's New Worlds team as de facto art director and graphic designer from 1967 to 1970, then became a consulting editor for Avon Books, acquiring work for their science-fiction list. In the 1980s, Platt edited and published The Patchin Review, a magazine of literary criticism and commentary emphasizing science fiction, which attracted contributions from such noted authors as Philip K. Dick, Gregory Benford, and Brian Aldiss. He is the author of more than forty novels and non-fiction books. More recently, Platt has been a contributing editor for Make, an American bimonthly magazine which focuses on do it yourself (DIY) and/or DIWO (Do It With Others) projects involving computers, electronics, robotics, metalworking, woodworking and other disciplines.

Hound Dog's Ear illustrations

by Lissanne Lake

Lissanne Lake is a full-time freelance illustrator, and has been one for over 25 years. She has done over 100 book covers, plus magazine covers, gaming card illustrations, and an entire Tarot deck (Buckland Romani Tarot) plus outdoor murals and figurine designs, and many other things. (Artists are a versatile lot!) She lives in North Bergen, NJ with her partner Alan and a small bossy dog. You can check out her paintings on her Facebook page, the Fantastic Art of Lissanne Lake, and you can find many Lafferty illustrations in the albums there.

The Man Who Made Models - Review

by Stephen Case

The Man Who Made Models: The Collected Short Fiction
by R.A. Lafferty

My rating: 4 of 5 stars

It's kind of fun to be part of a renaissance, even if you were late to the party. It's kind of fun to be part of something gathering steam, spilling open, being rediscovered. Right now, that's more or less what's happening to the writings of R. A. Lafferty.

If you don't know Lafferty, you haven't been reading my blog long, as I've reviewed at least two of his books already. You haven't heard there was this really odd guy in Oklahoma writing at the crest of the New Wave in science fiction who was—bizarrely—Catholic, conservative, and curmudgeonly. You're one of the lucky ones, because you get to discover his work from the ground up.

The collection *The Man Who Made Models* is the best place to start. I've written about Lafferty's novels before. They are, I would argue, an acquired taste (but one well worth acquiring). It is in his short stories though that his madness and exuberance come in more manageable bits. But these aren't dainty snacks; even as short stories they're bloody, quivering chunks of meat you have to unhinge your jaw to swallow.

Part of what makes a Lafferty renaissance fun to be a part of is that Lafferty's writings are so immense and scattered. Only one of his books is still in print, and his short story collections are treasures for which used bookstores are to be scoured regularly. Many of his later works were never published on a large scale and only appeared in now-vanished small presses. His short stories are spread across decades and lost in a farrago of out-of-print collections, unpublished manuscripts, and copyright litigation. All of which makes this particular collection so exciting: it's purported to be the first volume in Lafferty's complete collected short fiction.

And it really is a great place to begin the strange odyssey that is Lafferty, assuming you can sweet-talk your local librarian in getting her hands on it. There's a fantastic mix of Lafferties in here, though I don't believe this volume was designed to be a "best of" collection. (My single complaint about this volume is that the editorial afterword doesn't explain the selection process for this volume. It is not chronological, as the list of original sources at the volume's conclusion shows these stories range from the 1960s to the 1980s and appeared in everything from big-name magazines to small-press chapbooks.)

Models a pleasant patchwork, but that makes it sound comfortable and cozy. It's not. It's a patchwork of monsters. You've got stories in here that are among Lafferty's best and brightest: "The Six Fingers of Time," "Frog on the Mountain," and "Narrow Valley." These are the ones you want someone to read for the first time when you're trying to explain who Lafferty is any why people get so excited about him.

But when you want to go beyond that and highlight his exuberant monstrosity, you've also got plenty of choices here. You have "The Hole on the Corner," for instance, which I think is one of the best examples of what makes Lafferty tick: the Chestertonian joy of the gruesome, bizarre, and hilarious. There are some that are genuinely frightening, whether that means chillingly subdued like "Parthen" or riotously macabre like "The Skinny People of Leptophlebo Street." And you have the ones where Lafferty almost goes too far, leaving you with a simmering crackling in your mind, an effervescence that only hints at the things other writers feel they need to work into their stories such as plots or conclusions: "The Ungodly Mice of Doctor Drakos," for instance, or the concluding work of the volume, "Rivers of Damascus."

I'm not a literary analyst who can comment eruditely on the philosophical or theological things lurking below the surface of Lafferty's prose, like some of the contributors to *Feast of Laughter*. But I want to comment briefly on two of the stories in this collection, because it's not worth much to an outsider to simply say Lafferty is impossible to classify and leave it at that. Each one of his stories bears deeper analysis, and each one in some way forces eyes and minds toward a world where a multiplicity of options and universes await, something that is often off-putting for those coming to his stories hoping for tidy conclusions and explanations. Things are a bit larger than that here; it's like waiting for a cloudscape to fall into its final configuration.

But there are two stories in this volume I especially love. The first is "Days of Grass, Days of Straw," which is absolutely strange. On first blush this story seems to be an alternate reality tale, in which a man comes to awareness in a "weird western" motif where Indians have a thriving civilization on the Great Plains. This, it is eventually explained, is a "day of grass," an extra day in the calendar that doesn't count, as opposed to the ordinary, mundane "days of straw." Life in the day of grass doesn't have much narrative structure: the characters eat and talk and make war with buffalo and dance beneath a floating mountain. Simultaneously, in our own reality the characters discuss the nature of these lost calendar days, and Lafferty lists several of them for us, days we're led to believe he's lifted from obscurity from half a dozen ethnic calendars. The story ends abruptly with no real conclusion: we're left with only potentiality, a flicker of wonder around the edges of our own life, and some pseudo-philosophical discussion of time and potentiality. It's gorgeous.

And then there's "Thus We Frustrated Charlemagne," which features—as much of Lafferty's short fiction does— characters that form a recurring cast of sorts in many of his stories. A group of scientists has achieved the technological breakthrough of sending avatars back in time to alter the past. (One of the best things about reading Lafferty is the way he handles technology. His explanations, which border on the absurd, somehow have aged much better than some of the best "hard science" explanations for fictitious technology.) Each time they alter the past, the world around them is transformed. It's a trope that's been explored often in science fiction since, but here it's as fresh and new and hilarious as an actual real world popping into existence.

That's much of the deep magic here: new, real worlds.

Lafferty's science fiction is never about making fantasy worlds to replace this one. Rather, he writes to open our eyes to the weirdness and the wonder in this one. The world, Lafferty's fiction seems to say, is stranger than you can imagine. This one. The one you're sitting in. It's going to eat you alive. All of the fantasy– all of the horror and monstrosity and laughter and joy– is just him shaking your shoulders. Shaking them hard. Wake up.

Stephen Case gets paid for teaching people about space, which is pretty much the coolest thing ever. He also occasionally gets paid for writing stories about space (and other things), which have appeared in Beneath Ceaseless Skies, Daily Science Fiction, Orson Scott Card's Intergalactic Medicine Show (forthcoming), and several other publications. His first anthology, Trees and Other Wonders, is available through Amazon. Stephen has a PhD in the history and philosophy of science from the University of Notre Dame and will talk for inordinate amounts of time about nineteenth-century British astronomy. He lives with his wife, four children, and three chickens in an undisclosed suburb of Chicago that has not yet legalized backyard chickens.

"Shriek, shriek," said Mama Regina, but her voice was muffled.

R. A. Lafferty, "The Hole on the Corner"

Illustration © 2015 Anthony Ryan Rhodes

Past Master by R. A. Lafferty

by MPorcius

As I admitted in the comments to my blog post about *Utopia*, the main reason I read Thomas More's famous work at this time was as preparation for reading R. A. Lafferty's first published novel, *Past Master*, which I purchased in late November along with some other Lafferty paperbacks.

The back cover of my copy of *Past Master*, the 1968 Ace Science Fiction Special, includes lengthy and detailed praise for the novel from people much smarter and more successful than I am. Praise for Lafferty and this book, we are told, is unanimous! Dare I buck the trend? Luckily, I need not dare; the book is good! Almost every page of *Past Master* confronts the reader with a bewildering mystery, a strange oddity or a striking image, and I enjoyed it. The praise is still unanimous!

It is the 26th century. Humanity has colonized several planets, but by far the most populous and prominent, in fact overshadowing Earth, is Astrobe. The novel begins in a building on Astrobe that is under attack by "mechanical killers" with "ogre faces." Taking cover inside the building are three men, the three leaders of Astrobe: Cosmos Kingmaker, the wealthiest man on Astrobe, Peter Procter, the luckiest, and Fabian Foreman, the smartest. Each of these three men believes he is the true ruler, and is manipulating the other two.

The mechanical killers have come to destroy Foreman; their mind scanners can detect doubts about "the Astrobe Dream," the ruling ideology of the planet, and Foreman is going through a period of skepticism about how things on Astrobe are run. He knows a secret way out of the building, but before he flees the three leaders must come to an important decision. Astrobe, described by Kingmaker as "the last chance of mankind," is in jeopardy, and a man must be found who can lead Astrobe out of these troubles, or at least serve as the public face of the ruling clique as they strive to solve the crisis. It is decided to send an agent back to Earth and back through time to enlist a great man from history for this task, and the man they settle on is Thomas More, the English lawyer and Catholic saint, opponent of the Protestant Reformation and author of *Utopia*.

The agent is a man called Paul, a man experienced in dealing with danger, who is pursued by the same types of mechanical killers that are after Foreman. He fights and connives his way to a space ship and to Earth, which is 1.5 parsecs away. In one month the Hopp-Equation Drive on Paul's ship can propel a space ship 1.5 parsecs, a distance it takes light five years to cross, but such travel has unnerving side effects. For one thing, travelers are subject to "reversals;" during the voyage men become women, right-handers become left-handers. Space travelers also experience as much psychic activity in that one month as they would normally experience in five years. This manifests itself in thousands of vivid dreams, one following after the other. These dreams can be symbolic and even precognitive.

Lafferty's version of Thomas More is a charming character who, when brought forward in time one thousand years, embraces tobacco and mystery and science fiction novels, and asks Paul if the fishing is good on Astrobe. He tells Paul that he has been visited by time travelers before, and expresses dismay that so many people have seen *Utopia* as a blueprint for an ideal civilization when in fact he meant it as a satire and a warning of the kind of sick society he feared would result if trends he detected in early 16th century Europe were allowed to continue.

After landing on Astrobe Paul and More fight their way through their mysterious enemies, aided by equally bizarre allies, to safety. More is enthusiastically welcomed by the ruling class of Astrobe and begins to investigate the mysteries presented by the planet to him and by the novel to the reader. Life is easy in the well-organized cities of Astrobe, where poverty and illness have been eliminated, along with individuality. (The Astrobe Dream holds that a society is like a body, and all the citizens have to work together the way all the cells of a body work together. Following this analogy, an individual is like a cancer.) What exactly is the crisis that is threatening Astrobe? Is it the high suicide rate? The fact that a large proportion of the population has lost faith in the ideology of Astrobe and gone to live in reeking unhealthy slums or wild feral areas where they are in danger from ravenous monsters? Or is it Ouden, a sentient celestial nothingness worshipped as a god by the artificial people of Astrobe, who wishes to extend his dominion to include the natural old-fashioned humans?

The climax of the novel comes when More, performing the duties of a rubberstamp president, refuses to rubberstamp a single piece of legislation, one outlawing belief in God. More is sentenced to death, and his public execution inspires an upsurge of feeling among the citizens of the perfect cities and an attack by an army from the slums. Lafferty compares the death of Thomas More in the year 2535 with such epoch-marking incidents as the fall of the Roman Republic, the Protestant Reformation, the discovery of America, and the birth of Jesus. A new age is dawning, an old world is dying and a new world being born. Whether this new age will be better than the old Lafferty does not say, but he says we can and should hope.

This is a dense novel, full of strange characters with weird powers and mysterious agendas, dreadful fights, and allusions to religious and political topics, and sprinkled with bizarre dreams and tall tales. More himself, rather than some stalwart exemplar, is a complex, shifting figure whose faith in

Christianity comes and goes, and whose allegiance and objectives change back and forth. Lafferty is no doubt opposed to the atheistic and tyrannical Astrobe dream, but admits that the idea of a perfectly planned, perfectly easy life can be very attractive, so seductive that a man as wise as More might fall for it. But a life that is too easy is not worth living; the people of Astrobe are committing suicide by the millions and abandoning in droves the perfectly organized cities because a life without challenge or struggle is not a life at all.

Lafferty doesn't use words like "socialism" or "collectivism" or "communism," but I still think it is fair to see the book as, in part, a (hostile) commentary on socialism and an expansive welfare state. Lafferty employs one of the traditional criticisms of socialism, that it requires a brutally repressive enforcement apparatus that polices people's very thoughts, but I think it is interesting that he abandons one of the other traditional attacks on socialism, that the lack of property and price signals would lead to inefficiencies and poverty. Instead, Lafferty suggests that even if socialism succeeds on its own terms and produces plenty for all, that it is inhuman and soul destroying. Multitudes of people on Astrobe freely choose to work dangerous jobs in a polluted slum rather than live a life of total ease and absolute comfort in the shining cities.

Machines and artificial people (Lafferty never says "robots") are very important to the novel. It is these machines, which can do all the boring or dangerous jobs as well as read and even manipulate minds, which make the efficient Astrobe economy and oppressive Astrobe police state possible. The sympathy More feels for the Astrobe Dream is partly or wholly due to psychic probes, sent by the nihilistic leaders of the artificial people, which put thoughts into More's head as well as words into his mouth. (When More is aware of these probes he calls them "snakes.") *Past Master* may be as much a criticism of technology as it is of government intervention into private and economic life; when men become too reliant on soulless machines, Lafferty suggests, men lose their souls and become mere machines themselves.

Compared to the other Lafferty novels I have read, *The Devil Is Dead* and *The Reefs of Earth*, *Past Master*, in plot and style, is a little more in line with those of a conventional science fiction novel; there are well-realized and sympathetic characters, the presentation of futuristic technologies and societies, and a plot arc full of twists that generates suspense and ends with a climactic paradigm shift. *Past Master* has fewer silly jokes, though there are some good ones. *Past Master* is probably more "user friendly" than *The Devil is Dead* and *Reefs of Earth*, though it still is distinctly a Lafferty work, often folksy in tone and with numerous references to life after death, which seems to be something Lafferty is very interested in. (We are reminded more than once that More himself died a thousand years before his adventure on Astrobe, there is a scene in which hundreds of skulls in niches on a crypt wall respond to the approach of an immortal woman, and there is a character called Adam whom we are told has died many times.)

Highly recommended to fans of literary science fiction and to classic SF fans curious to read something new and different but made up of so many of those classic SF elements we all love, like space travel, time travel, oppressive governments, telepathy, robots, aliens, monsters and wars.

****

If you are interested in Lafferty and SF that is a little off the beaten path you should definitely check out valued commenter Kevin's great blog, Yet Another Lafferty Blog. Envy his Lafferty collection!

This work © 2015 by Mporcius.

Utopia by Thomas More
by MPorcius

Way back in my Rutgers days I was supposed to read *Utopia* by Thomas More in a class on Tudor England taught by Professor Maurice Lee. I must have had some video games to play or something, because I didn't read it. Maybe I was painting some Games Workshop tanks and artillery that week? Anyway, this week I downloaded an electronic version of *Utopia* and completed the assignment, less than 25 years behind schedule. I didn't let you down after all, Prof Lee!

More starts off his book, presented to the world in 1516, with a first person narrative about his diplomatic mission to the Continent. In the Low Countries he meets a wise and well-traveled man. At a friendly meal this traveler, Raphael Hythloday, starts criticizing the English and French ruling classes and their governing policies. Thieves, he claims, are driven to crime by hunger, hunger caused by the policies of the rich, and so hanging thieves is immoral and counterproductive. The nobility and their hangers on are idle and greedy. The French government is damned for maintaining a standing army, and the English upper class denounced for the "enclosure movement" we talked about ad nauseum in college, whereby farm land held in common was turned into private pasture for sheep, leading to increased efficiency and the dislocation of many rural people. Everybody, rich and poor, spends too much money on fancy clothes, on gambling, and in taverns and "infamous houses," writes More, the guy who wore a hair shirt and thought flagellating himself was a good way to spend his down time.

So, More has a lot of gripes about the powers that be (who doesn't, buddy?) and even ordinary people who want to relax with a little sex, booze, dice and cards. But does he have solutions? Well, he does; or at least he acts like he does. Hythloday relates how thieves are dealt with among the Polylerits, a fictional autonomous bunch of people in Persia -

thieves become slaves to the public, forced to wear distinguishing marks and follow complex rules that keep them from fleeing or fomenting revolution. More is so impressed by this idea that he proclaims Hythloday a genius and urges him to become a royal adviser, but Hythloday declares that his ideas are too radical to be welcomed by courts and kings.

VTOPIAE INSVLAE FIGVRA

Hythloday then drops his bombshell. There is no hope, he tells More, of a just and prosperous society until property has been abolished and equality enforced, as it has been in a wonderful land he visited and spent five years in, Utopia. More (the character) makes the obvious objection to collectivism: that with no prospect of reward, people will not work. Hythloday tells More that if he will spare him some time, he will explain in detail how things work in Utopia, a country with no money, no property, and a happy populace. Seeing as there are no video games yet, and Games Workshop has yet to be founded, More has time to listen to Hythloday's description. So begins the discourse on the fantasy land which gives its name to More's book and has been applied to the entire literary genre of exemplary ideal societies.

Utopia has a scientifically planned economy, with experts keeping track of how much food needs to be grown and what quantities of other resources are required and directing who is to produce them and where they are to be sent. These experts draft people to work in the fields, whether they want to or no, and everybody has to work on the farm for at least two years. The government determines what professions people can pursue, and directs people to those professions the experts feel are in need of more practitioners.

Every little detail of life has been planned out and is under government control. The island of Utopia has fifty-four towns, and they all are built on the same plan. In fact, even the houses and streets all look exactly the same. People are assigned where to live; if your family has lots of children some will be assigned to a family which has few children; if your city has lots of people some will be sent to a city where some disaster has lowered the population. Everyone wears the same clothes, and fashions never change. The government makes sure you spend an appropriate number of hours a day working, an appropriate number of hours sleeping, and a healthy number of hours at wholesome recreation. If you want to go visit some other town, you have to ask permission from a government agent, and since there is no money, while in that town you have to pay your way by working. No one is allowed to be idle or waste time and resources on things like making nice clothes of different colors or designing or constructing different styles of architecture.

Order is maintained in Utopia by compelling all men to live in full view where there is no opportunity to form political parties; there is no privacy (doors are not locked) and no such places as taverns or brothels. Government magistrates are forbidden to talk about politics in private; such a crime is punished with death. Lesser crimes, like leaving your town without permission, get you tossed into slavery.

The Utopians have no money, and Hythloday argues at the end of the book that most crime would cease if money were abolished. The Utopians have such contempt for gold and silver that they use these metals to make chamber pots, as well as chains for their slaves. Pearls and diamonds are worn only by children. For fun everybody reads and attends lectures; More tells us that the Utopians find gambling and hunting totally uninteresting, even disgusting—all necessary butchering and hunting is done by slaves.

More's vision of Utopia is so extreme and repellent that we have to wonder how seriously he is promoting Utopia as a model of a just and efficient society, and how much his image of a totalitarian state with no property and no money is in fact some kind of satire. (In the last paragraph of the book More muddies the waters and leaves us with a puzzle when he says he endorses some but not all of the policies and beliefs of the Utopians, without specifying which. Tricky!)

How much sense does it make for a guy to criticize how real life governments abuse power, and then propose a government with far greater power? How much sense does it make for More to decry the way rural people are forced off the land in the interest of efficiency by rich sheep farmers, and then argue that it would be great if the government, in the interest of efficiency, told you where to live and what work to do and if and when and for how long you could take a trip to the next town? Maybe More is attacking English government policies by exaggerating them and showing how terrible they would be if more universally applied?

On the other hand, I suppose it is not hard to believe that More, a successful lawyer and politician and a well-read and pious intellectual who thought it was just fine to burn heretical books and heretical people, would like the idea of smart industrious ascetic guys like himself organizing everything and enforcing their own prejudices, making the lazy work, the vain abandon their fancy clothes and jewels, and the vicious put down their dice and cards and pick up improving books. More probably looked at the world, which is full of wars and crimes and poverty and famine, and figured he, or a cadre of people like him, could do a better job of running things. More also didn't have the benefit we have of 20th century examples of countries where policies abolishing property and planning the economy were put into practice.

Can I recommend *Utopia*, even though I am emphatically opposed to Utopia? It's not exactly a thrill ride or a page turner, but if you are interested in politics, economics, religion, and European history, as I am (in my own haphazard and lazy way), it certainly is worth a little of your time. The book provides a view into another world, that of early 16th century Europe, and addresses important contentious issues, like the role of the state and relations between social classes, that have been at the center of Western civilization for thousands of years and are still at the center of political and social debates in our day.

This work © 2015 by MPorcius

MPorcius grew up in Northern New Jersey, attended Rutgers University and then lived in New York City for over ten years. Through a strange concatenation of events he now lives in genteel poverty in the MidWest. He posts regular fiction reviews at the eponymously titled MPorcius Fiction Log: (http://mporcius.blogspot.com)

R.A. Lafferty — *Apocalypses* (1977)
by Gene McHugh

The two novellas that form *Apocalypses,* a book by R.A. Lafferty, are wildly, comically angry about the state of things in the world. Like a Mark Twain novel blurring-by at fast-forward speed mixed-up with the apocalyptic seriousness of Kierkegaard and the anarchic zaniness of the Marx Brothers, each work is a grotesque, slapstick *cri de coeur* regarding the hyperreality of contemporary life and the easygoing relativism with which people approach serious moral questions. As with much of Lafferty, the stories may at first seem playfully madcap, but upon closer examination they are among the most heavy, ponderous works in the sf & fantasy canon. Be warned, though: Lafferty is a hardline social conservative and, especially at this point in his career, he doesn't feel the need to shy away from saying what he thinks.

In *Where Have You Been Sandaliotis?*—a close cousin of Lafferty's most famous novel *Fourth Mansions* (1969)—a man who is most likely *not* Constantine Quiche, "the greatest detective in the world," is tasked by World Interpol to examine the possible theft of the entire island of Monaco. As it turns out, though, it's not that Monaco is stolen, but rather that an entirely different world is placed right on top of it. This new world is "Sandaliotis," a pastiche of vaguely Mediterranean ideals and architecture along with the promise of desires easily attained and endless novelty and change. There are loose moral guidelines—for example, it's entirely permissible to be married and divorced four, five, any number of times in the space of a single day (an idea that would particularly irk the conservative Catholicism of Lafferty). Further, the religion that does exist in Sandaliotis is couched in the form of sicko spectacle. In one of the most intensely surreal scenes, Quiche and a group of other men are hung from the walls of a thirteen-sided dungeon and are made to relive the crucifixion of Christ, but all their lines are being fed to them via bizarre teleprompter-like machines while a particularly evil "Director" orchestrates the whole thing for a movie that will be edited and broadcast that same day. In short, there is nothing concrete and eternally true in Sandaliotis; it's a pleasant, even fun place on the surface, but that's all it is—surface. Surface and endless novelty. Indeed, the only thing people seem to care about with any passion is speculating on real estate.

For most of the novel, Quiche wanders around, gets into various odd horrifying/comic situations, and tries to come to terms with whether or not Sandaliotis is, in fact, real. All around him, there are signs that, for all of its falseness, Sandaliotis has existed for a very long time, has its own history, archives, and ways of doing things. And the residents of Sandaliotis certainly don't think twice about it. However, what is eventually revealed is that it is indeed all a vastly complex hoax. Sandaliotis is literally hollow. It was built up through anti-matter or the energy of evil materialized as a sort of foam. Lafferty sets up a Manichean universe of good and evil, light and dark, matter and anti-matter, and he portrays the masses of humanity salivating at the chance to settle down in a simulacral world built on evil. Bleak, bitter, and cranky— to a fault—but also wildly inspired, with passages equal parts haunting, beautiful, and ridiculous.

In the second novella, *The Three Armageddons of Enniscorthy Sweeney,* the eponymous Sweeney, a man with a perpetually peeling, sunburned face who may or may not be the devil (or possibly even God), appears to be the source of all major world events. As he envisions things, they happen; there's even a groundbreaking mathematical formula discussed at length that proves this. As he writes his epic opera cycle—*Armageddon I, Armageddon II,* and *Armageddon III*—the world, it seems, enters into devastating world wars that correspond to the visions in his operas. Sweeney himself is, if not totally naïve, at least somewhat dumbfounded by all this. In his mind, if the world is becoming more violent and chaotic because of what he imagines in his operas, it's not necessarily his fault; he's simply showing people the gate of Hell and allowing them to choose whether or not they want to enter. For him, it's a no-brainer: choose goodness obviously. But for

Lafferty, the world is filled with thankless sinners, the "beasts of Armageddon" that gleefully choose to live in a seedy Hell rather than a clean-living heaven. Pornography and violence abound right alongside unlimited greed and the murder of the unborn (which is equated here to the Holocaust). It all comes to a head with Armageddon III—the end of the world. Lafferty's take on all this, though, is that, incredibly, no one is even worried about the apocalypse. The end of the world is something the mass of humanity couldn't care less about. Related to this is an interesting idea that the previous wars and violence and other historical atrocities that people discuss and study in school never actually happened. Lafferty devises a test to prove this unlikely premise. He says that a war is only real if people act as though it happened and change their ways; however, when he looks around, he sees no evidence of anyone acting as though they have seen trauma before or understand what apocalypse or the horror of war could be. If they did, they would surely act differently. The Christian Hell and the idea of war are just words now—symbols meant to fill in portions of conversations rather than actual, real things in peoples' lives. Therefore, wars and atrocity never happened; they are not real.

Like a gigantic McMansion, the world in *Apocalypses* seems to be the inheritance of something old and deep, but is, in fact, a thinly-veiled imitation of anything approaching these qualities. Culture and spirituality are cheap and, yet, most of his characters willfully participate in this cheapness because it makes hard things seem easy and they can all pat themselves on the back for being on the side of corporate-sponsored diet soda salvation.

The combination of extreme Saturday morning cartoon wackiness and extreme Sunday morning sermon gravitas has left the books caught in the middle of any pre-existing audience. They don't really fit into sf and fantasy, either, although I'm not sure where else they'd feel more at home. This is a shame because he is truly some sort of homespun visionary wonder. The more of his work one reads, the more this seems to be the case (and plenty of the most respected sf and fantasy writers of the past fifty years have said as much). However, his scolding of the vast swathe of humanity for their moral lackadaisicalness, especially in *Apocalypses*, may ultimately come across as more the ravings of a "cranky old man from Tulsa, Oklahoma," as he called himself, than wholly accurate or insightful (I suppose, in Lafferty's terms, though, that won't be settled until the Judgment Day). In any event, R.A. Lafferty's work goes deep and is worth seriously considering and appreciating.

November 29, 2011

This work © 2015 Gene McHugh

Gene McHugh is the author of Bang Bros: A Science Fiction Novel (forthcoming from left.gallery), Post Internet (Link Editions, 2011), and the producer of Net Art Hell, a recent podcast focused on individual works of net art. He is currently Head of Digital Media at the Fowler Museum at UCLA, and, prior to that, was the Interpretation Fellow at the Whitney Museum of American Art, and the Editorial Fellow at Rhizome at the New Museum. His writing on digital culture has been published in, among other venues, Artforum, Aperture, Garage, and Rhizome, and the anthologies You are Here: Art After the Internet (2014), edited by Omar Kholeif, and the forthcoming Mass Effect, edited by Lauren Cornell and Ed Halter. He is also the curator of several exhibitions, including projects by Nate Hill, Ann Hirsch, and the duo Bunny Rogers & Filip Olszewski.

Three Poems
by Bill Rogers

DOMOVOI

I am the Anableps Of South Hubert Ave.
Unseen and gigantic
Marching down the center of the street
Passing by garden gnomes
And donut ring sprinkler guards
Tonight I am caught
Between dogwood and lilac skies
My left eye is half of a plastic ping pong ball
Opaque, round side out
This eye looks out onto a field of chalk
My right eye is the purple candy shell of a marshmallow easter
  egg
Marshmallow inside, butt end out
It gazes on dragonfruit

My body is tall and thick and made of jade
My forehead is stretched and my back is bent
My forehead like the god of long life
My back like Punch or Kokopelli
I am a cactus god buoying on a cement sea
I love the rhythm of my hooves on the sidewalks
No one hears them: clop clop, clop clop
I look down and my arms are like wood
I could topple an SUV or shatter windows
But I want to edge the yard
I want to talk to dogs and squirrels
And repair broken mailboxes at night
I am the Domovoi Of The Place
I pass by at dusk or in the lost minutes of the day

I saw the package delivered
I saw the newspapers arrive
I saw the last jack-o-lantern fizzle out
And the last Christmas tree laid by the road
And Pin-the-tail-on-the-donkey
And Hide-And-Go-Seek

Some had discovered me
I don't know how
But they built little houses
They used them to communicate with me
They sent messages to me
I sent messages back
Some erected a line with tin cans dangling
Others put out crappy lawn decorations
Or left the old rope swing up for me
Even after the kids had grown and gone

Sometimes I ache when a door slams
Behind harsh words
Or if I look into windows
And hear no conversation
Or discover a particular sadness there

At times
I want to be the very long, very red ridge beam in the ceiling
The creaky step on the staircase
Or the grand-daddiest rock on the mantelpiece
My ambassador an iron cricket that maps the minutes with his
        shadow on stone
My implements a shovel, broom and stoker
With such an armory
Some might take me to be Neptune or Lord Murugan
But I would not require such fame
I would be quite content
As a hook in a wall
As a broken doorbell
Or as a window pane
My cousins are all of these
And it's only a small thing for me

As I proudly remain the Goblin Of The Street
Kicking aside the acorns
And committing my flounderisms
On the lines between times and neighborhoods
Running from cars
Stealing the sidewalk cracks
Disappearing into shadows
And though not seen
Always waving
As I pass

Bill Rogers
January 19th, 2011
Artwork available at:
http://giveawayboy.livejournal.com/477731.html

THE GREEN MORNING

The balcony window is open
Above mosquitoes and thieves
Above the Ho Ho Here We Come
Of bump-keys in the night
Above the followers-home of late nighters
Stirring in oak infested side-yards
Waiting for moments of hostile access
Above alienated neighbor kids
Entering lawns they once might have mowed
To hang their cocks over long grass
And piss on rotting sheds
Above local thugs stealing faux crystal from the front porch
And brazenly trying the knob

But here twenty stories up
The sound of the surf becomes our woodpecker drum
Knitting us into
The secret things that grow in darkness
The next thing I know is a long green silence
A snowy owl under glass
And mid-size land tortoises stealing night salad
Behind the red lamp of the Holy Infant Of Prague
We descend to the waves below
Going twenty stories down another way
To darkness but not to heat
To barnacles and warm water on cold sand
The foreheads of human tigers crash into our flesh
They walk on our bladders and bite the sides of our hands
Our bodies confer a glowing imprint onto black cloth
As we fall into to the dark back half of the world
Where clocks tell off the hours
With the tongues of birds
Like phantom sentries drawing magical seals on a night beach

During the coffee hour
The couch becomes my lotus throne
Cool air awakens my naked skin

In pointillist carpets of awareness
Beyond a planar world of angels and Egyptian gods
Past where owls alight on dowel rods
And the least killies congregate under warm towels
Here the national bird of Myanmar struts under oaks and thick vines
I gaze both fuzzy and clear into this cube of living green
Transforming all I encounter into a kind of Śarabha with the head of Ricky Nelson as a youth
He carries a twin-serpent crozier in his right hand, a Thomson's Gazelle in his left
His forehooves tame the god of fear
And the locus of this work is a secret ring of heat
Formed where a hot mug rests on my left inner thigh

And then off we go
To a house built of cedar
To gaze through the Charbel window
To be drowned in and buoyed up by a Syriac ocean
Before the long lazy middle hour of the day

~Bill Rogers
May 17th, 2012
(originally conceived in October of 2011)
Artwork available at:
http://giveawayboy.livejournal.com/493787.html

MARTINMAS WEEK

Right before we got to the new sukkah on Lincoln
Everything went flat
So I turned about, threw my jacket over you and took you
    under my left arm
Losing the vision of Hillsborough Bay
of the external bay
We walked across the sidewalk slabs
All slightly ajar
Their various orientations affected ever so gently
By time and forces
The slightest mismatches of alignment
Revealing phalanxes of entry
And I became like a bear going resolutely into his cave
What would have once been anger in me
Had been subsumed
Into a kind of resignation
Opened onto the plain of joy

I sometimes wonder when I see a man wandering alone
Having a conversation with himself
Is this madness or is this just a human modality
That of generating an other when no other is there?
I felt the fact of your presence in my wrist and upper arm
The sting that revealed to me I was not alone
And the sound of you became the music of our mutuality
The cadence of your broken potential
The struggles of your exhalations
The chafing of rubber on rubber
Of a once buoyant intestine
And the rhythm of the wheel
Marked out a secret moment half way between All Saint's and
    Saint Martin's
I treasured your weakness and it became my own
And your broken breath on the cool air
Awakened my heart

We looked out over mini-vistas of imported grass
Over the signs of politics and real estate

Over expressive mail box housings
Old plastic hummingbird feeders
Rotting jack-O-lanterns
And faded American flags
Your balance against mine
Achieved a kind of synthesis
A new energy that had not existed before
Others passed by us
Cautiously or indifferent
Or looked curiously up
From front porches or windows at stop lights
We passed by a stack of tires covered in a vinyl sheath
And a grinding electric bubble machine that was low on soap
Others were racing by
Others were selling things
And I knew our story
The one without destination or prize
Could never fully be told
Without the stamp of madness on it

Bill Rogers Nov. 14th, 2010
Artwork available at
http://giveawayboy.livejournal.com/474528.html

This work is © 2015 Bill Rogers.

Bill Rogers, aka Giveawayboy, spends most of his time drawing and painting solo works or collaborating with his art partner in crime Revansj. The bulk of his days are steeped in tall tales, dreams and mythology. When he is not creating new drawings or paintings or writing poetry, he walks about in the barely known and re-enchanted landscape of Tampa Bay. Bill's first encounter with Lafferty's work was Annals Of Klepsis.

The Lost Children of Boo-Hay World

by Daniel Otto Jack Petersen

"Reminds me of something," the xenologist murmured.

"The meteorologist would have loved this," said the captain.

As their ship approached the little planetoid—no bigger than a very small country really, but spherical - certain atmospheric features coalesced. Up toward the planet's north pole, two gigantic black storms held steady sway, spaced evenly apart in the east and west, each one a roughly circular mega-cloud.

"I don't know," said the ship's cook. "I think the meteorologist might've had a problem with those storm clouds being black, not to mention their size and distribution."

Two lesser storms—which were nevertheless also vast and black, were spaced closer together toward the equator, and of a shape more oval, with their southernmost ends tilting slightly away from one another. Down toward the southern pole, no clouds in sight, a chain of almost square-shaped mountains stretched right across the face of the planet as seen from the ship's approach, like a row of teeth.

"Wait, wait, it'll come to me," said the xenologist.

Then it was gone. They had pierced the planet's atmosphere.

As their ship nuzzled into its landing, a square mile stretch of cobwebbed gravestones hove into view.

Epic Manson laughed. A derisive noise. And a grand noise too. Everything about Epic was epic. (Almost.) The ship's captain.

French Rafferty rubbed his hands on his apron and then rubbed his eyes some more. The ship's cook and machinist.

They had all been rubbing their eyes as the ship settled

on the rank luxuriance of the grassy pampas that led up to the incongruously tidy graveyard. The gravestones were crumbling and cobwebbed and yet in a way that seemed manicured and immaculate. What's more, the graveyard appeared to dance a little in their vision, glitching with squiggly black lines.

"Bad reception like that only happens when you're still in orbit," Rafferty said in bemusement.

"We're looking through the command window, not one of the viewscreens in your kitchen, Raff," Epic retorted. How could a man so obsessed with mechanisms be so absent-minded about whether he was using one or not? Captain and cook could not be more different Epic often thought to himself.

Gooseneck Gorbaldine went to work on it. Analyzing. Her long neck was a study in studious intent as she bent it to the task of analysis. She was snapping drone-shots on her palm as she stepped lively to the airlock. The ship's biologist.

Professor Prodigious Deftstroke reserved his judgment. But when he eventually gave it, it would be swift and decisive, sweeping yet acute. The ship's philosopher-theologian and cosmologist.

Likely Shrikely smiled darkly. Well, she made all her faces darkly. Her skin was rich ebony. She was also the clown of the group so she smiled a lot, with her rich green eyes as well as her dusky mouth. The ship's xenologist.

Pressure-suited and already immersed in the landscape, Gooseneck caught one of the many black spiders crawling about on the tombstones and held its wriggling shape up to a drone hovering about her. "These were the squiggly lines we saw," she said. "Each one appears to be exactly the size of a fifty-cent piece."

"A what?" said Epic next to her now. He was the second to suit up and get to ground.

"An ancient coin. Hobby of mine. Never mind," she mumbled absently in response, busy at her work. Containered and scanned, she pronounced of the spider she had caught: "It's plastic!" She said so in the very voice of incredulity.

"You mean plastic on the outside," French said, having

joined them now. "There are obviously mechanical and electrical parts on the inside to make it crawl. Or have they managed all-plastic technology? Well, that'd still be mechanical, wouldn't it? Yeah, yeah." Rafferty frequently held conversations like this with himself. He never felt lonely slaving away over the crew's meals in the kitchen. Or at least, he never sounded like it.

"No," Gooseneck said. "It's just plastic. Right through. Its crawling is impossible."

Epic rolled his epic eyes at this. He was huge all over, a grotesque man really, to be so large and so proportionately proportioned. "Your method must be flawed," he said to Gorbaldine. Epic was the least smart of the crew, he knew and accepted that. Yet he was no dummy for all that. They were all exceptionally intelligent persons on the team. Epic Manson, however, despite being epic in all other dimensions, was, intellectually, just plain intelligent. The others were out and out geniuses.

Gorbaldine ignored the captain's interjection, confident in her analysis.

Then, a creak and a clang behind them. They looked back over their shoulders toward the sound and saw that an ornate, large-gated, and ivy covered iron fence stood between them and their ship. Indeed, it surrounded the whole graveyard.

"Um, that wasn't there before, was it?" said Likely. She was suited up and among them now too, scanning epitaphs.

We forgot it. Sorry, whispered a voice that sounded very much like that of a child.

"Who said that?" asked Gooseneck. "Likely, are you playing games?" The two women of the crew got along well enough most of the time, and even liked to play games of all sorts with one another (and the men), but Gorbaldine could get mean when she'd had enough. And Likely didn't have much of an off switch when it came to being roguish.

"That wasn't me!" protested Likely. "Would I ask a question and then throw my voice and whisper an answer to it?"

"Most certainly, Likely. You would indeed," said Deftstroke in their headcoms. He was still observing from the ship.

"Ok, I would," she admitted with a winsome grin. "But it wasn't me!"

"The gates work fine," said Epic. He had sprinted over to check the high and wide gates, planning to vault them if needed. He was a little disappointed when that proved unnecessary. "It's rusty and noisy, but swings open and closed just fine." They listened to the creepy creaking as he demonstrated. But its creepiness was a little clichéd they thought.

"By all means prop it open, Epic. Let's not take chances," commed Deftstroke.

Shrikely turned back to the epitaph of the tombstone she'd been examining. Gorbaldine had gone straight for the apparent lifeforms and missed the aspects of the tombstones altogether. Shrikely, on the other hand, was reading them right off.

"The writing's very, very wrong," said Likely. "Impossible. It's in our language. Name on this one says Ted N. Buried."

She stepped to another.

"Name on this one says Deadman. Under that is chiseled 'Nuff Said'."

She swept her gaze more widely, saw weeping angels, leering gargoyles, crosses and arches and pillars.

"This one's got crossed six-shooters. Those are ancient—"

"We know what cowboys and gunslingers are, Shrikely," rumbled the captain.

"It says:
Here lays Butch,
We planted him raw.
He was quick on the trigger,
But slow on the draw."

"Here's another one with a single pistol of some sort on it," said Rafferty. "It reads:
LESTER MORE
Four slugs
From a forty-four
No Les no more
   Humph."

"I've got a suspicion," said Likely.

219

"Well?" said the captain.

"These—all of this - it's somebody's clichés. From an ancient horror-holiday."

"But they're ancient clichés," said Gorbaldine. "From sometime Before Galactic Era. How would they have got out here to an uncharted planetoid?"

"I didn't say it made sense," said Likely. "But let's call it Cliché Planet!"

The ship's meteorologist having died on a previous planetfall, the crew was only just now noticing that the sky was slate-colored as if in preparation for rain. It had been like that the whole time. It wasn't as dark as one of the mega storm clouds they had observed from orbit, but it was definitely the color before a downpour. Yet nothing in the air felt like the unmistakable electric sort of feeling that precedes a downpour. So they were surprised to see a bolt of lightning fork down the slate sky. They were more surprised still that it didn't flash. It took its time. They felt like they were watching that old and (ironically) short-lived Slo-Mo era of experimental cinema where whole features were in half time (or slower), deep-voiced dialogue and all. They recalled those movies now because the lightning bolt streaked down slow enough—took it a good handful of seconds, like a giant palsied hand drawing a line down a giant blackboard—that they could watch the bolt of it fork into two more jagged lines and spread the rest of the way down to the planet's surface somewhere in the distance. And it was all strangely silent.

Gooseneck even had time to engage her size-eyes. She focused on the lengthening end of one of the forkings of the lightning and gasped.

There was the unmistakable blur of a tiny running pair of lightning-white legs at the tip edge of the spreading streak. She dizzied herself jerking her enhanced gaze to the descending edge of the other forking and saw there another blurry pair of blazing legs. They hit the ground running and left the lightning bolt behind. Then she lost sight of them. Dialling back her size-eyes, she looked to her crewmembers, unsure if she should tell them what she thought she saw.

"I'm no expert, but I don't think this planet has the right meteorology for lightning," she said, somewhat to herself.

"Conditions are right for plenty of rain, but no lightning. It's like a whole planet of Scotland or Ireland. Earth places," she added to Epic and Gorbaldine, the only crew members not from or overly familiar with Earth. "But here we've apparently just witnessed the opposite: lightning and no rain. Like a dry thunderstorm in a desert. But this isn't desert."

Likely grinned. "Let's call the planet Celtic Arabia!"

"Those black mega-storms we saw from orbit surely contain rain as well as lightning," said Epic. He looked to each horizon as if he might spot those great black raging monsters.

"We're right between the eyes of those storms," said Rafferty, noticing the captain's gaze. "Can't see either of 'em from here."

"That's it!" shouted Likely. "Not eyes. Eye sockets! And two nostril cavities, the smaller storms below the two giant ones above. And the mountain ranges were the top row of teeth, and no lower jaw, as it should be aside from rigged up specimens for medical students. Let's call it Skull Planet! Or Golgotha World!"

"And there should have been thunder already. Almost simultaneous with a bolt that visibly close," said Epic.

They all heard a few swift whispers then, in the air about them.

Dammit! You forgot again! A girl's voice.

Oh yeah! A boy's voice.

Gooseneck quickly scanned the horizon through her size-eyes. She gave another gasp as she caught sight of the running blur again and saw a tiny lighting-white arm shoot out of it holding an old-timey megaphone. The arm clamped the megaphone over a tiny mouth and shouted through it:

CRACK!

It was the actual word "crack" they heard and it was loud enough to make all of them jump. Gooseneck herself was jolted out of using her size-eyes. When she activated them again, she saw no trace of the little white blur. The riven lightning streak did another strange thing then. Or rather, it didn't do something it should have. It didn't fade.

The crew let that mystery be for the moment. They continued their survey under the permanent bright sky-fork stuck gigantically into the ground in the distance, looking for all the world as if the planetoid were an Olympian roast being checked for readiness. The gravestones and "cobwebs" turned out, under scan, to be of synthetic material also. So did the dirt and sod of the graveyard. And so too the zombies that began bursting forth from it.

The zombies mostly just milled about moaning quietly. But a few of them made short work of the nearest crew member.

"I didn't think synthetic stuff could all out kill you like that," Epic said as he looked down at the half and soon to be wholly eaten body of Rafferty.

Don't worry, we'll use him again later, promise! giggled a young voice.

"And he's the ship's cook!" said Gooseneck out of a swollen face. "Oh the irony!" she cried thickly. Wait, why the swollen cry and thick face? One of those all-plastic spiders had bitten her face when she held it close to peer at it (wanting a natural look before she engaged her size-eyes for a macro-lense view) and its plastic bite had poisoned her quite impossibly.

"Yes. They eat the one who feeds us and deform the one most beautiful among us," said Deftstroke in coms. "It's almost like some intuitive ecology that behaves symbolically toward invading organisms."

"Hey, I'm right here!" interjected Likely.

"Oh," said the professor placatingly. "I didn't mean to offend your homeworld indigenous sensibilities, dear Miss Shrikely."

"I'm talking about the first thing you said, Prodders. And anyway 'I am dark but lovely'," Likely quoted, not for the first time. "And green-eyed! And lovely-eared! Do none of you have eyes to see these lovely ears? No, there's not a Solomon among you." A complaint she voiced often, though she knew it wasn't true. She had spurned the furtive advances of the reedy Professor more than once.

"Solomon didn't say anything about the Shulamite's ears, did he?" said Rafferty's head, which was a few meters from his body now. And then the zombies at the ears off him. They were thorough. Rafferty stopped talking soon after. He was dead at last, and munched down to scraps.

"By extrapolation," Deftstroke hastened to continue, embarrassed by the subject matter of the interjection, "the eco-symbology of this place will make me, the smartest, become the dumbest, and you, Epic, the largest and strongest (and ugliest)," this last was under his breath, "the smallest and weakest, though I can't imagine how as to size. Strength is easy enough to deplete."

They gathered their samples, readings, bewilderments, intumescences, and what scraps they could of Rafferty and returned to the ship for further analysis, reflection, and repast.

Over lunch, they spontaneously started calling it Halloween Planet. Halloween, or its equivalent, was a tradition still celebrated in one form or another in some pockets of the galaxy. Then they argued about whether Samhain Planet or All Hallows' World would be more appropriate. They realized that for all their knowledge, they had almost no knowledge of the real origins of that ancient holiday.

"It's coming out of our minds? The planet's getting it all from there?" Epic inquired around a mouthful of roast warphog. They were glad they'd frozen extra specimens of these delicious bi-locational boars from their hunting expeditions on the planet just before this one. And that the late ship's cook had already prepared them. The roasts only needed re-heating. (They placed Rafferty's remains in the freezer when they took the warphogs out.) Halloween Planet appeared to have no game of its own.

"Yes, ancient Halloween tropes in our heads, from sometime BGE apparently" said Deftstroke.

"Like on Bradbury Planet," suggested Gorbaldine, still swollenly, sucking a hog shake she'd made through a straw.

"Except that planet showed nice things to the explorers, then did mean things to them when they were lulled and happy," said Epic. "Maybe here they'll do something nice at the end, after all this meanness."

They all looked at Epic. It was an incredibly boyish thing to say and Epic never took any such view. The planet was doing its work on him too.

"But that was just a fiction," said Likely between licking

shiny fingers, a habit Deftstroke found it hard not to ponder.

"Fiction?" said Gorbaldine.

"You know, *The Silver Plague* by Bradbury Rockwell? That's the novel that features his made-up world, Bradbury Planet," said Deftstroke, yanking his eyes from Likely.

"Oh, Brad Rockwell, gotta love his stuff," said the captain.

"I thought he was a painter," said Gorbaldine.

"Yeah, and writer of stories too," said Likely.

"I thought that cycle was called *The Silver Cicadas*," said the captain.

"Yes, and some say *The Silver Crocus*," said the professor. "The evidence is mixed. No one knows for sure what the original title was."

"I didn't take Mid-Medieval Lit in college," admitted Gorbaldine with no shame or regret. "Too hard when they won't let you read modern translations."

"Well, I wouldn't have thought that even us medievalists in the crew would remember enough Halloween tropes for some place like this to work with," said Shrikely.

"Apparently we do," said Deftstroke. "Did you know that the people living in the Mid-Medieval period called their own era the *Modern* period? As if every period isn't called 'modern' by those living through it. And what we call the Late-Medieval period, when colonization of the Solar System was completed, they called 'the Space-Faring Age'!" He chuckled as he said that last phrase.

"I'm not interested in a lecture right now," said Gorbaldine. "Let's analyze this stuff."

"You can't analyze tropes," said Likely.

"Like hell you can't!" said the professor warmly, a rare moment of annoyance toward his dark and lovely crush and a rare moment of demotic colloquialism. Deftstroke was a celebrated trope theorist in the terrestrial discipline of analytic metaphysics as well as a notable figure in the study of artistic tropes in literary theory.

"She means the way *I* analyze," said Gooseneck. "With machines and measurements."

"Hm," mused Shrikely, getting on with the analysis that a biologist couldn't do. "Our Ethiopian version of Hallows'

Eve was Buhé and we didn't dress up. It was about Lost Children being found again by torchlight and given bread to eat. (Hoya hoye! The *injera* was so delicious on that night!) Maybe Euro-American Halloween was really about that too, but they'd lost their way even from their lostness."

At this, Shrikely's mouth and nose, just for a split second, pushed themselves out into the bare beginnings of a snout.

"Is the planet doing that to you?" the captain asked her sharply.

Not us! cried two young voices in unison. But that couldn't happen, so the crew pretended it didn't.

"Only my home planet," said Likely with the hint of a grin.

"What *are* you?" asked Gorbaldine.

Deftstroke looked crestfallen. "You're no genius!"

"Or maybe I'm the only real one among us, a tutelary spirit, a guardian deity, one with prophetic skills."

Hey, what about us? said one of those child voices no one admitted hearing.

We're those things too, you know, said the other.

Likely's wry smile beamed now. She had her own tropes this planet wouldn't figure out so easily.

But there was someone else at the lunch table who was going through a more permanent transmogrification than Likely. Gorbaldine's formerly smooth and well-proportioned face had widened to about twice its former size and it seemed to be all in shadow now. It was a bristly shadow. When she felt it on her face as she wiped at her lips, she fled from the mess hall with something between a sob and a chortle.

After lunch, in the spacious common room, Epic saw that Gorbaldine's fine legs were covered in bristly black hairs. She'd done the obligatory strip-down-to-your-underwear-since-there-

are-monsters-around scene. (That might have been one of the ancient tropes too.) No amount of neglected shaving could produce such a winter crop, Epic thought as he looked at her legs. It was thick, furry spider hair. His skin crawled at the realization. She realized that what would normally have been a leer from her captain was now a look of horror.

"Listen," she said to him in a widening accent out of her ever widening mouth. 'I want to ask you to do something for me before my mouth's too big and weird for me to speak in a way you can understand anymore."

Epic gulped, couldn't meet her eyes (those eyes! what was happening to them?), muttered "Yes?"

"While I eat you up," said Gorbaldine with a clicking noise amidst the thickened sound of her voice now, "I'll start with your legs, don't worry. But when I eat you up, I want you to shout 'Shriek, shriek. My wife is a spider! Shriek, shriek.' Would you do that for me, Epic?"

Epic looked at her uncomprehendingly a moment, then looked away with a shudder. Her eyes were something horrible now and her mouth too, like there were too many of them - eyes, mouths - too much visage and oculi and munching maw. Even those once delectable legs had multiplied, every one as bristly as its sister.

"It's something I read in an ancient story once," she explained, all thickly hissing and clicking voice now, the meaning of her words more in his mind than in the sound of them. "I never liked that old stuff, but this one was in translation and it somehow always stuck with me. It wasn't a real scenario like this is, of course. It was a story all about dimensions, different versions of possible worlds. It was Total Modal like my college boyfriend liked to say. He studied philosophy. Anyway, that story wasn't something simply happening like this is. It was a could've happened sort of thing, you know? I never liked philosophy any more than I liked literature, but that story tickled my fancy somehow, I guess. But I think it'd be fun if we recreate it. Poor Epic, I know I'm not really your wife, and I know you always wanted to be the one eating *me* up. But it's not going to be that way."

Epic ignored this chatter and kicked her hard in the masticating mandibles and then pounced with both big booted feet onto her fattening abdomen, with crunching effect. Even thus crippled, she bucked him, leapt upon him, took a goodly chunk of him in one big gulp. He produced his huge captain's knife and trimmed her by a joint or two. And in this manner they finished each other off.

Ew. That was a little gross, said a girl voice.

It's supposed to be! It's a gross-time holiday, said a boy voice.

Professor Prodigious Deftstroke came from the mess hall into the common room on his way to the ship's command deck, to which Likely had already repaired. He skirted the mess of Epic and Gooseneck on the floor with some disgust.

"Well, I guess it's just the two of us now," he said to Ms. Shrikely. Then he followed her gaze out of the window.

The zombies had gotten more organized and more numerous and were all over the ship now. They had been joined by wolf men and lizard people and a host of other zoomorphs and unnamables. The forked lightning streak was still out there in the distance, the sky still slate with no rain.

"At least they can't get in here," said the professor.

Likely barked a little laugh. "Don't count on it."

A red light formed in the sky directly overhead, grew into a hurtling ball, a huge rock that actually diminished in size as it come down directly at the ship's command window. A host of monster hands pointed up to it and a chorus of creatures cried in unison: "The Night of the Comet!" Close enough. Night of the Meteor doesn't sound as good anyway.

Good throw! said the boy voice.

I always was a better arm than you, said the girl voice.

When the meteorite struck the ship's window, it was only the size of a probe-pod but it hit with such force it shattered the thick flexi-glass into great gelatinous globs, and the flesheaters all swarmed in. They lifted the last two crewmates out into the planet's atmosphere, in an almost processional manner. They slashed and gashed them, ate enough of them to be polite and decorous. Likely herself quickly bled out and went glassy eyed.

Then her fresh corpse said, "Well, I'm not really dead. I'm just going to have to give up this form. Too bad. I liked it. Even if none of you (sorry professor) appreciated it." Her nose and mouth began to push forward into the beginnings of the snout they had seen earlier, which formed fully now and stayed put. The rest of her followed suit: pads formed and claws pushed out of paws, legs cracked backward-jointed, teeth elongated and sharpened, a bushy tail sprouted, her eyes remained green, and her lovely ears rose and became the high proud ears of the sleek Ethiopian wolf. Except that this one's pelt was an uninterrupted midnight black. All the wounds of the other body had vanished. She barked "Bye!" and loped off, instinctively sniffing out some non-synthetic terrain in which to den for a while, until things became clearer. Her crewmates never saw her again, in any form. They might be used again in the next version, but she was different material and worked in a different way.

Prof Prod lay on his back, dying, the light fading from his eyes.

Wait! A voice from the sky, female. *You can't all die yet, we haven't finished all our tropes.*

"I'm still alive!" Epic cried out happily from the ship's hatch. "Guess I win!"

Thought he was dead, said the male voice.

Enough chunks out of him to be, said the female voice. *Guess he lives up to his name. Goody!*

"So now you talk plainly, do you?" the expiring professor wheezed at the sky.

So now you listen plainly, do you? the girl voice called down.

Deftstroke couldn't resist making an intellectual point with his dying breath: "As to your alleged tropes, young lady, the whole universe is made of tropes." The dying old professor laboriously craned his head toward Epic, blood trickling from various holes in him, both original and new. "That man's gargantuan red boot is one instance of redness and his other boot is, in its turn, its own distinct redness. Two rednesses, each its own discrete thing, no mystifying 'universals' allegedly tying them together. Abstract particulars, not concrete particulars, are the real stuff of the world. It's tropes all the way down."

"Professor, you do have a lot of discrete rednesses coming out of you, I'll give you that," commented captain Manson commiseratingly.

Stop looking at boots and bloods and look up at the sky! said the boy voice from above. Prodigious and Epic both looked up and saw that the sky was spitting down a host of long, straight, thin drops of wooden rain ridden by hook-nosed women. The wooden raindrops had stiff little bursts of straw-colored flame sprouting from behind.

"Oh, I see," gurgled the professor. "Witches on broomsticks. Very good." And then he died, his dead eyes still staring up at the witch-spitting sky.

What are we gonna do with all this extra stuff? said the boy voice.

I dunno, just drop it anywhere. We'll pick it up later, said the girl voice.

Okay.

Then the windows of heaven were opened and all the leftover tropes came clattering down in immense cataracts of cliché and convention. Ghosts and their rattling chains, jack-o-lanterns aflame and laughing hideously, hockey masks, chainsaws, bloody axes, and thousands more dime-store horrors and monstrosities crashed to the ground and formed into great heaps.

Epic said again, "I win then, right?" A big uncharacteristic grin split his bruised face. "What's my prize?"

Voice from the air again, female: *Wait for it. This is the coup de grâce.*

Then a small child came up to Epic. Quite suddenly, out from behind one of the mounds of tropes he supposed. Came right up to him. Up to about his knee, that is. Epic couldn't tell if it was a boy or a girl. It looked like the Generic Child. It held an empty sack in its left hand. It raised its generic right arm and pointed its generic finger in the air about at level with Epic's thigh, and held it there, as if frozen in a mime. It opened its generic mouth, wide, and held it open there.

"Gonna catch flies," Epic said with a friendly grin at the Generic Child. "That's what my pop always said."

A muffled voice came from the general vicinity of the Generic Child, Epic couldn't tell quite from where. "Hang on!" it shouted, its voice sounding as if it were calling up from the bottom of a set of cellar stairs.

Epic had a notion and he spoke it. "Is that sack for candy? But where's your costume?"

Then a tiny huffing person popped out of the Generic Child's generic mouth and stood on the Generic Child's generic bottom lip. The tiny lightning-white person was a real boy and he cupped his tiny hands to his own tiny but very lively and living mouth, and shouted in a voice of surprising resonance: "DING DONG!"

Epic's mouth was wide open now.

The tiny boy stage whispered behind his tiny hand: "Gonna catch flies!"

Then he disappeared back inside the mouth. Epic could hear, in the vicinity of the Generic Child's neck and shoulders, the faint sound of tiny feet running down tiny stairs. The Generic Child's right and left hands came together at its waste to hold open the mouth of the empty sack before Epic in what was clearly a gesture of importunity. Then the outlines of a sort of doorway or hatch appeared in the Generic Child's belly (the generic shirt it wore was seen to be of a piece with its person) and this hatch opened outward just above the proffered sack and the tiny boy now reappeared here, red cheeked, and shouted with only one cupped hand this time: "TRICK OR TREAT!"

Epic closed his mouth, then opened it again to release an epic belly laugh. Then he clapped applause at the Tiny Real Boy with his Generic Child costume.

A few moments later the boy and the girl were standing together on Epic's epic palm. With genuine wonder, Epic asked, "What *are* you?"

"We're elementals, the spirits of this world," said the girl with the tone one uses for a small child. "The planet's our skin."

"It's our whole body really," amended the boy.

"How many spirits are you?"

"Well, how many do you see?" said the girl, exasperated. "Only the two of us! Just how deformed do you think we are?" She climbed up his arm.

"Deformed?"

"Worlds just have one spirit, but this one was born with two," the girl explained from atop Epic's shoulder now.

"We're what you'd call a freak," the boy chimed in.

"Oh. I don't think you're freaks," said Epic. "I mean, a freak."

"Aw. Thanks!" sang out both little voices.

"Do you wanna finish playing then?' asked the sister hanging from the ridges of Epic's face now.

"Yeah, you wanna?" asked the brother from his palm.

"Oh boy, do I!" said Epic and laughed happily.

When Epic laughed his happy epic laugh, the sister climbed into his mouth and down his throat. There were no stairs yet, so you could only hear her tumble and tunnel down. It was a longer way to go in such a huge man and the boy spirit started to whistle while he waited for his sister. He hopped off Epic's trembling hand - just before it squeezed into a fist, maybe in a gesture of pain - and back onto the Generic Child costume. Epic turned a bit green in the face. He was also beginning to look a bit more generic. Like the Generic Man.

Then, after a first few running attempts that bulged his skin out a bit, the tiny girl burst wetly from the captain's stomach in a puff of reeking steam and shouted a ruddy bloody "TRICK OR TREAT!" An instant later, a red stream gushed from behind her and knocked her right down to the ground, a good ways to fall. And it kept spilling hotly on her for a good minute as she sprawled on the ground trying to catch her breath and slipping in the sticky sweet stuff. She and the boy both laughed and laughed at that.

Many months after this, the tropes were long since tidied away, except scattered trinkets of horror missed here and there in the planetoid's landscape. Just outside the graveyard fence a small, tended garden now grew. There was something in the shape of a French Rafferty plant growing nicely there in the shade of an Epic Manson tree. A Gorbaldine Goosneck vine was creeping towards the tree and would begin climbing it any day now. A great orange gourd of the Prodigious Defstroke variety thrived there too.

A young voice from the sky, male. *What will we do until someone else comes? Hey, I know! Where's that black puppy? Did you see the lovely ears on her?*

Another young voice from the air, female. *And how about those Halloween tropes inside her head? She called it Boo-Hay. That's an even better name for it. That stuff'll be more fun to make anyway. Let's figure em out now. Just think of the huge masks!*

The Hyena! The Mud Turtle! The Elephant Shrew!
Yeah! Here puppy, heeeeere puppy!

Who Was That?

by Martin Heavisides

a. I Wasn't Myself

For the past three months I've been occupied by a personality I recollect nothing about—one at least and let's keep the dimensions of the problem manageable? at least until we find out they're permanently (or multi-temporarily) not?

They remember me in Fungo county, where I rescued seven people from the jaws (jaws? that's what it says in the dispatches) of a flood that regrettably claimed scores of other lives. It was, said survivors, as if I were everywhere at once. If that's true I was inefficient or worse so I prefer the hypothesis that I was able to be some places but not others.

I'd be in Fungo county for celebrations and parades in my honour even as we speak if it weren't for the fact that they have an enforceable extradition treaty with Mungo county where I'm wanted in connection with the slaying of two. I'm safe in Lungo county where I'm neither notorious nor famous for anything in particular, where in fact I may never have been except in present form.

Assume the worst/best: that I am responsible for both sets of actions. Wouldn't you say I'm ahead on the percentages? Not only that, but if somebody capable of so heroic a rescue did slay two he probably had his reasons? (In Mungo county opinion is considerably divided on this question. There are actually pro- and anti-double murder factions.) And I may not have done it! The evidence is largely circumstantial.

I'd return to Mungo county like that! (I'm snapping my fingers even if it doesn't sound like much, how do people make that noise anyway?), clear my good name in no time only they don't simply retain execution there, the method is by being lethally set in Alfalfa flavoured gelatin. It's a particularly horrible death for an allergy sufferer. The method's considered almost equally abhorrent in both Fungo and Lungo county (by citizenry and officialry alike), but I'm safe in Lungo county where enthusiasm for my case is tepid at best, as trade disputes keep relations between Lungo and Mungo county cool. "We wouldn't extradite the worst imaginable butcher to the tender mercies of that bunch of thieves," say the legislators of Lungo county, "and proof is inconclusive as to whether you're anywhere near as bad as that. It's actually as likely as not you had your reasons." Fungo county on the other hand is no respecter of persons when it comes to the iron rule of law. "We'd extradite our own grandmother if there appeared to be a case requiring answer in a court of law, to Mungo county with its sneezy execution style or any other county." And opinion is furious against me among at least half the populace in Mungo county, how could I guarantee they wouldn't preponderate on the jury panel? Not even if the gel were Lobster Newberg with the piquantest of sauces.

If I did face my accusers in Mungo county, given that I have no recollection of committing these actions, or not (what would be a decisive memory of not doing something?), and have no access to the motives of the personality then occupying me (as photographs attest), would it truly be 'my' accusers I was facing? (Being a changed person is an acceptable though by no means infallible—because not easily proven—defense in Jungo, Wungo and Fungo county itself, but not in Lungo or Mungo which makes the antipathy between these neighbours doubly my good fortune. And I have to think my ability to mount a proper defence would be seriously compromised.)

To top it all off I'm considerably strapped for cash. Assets I could live on handsomely in Mungo or Fungo county cannot be accessed abroad pending settlement of legal actions, and in Lungo county I have very nearly squat. (I have been able to secure employment temporarily as a lifeguard, but with half the beaches closed due to toxics and the other half in imminent peril of being so, it's six of one, half dozen of the other whether this is a job at risk or simply far too risky a job.

And should I be taking responsibility for these mortal acts at all? For the flood rescues of course, that's only self-evident; but who really killed (as the prosecutor alleges) these two people in Mungo county, even if it should be proven that 'I' did, if I—literally—wasn't myself? Nobody's ever successfully argued that point in a Mungo court, and people have tried. (Mungo county has the third highest incidence of personality obtrusion and even extrusion of any county in the nation. You'd think in consideration they'd cut their citizens some slack, but no.) I'm simply not prepared to take the risk of such an unholy clotting of nasal passages at my last breath. Would you be? Whoever you happen to be at the moment?

As to the goings-on in Jungo, where it's rumoured 'I' am still at large—can't think about that now—not until I've had another drink or three. Well thank you very much kind friend, double Ballantine's Charley please, rocks? As you can imagine, on a lifeguard's salary. . . these can mount up pretty quick, I'm grateful for help from a stranger with a sympathetic ear.

b. Did I Say 'I'?

Right then, in Jungo county somebody with my face and body and I think you could say, genetic particulars, is trying to carry out a bloodless coup. This would have been inconceivable back in the old days when counties had much less local autonomy. Be that as it may.

This plan of 'mine'—though I swear to you I don't know a thing about it except what I read in the papers—has gone wrong in two important ways. 1.) It's grown rather bloody and while he's not solely responsible for that, it has led to a considerable swing of public opinion against him. 2.) It seems far less likely to achieve an overthrow of present authority and the institution of one more in keeping with the will and silent aspiration of the people than to end in a complete utter rout. Things aren't looking too promising for me there—whoever that might be. I understand the only reason county militia haven't crushed the uprising outright is that they want to capture the ringleaders alive "so we can have the pleasure of trying and painfully executing their sorry asses."? That's a direct quote, I'm not making it up. Shocking in a family newspaper. Amazing how vindictive people can turn when they make politics or the military their career, so you can imagine how it is in Jungo, which is a military oligarchy so the politicians are all also soldiers.

This may have been a fatal flaw in—well, I can't say 'my' plans, whatever the appearances, though I've read the manifesto and I must say the points made seem fair enough and the plan for restoration of civil order once the coup's succeeded—ha! bloodlessly, is equitable and just to all parties, even the tyrant landholders who'd be stripped of their possessions but compensated at a fair rate for the inconvenience this entails. Sort of wish I'd written parts of that manifesto myself. But living under an oligarchy with military parades in the public square every second day, I suppose you grow a little cynical about the prospect of meaningful change. And who's to say, with the best will in the world, he wouldn't have ended up in a worse jumble of corruption and arbitrary force than his predecessors? It's not as if the best laid plans of mice and men don't way aft gang agley.

But the fatal flaw in his scheme—"mine" as you might say—it seems to me is this: whatever the prospects for a bloodless coup based on reasonable power sharing among the populace at large in other circumstances, it is not the approach to take with a bloodthirsty gang of Generals with the title of Mayor and Colonels staffing the aldermanic chambers. I'll grant you there've been seven successful coups in the past decade in Jungo as well as seven that failed. What characterized all of these, the failures as well as the successes, was a realistic estimate of faction and power shift behind the scenes, the willingness to cultivate a faction of your own and strike ruthlessly and swiftly at those likely to oppose you no matter what. More than anything else what distinguished the successes from the failures, and not by much, was the swiftness and ruthlessness with which a secret plan was carried out.

(Maybe a hundred co-conspirators were in on the secret but you know what I mean.) Compare and contrast with the method I used; arrive at the county's chief legislative hall/military college with a slate of reasonable demands and a hundred or so unarmed followers to bolster our worthy cause. You can imagine how that went over, it's a miracle we weren't all slaughtered on the spot. Certainly the few who were carrying concealed weapons didn't prevent that, they only gave the government an excuse for reprisals in disreputable areas whose citizens, for the most part, wot not of our plans in the least if you want to know the truth.

Did I say 'I'? slip of the tongue. That's the worst of these extruded personalities, you tend to take an unhealthy interest as if their goings-on had something to do with you. Be thankful you've never suffered from one. (I mean what interest could I have in overthrowing the government of Jungo? though bloodlessly would certainly be my preferred method, I get squeamish around blood. Don't much like spilled water even. I don't even want to visit there! who would unless they had urgent business that required their presence and stood to earn them lots of money? Even then you'd bring bodyguards, not just to defend against bandits—who're usually poorly armed—but against the legislative assembly. I'm certainly not going to travel there any time soon, blessed as I am with these features, this frame, and DNA specs to die for horribly. Worse than Alfalfa in Jungo county.)

If I were him I would have changed my story completely the moment I saw the turn events were taking. I would have claimed this was a government-funded art-civics project. A judge with a sense of humour wouldn't have sentenced anyone to more than ten years' hard labour, a few of them might have survived that. One of those, who knows? might even have worked out a plan that succeeded, some of Jungo's most prominent coupsters arose from just such "schools".

I must say I'm surprised you're not more informed about all this, or is it simply 'my' role—in a manner of speaking—you wot not of? Well I suppose it's not surprising you're only dimly aware, meaning no offence, it isn't exactly front page news anywhere but in Jungo, though it's possible the official reports take certain liberties with the facts if you know what I mean—practically the only liberties, by all accounts, anybody takes in those parts. I have to hunt up the story on the inside pages, smaller and smaller columns further and further in each day. I wouldn't bother if I didn't feel—even at some remove—a certain personal interest in the unfolding course.

Actually I suppose what it would be accurate to say about Jungo is this: civil liberties don't get much play there, but uncivil liberties of all sorts are taken, on a schedule so regular you could set your clock by it. 'I' thought a well reasoned argument of no more than 3¼ single spaced pages, in language so plain any court of law would instantly disallow it, was enough to make the scales fall instantly from the eyes of these well-armed perps who happened to be the law, so that they would surrender all their percs and blend in with a populace permanently united in harmony, peace, justice and mercy. That last word must have particularly rankled; scarcely an official could read that word on the page and not see its implications as personally insulting. Deadly insulting, and according to latest reports 'I' have been captured and await the pleasure of my executioners, who are likely to take considerable pleasure in being as spitefully creative as they possibly can on my sorry ass. It's enough to drive you to drink. . . really sir? Don't mind if I do.

c. Coming or Going

Have you ever been certain you were right about something, even though you didn't have any evidence, in fact the evidence you did have seemed to point to some other conclusion altogether? And then it turned out you were right? nah, doesn't happen to me much either, but I sometimes think—if you see what I mean—that I could trust my instincts more if I only knew with something resembling certainty, most times, whose instincts those'd be I'd be trusting. Some of the personalities I've been infested with have no such doubts and hesitations, or that've gone off walking on their own to establish wholly independent lives and deaths. (I see by the late editions there's been a multiple execution in Jungo county, public and ceremonial to make a stirring example of the foolish rebel pack 'I' led. Raise your glass in mourning. It's some consolation to read how nobly 'I' suffered my end, chatting amiably with my torturers, sweaty at their work of making my death as drawn out and grisly as possible. Reduce me to a gibbering idiot but they couldn't do it! so there! See the execution of Balthazar Gerard for a close parallel (you don't think they'd give the details, let alone photos in a newspaper foldout children might see? like this one, eight colour pages? the press today, it'd have to heave itself up mightily to reach the gutter.)

Anyway Balthazar Gerard was shite in the formal dress of a beggar, he bought gun, powder and balls with money given him in charity by William the Silent to clothe and feed himself, and ripped open the chest of William the Silent at close range with those balls discharged. That'll do fatal things to a man who hadn't thought to strap on his armour over breakfast. He died, Balthazar, surprisingly well though.

What I'm worth as a man or a shite is for others to determine, but I'll tell you this when it's my time to go—though I see by the papers I might be doing staggered duties in that respect—I intend to go cowardly and whimpering, postpone it to the last possible minute and second thank you very much. Raise your glass in mourning sir? don't mind if I do another of these please Charley what's that sir? Oh Charley! make it two.)

That's the worst of these personality invasions, and personalities walking off on their own clear out of you to make their way in this dangerous world. You don't know whether you're coming or going and where's that exactly when it's at home?! (if you see what I mean). AND THEY CLAIM IT ISN'T A MEDICAL CONDITION! that's just to cut down on the health card claims and I suppose you can't really blame them. We'd bankrupt the system all by ourselves, them treating us according to a thousand schemes in futile search of a cure. I could easily see them making it worse, not better, and my case is quite bad enough already giving thanks to the powers that be.

There's a me running around in Slungo county you should steer clear of if you ever get the chance. The horrible things that man has done! some of them prurient and entertaining I'll grant you, but most of them just dull, grinding and repetitive—as to effect I mean, he has a certain talent for variety of means. Of course Slungo county's a slum altogether and he lives in the worst neighbourhood, the one the hardmen themselves for the most part shun as too dangerous, in the capital Slimeturd City itself. What do you mean? Charley d'you have a map back there? thinks I'm making the name up but it's on all the maps see? though sometimes they put a dash through a few of the letters out of respect for refined sensibilities see? see what did I tell you? S—ETURD CITY. I gather you're not from these parts.

Anyway growing up as he did, where he did, his plan of life is perfectly in accord with his surroundings and so makes perfect sense. Does that excuse it? wiser heads than mine, but it seems a waste. The cleverness of his schemes sometimes, the busy and intricate calculations! Wish I had half his brains, wonder how many of mine he took with him when he went and what does he do with it all? Help bring about a better world? no, a worse slum, one he can manipulate better. I doubt I'd be any different in his place.

No, I won't go into any more detail isn't it enough the way it clots my own brain at times, a whirling chaos, bodies leaking fluids, the luckiest of them dead and that's on a slow day! clotting my brain here, behind the eyeballs and the earlobes and the lower jaw. The lower jaw? isn't that a wee bit down for the brainseat to reach? Should have said mouth anyway as it's more properly an orifice. That's the greatest danger of oral sex by the way: fucking your brains out. (If I could only remember, that has a beautiful lilt in the Latin. Strong drink is raging and buggers up your recollection of tongues. Of COURSE I'll have another Charley! and yourself sir? You seem to be falling behind me in the count.

What did you say? repeat that please! Lord God and some of his saints, I'd never have spoken out as freely as I did, however much plied with firewater to lubricate and loosen tonsils and tongue, if I'd known I was spilling inmost secrets, and outmost secrets too, to a WRITER!!! Do you suppose there's any money in my story? I'd be happy to go halves. I might lose my job as a lifeguard soon or the conditions of employment might kill me. Likely not all of me but still! it'd make an appreciable dent. I'd feel the loss most grievous.

This work is © 2015 Martin Heavisides.

Martin Heavisides is a contributing editor to Linnet's Wings (most recently introducing a handpicked selection from the poetry of William Blake) and author of a novel, Undermind. One of his seven full-length plays, Empty Bowl, was given a live reading by The Living Theatre in New York and published in Linnet's Wings (Summer 2008). Mad Hatter's Review, Gambara, Cella's Round Trip, Journal of Compressed Creativity and FRIGG are also among the sane and sensible journals that have accepted his work. http://theevitable.blogspot.com http://movingpicturewrites.com

People are Strange
by Christopher Blake

It was not so long ago now, in a place that could have been almost anywhere when the sun, spilling like brandy through the town of Apple Creek, rose up over a mountain range that'd been thrown together overnight.

On this morning, the 31st of August, Joe Runciman was out for his weekly walk. He ambled along on his old-man legs but inside he skipped (hippity-hop!) through the summer sunshine.

At the corner he met his friend Alec Ohls who he could tell was prancing (clippity-clop!) despite his legs being even older than Joe's which, truth be told, were already quite old themselves.

"Hello Alec," said Joe.

"Hello Joe," said Alec.

"Trying to be smart, Alec?"

"No more than average, Joe"

"Ha," said Joe, "Ha."

"Chortle, chortle," said Alec.

They walked on in silence, Joe's gray hair flapping and Alec's white beard twisting in the breeze. Joe was waltzing now so Alec cantered beside him to keep up. He whispered to himself the first three primes in ascending order.

"<u>One</u>, two, three, <u>one</u>, two, three," he hummed.

"What's that?" asked Joe.

"<u>Not</u> a thing, <u>not</u> a thing," said Alec, keeping time.

At the corner was a sign and Joe paced to a standstill beside it. Alec noticed too late and nearly tripped over his own legs but reared up just in time and stopped beside Joe.

"You remember these?" asked Joe.

Alec leaned backwards and perched his glasses at the tip of his nose.

"Report Illegal Aliens!" proclaimed the sign enthusiastically. It was a border town after all. <u>Was</u> a border

242

town.

"Well where are they?" demanded Alec, looking around.

"They're gone," said Joe. "Been gone for years."

"Turn 'em in!" shouted Alec. "That's what I always say."

"You're not listening," said Joe. "There's no such thing as Illegal Aliens anymore. They're gone. Finished. Kaput."

"Says you."

"Says the world."

"Piss off, says Alec."

Joe turned on his heel and pussyfooted to Mrs. O'Malley's prize winning blue hydrangeas (the secret, she says, is in the soil's acidity) then relieved himself luxuriantly. He sauntered back to Alec who was pointing at the hydrangeas and choking on his giggles.

Joe turned back and looked at Mrs. O'Malley's prize winning blue hydrangeas which were now her as yet undecorated pink hydrangeas.

"I always said you were a base fellow," said Alec.

"Tee," said Joe, "Hee."

"Snicker, snicker," said Alec.

A screen door burst open and Mrs. O'Malley herself appeared on the porch, brandishing a rolling pin that dripped with blood and dangling intestines.

"Cripes," said Alec. "It's Crazy Kat O'Malley!"

"The witch!" said Joe, "Run away!" and they broke like eggs and scrambled down the street, Alec in the lead at a gallop with Joe jitterbugging behind him.

"I'll send your sons after you," yelled Crazy Kat.

"And see if we care," hollered Alec.

The mad harridan thrashed the air and great plumes of steam shot from her ears but the boys were already gone and the old witch had no one to shout at but the formerly prize winning hydrangeas which had stopped listening to this sort of thing a long time ago.

They raced to the corner, then stopped when the imagined pace became too much and hobbled out of sight of Crazy Kat and her pink hydrangeas. They strode along in silence for a while until they reached the crest of a hill and stopped to look down at the town below.

"Same old Apple Creek," said Joe wistfully. "Never

changes."

"Other than all those people," said Alec, "And the houses, and that mountain range."

"Well of course other than the people and the houses and the mountain range," said Joe. "But aside from that..."

"Same old Apple Creek," said Alec, "But say, where are we going anyhow?"

"To adventure," said Joe. "I can feel it. Today we're going to adventure. Like we used to."

They smiled at one another and together they marched arm in arm into the valley where the town of Apple Creek sat and picked its teeth in the August sunshine. But though they'd lived there all their lives, they soon got lost, so they stopped to ask directions from a short fellow shouting the stock of his fruit-stall to the bustling street.

"Hello," said Alec, "We've never been here before and we've managed to get lost."

"Well of course you've never been here," said the little man. "It's a new street, just laid last night. Apples, Mangoes, translucent Pears!"

"Very industrious of you," said Joe, "To lay a street overnight and to build all these houses and shops to go with it."

"No point to a street without shops and houses," said he. "Pineapples, Oranges, slippery Melons!"

"Tell me," said Alec, "Where did you all come from?"

"From China, of course," said the Chinese man. "Avocados, Plantains, flaccid Bananas!"

"But what great English you speak! And are you all fruit sellers?" asked Joe, gazing up the street at the line of equally enthusiastic fruiterers.

"No," he said, "Most of us are here to manufacture fortune cookies. Dates, Papayas, sparkly Limes!"

"I thought those were an American invention," said Alec.

"Of course," said the man, "But we lend them authenticity. Tangerines, Lemons, velvety Kiwis!"

"Sounds sensible," said Joe. "You're all clearly very quick workers. I imagine you'll have quite the industry here before long."

"Which way did you say the town square was?" asked

Alec.

"Up the road and to the left, then first right then left again. From there it's straight ahead. Blackberries, Blueberries, turgid Raspberries!"

They thanked him and bought two slices of slippery melon, then scampered through the throng along the route the little man had told them.

"Nice man," said Alec and munched his melon.

"Very nice," said Joe. "Incredible work ethic!"

"The benefits of open borders!" said Alec.

"Indeed," said Joe. "No illegal aliens from anyplace."

The crowds began to thin and the boys sauntered forward, at last catching sight of the old town hall and the square it fronted. A flag flapped lazily before them and behind it all the new mountain range loomed majestically above.

In the centre of the square were a flock of people and a man with a wolfish nose who was speaking to them from a bandstand.

"What's this?" asked Alec of the nearest man.

"The mayor is giving a speech!"

"What about?" asked Joe.

"The Chinese," whispered the man.

"What about them?"

"How we've got to get rid of them!"

"Get rid of them? We thought they were rather nice."

"So did I. Until the mayor told us about those strange ways they advertise their fruit."

"He's right," nodded Alec. "It was a bit strange the way he shouted his wares."

"But the slippery melon was delicious," said Joe, "And slippery!"

"Quite true," said Alec.

"Well, you can't get rid of them," said Joe. "Open borders and all."

"Oh, we don't mind if they're here, we just don't want them here."

"I see," said Joe.

"Well, we best be going," said Alec.

The man nodded and turned back to face the wolf nosed mayor who was now howling incomprehensibly. With his hairy hands, he gestured wildly towards the nascent Chinatown, then dove through the audience and bit savagely into the neck of a spectator.

The crowd applauded madly. Alec and Joe wandered off.

They ambled on towards the mountain range, Joe sashaying and Alec trotting along beside him. They passed through foothills where fresh grass lounged idly and over streams where the melted frost of the night before trickled truantly down the mountains.

They were deep in the forest now, far from towns and roads and civilization, but soon enough they came to a little stand where two boys sat, looking down with deadly focus at a piece of paper placed between them.

"'Morning," said Joe.

"Shush," said a blond haired boy, drawing an X into the top left square of a three by three grid.

"The Gainesville Gambit!" shouted the other. "You wouldn't!"

"I have," said the first. "How do you reply?"

Just then, a third boy appeared from a hole next to the stand and looked down at the game.

"That the Gainesville Gambit?" he asked.

"Sure is," said the blond boy.

The newcomer whistled through the hole left by his missing tooth.

"How you going to respond to that?" he asked the other.

"Well give me a second, will you? I'm considering my options."

"Now what are you boys up to?" asked Joe.

"Running a business, Sir," replied the third boy.

"And what kind of business is that?" asked Alec.

"A lemonade stand!" announced the third boy proudly.

"Well, where is it?" asked Joe.

"What?" said the blond boy, irritated by the disturbance. "The lemonade?"

"Oh, we sold it all this morning," said the third boy, "There was an early rush."

"An early rush out here? In the middle of nowhere?"

"Not the middle of nowhere Sir. This is prime real estate."

"On the doorstep of the biggest infrastructure project of the century," said the blond boy absently.

"What infrastructure project?" asked Joe.

"Aha!" shouted the blond boy's opponent and scratched an O in the middle square.

"The Runnymede Riposte!" said the third boy. "A prudent move."

The blond boy looked down at the paper and scratched his head. His brown haired opponent laughed.

"We've been digging a hole for most of the summer," said the brown haired boy, "To increase the traffic. Things really picked up steam when Roy arrived yesterday, though. He's been a godsend."

The third boy smiled.

"It was nothing really," he said.

"Where's the hole go?" asked Joe.

"Well China, of course," said the brown haired boy. "You know how many people they've got over there? Big market for lemonade."

"You can't get to China from here," said Alec. "You gotta dig from Canton, Illinois to do that. It's antipodal. That's why they named it Canton, Illinois."

"Actually," said Roy, "If we dug straight down we'd wind up in the Indian Ocean. We had to make a turn under Russia and even then it was real chancy for a while."

"That so," said Joe.

"Yessir," said the brown haired boy.

"Let's see this hole," said Alec.

Roy led them away while the blond boy sweated over his next move and the brown haired one leaned back in his chair and chewed a blade of grass.

The hole, when they reached it, was 10 feet wide and perfectly round and dove straight down through the earth.

"Some hole," said Alec.

"I'll say, said Joe.

"So that's where the mountains came from," said Alec.

"Had to dump the soil somewhere," shrugged Roy.

"And what about when you hit the liquid mantle of the earth? I hear it's pretty hot down there."

"Aww, it wasn't so bad. The others passed me down

lemonade when I got thirsty."

Back at the lemonade stand the blond boy had just placed an X in the bottom right square.

"The Toulouse Trap," said Roy. "Oh wise, oh very wise."

"You all look so familiar," said Alec. "What did you say your names were?"

"Well, I'm Roy," said Roy. "The blond boy is Joe Runciman and the brown haired one is Alec Ohls."

"Alec Ohls!" said Alec Ohls.

"Joe Runciman!" said Joe Runciman.

The boys didn't look up from their game.

"Mmhmm," they said.

"Must be our grandkids," whispered Joe.

"I won't have grandkids of ours setting up lemonade stands," muttered Alec. "It's indecent!"

"Alec Ohls III," said Alec Ohls, "You put a stop to this lemonade nonsense right now."

"And Joe Runciman III," said Joe Runciman, "Fill up that hole to China. It's a death trap."

The boys looked up from their game.

"Who are you shouting at?" asked the blond boy.

"You," said Alec and Joe together.

"You've got us confused," said the blond haired boy. "Joe Runciman III's my father. I'm Joe Runciman IV and that's Alec Ohls IV."

Joe and Alec studied them.

"They did look a bit young," said Joe to Alec.

"Who's he then?" asked Alec and pointed at the third boy.

"That's Roy," said Alec Ohls IV.

"Roy who?" asked Joe.

"Just Roy," said Joe Runciman IV. "He's the new kid."

Roy smiled and stuck the tip of his tongue through the hole in his teeth.

"Well, if you're our great grandkids," said Alec, "I've got no problem with the lemonade stand."

"Or the hole," said Joe.

"Or the hole," agreed Alec.

"You got a couple extra chairs back there?" asked Joe.

"Sure thing," said Alec Ohls IV and he motioned Alec

and Joe around, then scratched an O into the bottom middle square.

"The Saratoga Swipe," said Roy.

"The Saratoga Swipe," repeated Alec Ohls IV.

"Say Roy," said Joe. "You remind me of a boy Alec and I knew back when we were your age. He had a real flair for engineering too. What was his name, Alec?"

"Roy," said Alec.

"So it was," said Joe, "Hell, now that you say it, Roy must be his great-grandson. He's the spitting image."

"No, no," said Roy. "My great-grandfather died a real long time ago."

"Might seem like a long time ago to you, but its only yesterday to us," said Alec.

"No," said Roy, "I mean a <u>long</u> time ago. Must be 3,000 years ago now."

"Of course!" shouted Joe Runciman IV, and he placed an X in the top middle square.

"The Pensacola Parry," said Roy. "Beautiful play, just beautiful"

"Then you're," said Joe.

"An alien!" shouted Alec. "Turn him in! Turn in Illegal Aliens!"

"Shush!" said Alec Ohls IV and Joe Runciman IV.

"That explains the goofing with the hole," whispered Joe. "They were always monkeying around with some kind of mischief."

"I told you they were here," said Alec. "I knew it all along," and he turned away from them.

Joe studied Roy. He looked just like any other kid: blue eyes, brown hair, the standard number of arms and legs with bruises and scrapes in the right places. A smile lit up Joe's face.

"But then you must be Roy," said Joe. "I mean, our Roy, from way back."

"Sure am," said Roy. "I didn't recognize you two at first. You got old."

"And you've stayed young."

"I was old for a while. I got young again."

Alec turned back towards Roy and his eyes were red and glassy.

"Why'd you have to go, Roy? Why'd you have to go? We were friends. I missed you."

"I grew up," said Roy. "I didn't have a choice."

"But where have you all been?" asked Joe. "There hasn't been an alien seen in years."

"Everyone else grew up too. My people have two stages and we go back and forth between them now and again. The first stage, what I'm in now, well, we stand out a lot more than the stage twos, what with our fooling around and all. It took us a while after we landed to figure that out, but once we did we shipped the stage one's off world and moved the stage twos away before they reverted. That's why no one's noticed us. We've been hiding."

"Then how are you back?" asked Alec.

"We usually revert at a pretty fixed schedule, but somehow I turned back early and of course," he grinned, "I didn't want to leave. So I came looking for you two. I found your great-grandsons and it was just like old times."

"Like when you built us those wings," said Joe.

"Or when you made the state into an island," added Alec.

"Just like that," said Roy, "And even better now that we're all together again."

Alec shuffled over to Roy, then knelt and hugged his old lost friend. They held each other tightly and a tear strolled down Alec's cheek and got lost in the hairs of his tangled beard.

"Gotcha!" shouted Alec Ohls IV, and he placed an O in the upper right hand corner of the board.

"The Beijing Block and Sock," breathed Roy and his features glowed. "Inspired, simply inspired."

They all smiled. Alec stood up and returned to his seat. From the distance came the sound of rolling thunder and a great dust plume was dancing on the horizon. The chaos charged forward and the dust was sucked high into the air, then scattered down over the new mountains.

"Stampede!" bellowed Alec.

"Customers!" cried Joe Runciman IV.

"I thought you were out of lemonade," said Joe.

"Roy can whip some up," said Alec Ohls IV and in an instant two huge casks appeared next to the stand.

"Good work," said Joe Runciman IV and Roy gave a little bow.

The crowd was drawing nearer now and after a moment Joe and Alec made out the leaders of the pack. They were the settlers from the newly built Chinatown and the men in front ran back and forth and laid down new stretches of road as their fellows followed, wheeling their houses and shops behind them.

When the leaders reached the hole, they hurled their lengths of road before them, then hopped down and followed them as they fell. After a minute of this constant caravan, Alec spotted their friend, the fruiterer of the slippery melon, and plucked him from the crowd.

"You must be thirsty from all that running," said Joe Runciman IV. "Here, have a lemonade on the house."

The fruiterer took it and knocked it quickly back.

"What's going on?" asked Alec.

"The town's throwing us out. Said we were unfairly disadvantaging the local fortune cookie industry. Grapefruits, Limes, saturnine Lemons!"

"No thanks," said Alec Ohls IV. "We're all right for citrus."

"But we don't have a local fortune cookie industry," said Joe.

"No matter. We know when we're not wanted. It's time to head back. Clementines, cherries, buttery Coconuts!" said the fruiterer, and he hopped into the hole.

"Nice man," said Alec.

"Very nice," said Joe and they stood and sipped their lemonade as Apple Creek's short lived Chinatown packed up and trundled by, then disappeared into the hole.

"None of them are stopping for lemonade," complained Alec Ohls IV.

"They're very industrious," said Joe. "Probably no time for lemonade."

"How's that!" said Joe Runciman IV and scratched an X into the bottom left hand corner of the game.

"The Roncesvalles Rearguard," said Roy. "A desperate play."

Joe Runciman IV ignored him and they all watched, rapt,

as Alec Ohls IV considered his next and final move.

"Alec!" came a shout.

"Joe!" came another.

Alec and Alec and Joe and Joe turned 'round.

Four men and a monster were walking towards them. Two of the men were middle aged and two others were older. The monster was of indeterminate age but was dressed in a very snappy three-piece suit that set of his green skin wonderfully.

"There you are, Dad," said the monster, rushing over and lifting Roy into his arms.

"This is my son, Roy junior," said Roy the boy. "Son, these are Alec Ohls and Joe Runciman and Alec Ohls IV and Joe Runciman IV."

Pleasantries were exchanged.

"I believe I've already met your sons and grandsons," said Roy junior to Alec and Joe.

"I apologize," said Alec.

"Yuk," said Joe, "Yuk."

"Chuckle, chuckle," said Alec.

"My last move," breathed Alec Ohls IV and he placed an O in the left middle square. "The Rubicon."

Joe Runciman IV cursed under his breath. Roy looked on in awed silence.

"Alec, Joe," said the youngest of the approaching men.

"Hello, grandson," said Joe.

"Hi gramps," replied Joe Runciman III.

"I hope the boys weren't too much trouble, Mr. Runciman," said Alec Ohls III as he stood behind his son.

"Don't be ignorant," said Alec.

"Hi granddad," sighed Alec Ohls III.

"What's this I hear about you peeing in Katherine O'Malley's hydrangeas, Dad?" asked Joe Runciman junior.

"Alec provoked me," said Joe.

"Is that true, Pop?" asked Alec Ohls junior.

"Damn right," said Alec, "And I'd do it again."

"Well, the two of you've got to apologize," said Joe Runciman junior. "Mrs. O'Malley's in a complete tizzy."

"All the more reason to stay away," said Joe.

"Dad, aren't you proud of us?" asked Alec Ohls IV. "We

set up our own business and dug a hole all the way to China."

"Well, that's very impressive son, but I'm afraid you're going to have to close it up. School starts on Monday and we can't just leave a huge unattended hole to China back here—it's a recipe for a lawsuit."

"No!" shouted Joe Runciman IV and he and Alec Ohls IV grabbed Roy and ran towards the hole.

"What is happening to our young people?" said Joe Runciman III. "They disrespect their elders, they disobey their parents. They ignore the law. They riot in the streets inflamed with wild notions. Their morals are decaying. What is to become of them?"

"Who said that?" asked Alec Ohls III.

"I did," said Joe Runciman III.

"Oh, let the boys have their fun," said Alec.

"They're not hurting anyone," added Joe.

"That's not the point," said Joe Runciman III. "They turn ten this year, and it's about time they grew up. No more of these childish games," and he and Alec Ohls III grabbed their sons and hauled them back to the lemonade stand.

"You too, Roy," said Roy Junior, the monster. "Until you grow up again, you'll just never fit in here the way I do. You can't stay, but before you go you need to close up the hole like the men asked."

"Come on Pop," said Alec Ohls junior.

"Time to go, Dad," added Joe Runciman junior.

Alec and Joe looked at each other and at their sons, grandsons, and great grandsons and at their old friend and his well-dressed son, the monster. By now the sun was perched in its noonday nest and its light swam straight down the magnificent hole which sparkled and glittered into the depths.

"Roy," said Alec, "Do you remember how to make those wings from when we were kids?"

"Of course," said Roy.

"How about a last couple pairs for the road?" said Joe and as he spoke great golden wings exploded from his and Alec's backs and they fluttered up through the syrupy sunshine.

"You get down here this instant!" shouted Joe Runciman junior.

"Or what?" bellowed Joe and laughed and frolicked in the thermals.

"Goodbye, Roy," said Alec, and he flapped by and tousled Roy's hair. "I'll miss you."

"Don't worry," said Roy, "I'll be around."

"Can't we come with you?" shouted Alec Ohls IV.

"'Fraid not boys," said Alec. "Whether you like it or not, you're about to grow up. But maybe one day," and he flew corkscrews and loop the loops above them.

"I've got it!" shouted Joe Runciman IV, and he placed his last X in the right middle square.

"The Sausalito Stalemate," said Alec Ohls IV. "Another tie."

"Another tie," agreed Roy and squinted into the sun at the winged figures.

"So long boys!" shouted Alec.

"Don't close her up 'till we're through, Roy," said Joe.

"Yessir," said Roy and gave them a childish salute.

Alec and Joe did a few last barrel rolls and somersaults, then pounded up into the sky in a double helix of golden air. They flew so high that it seemed they might be melted by the sun but their golden wings held strong and at last they ceased their flapping and dove straight down towards the hole.

They made rude faces as they passed the lemonade stand at which the boys laughed and the men scoffed and then they disappeared into the hole and left the town of Apple Creek forever.

The others were motionless, each father standing beside his son, listening as the whoops and hollers of the old men echoed up to them.

But the day was growing older and the walk ahead was long and so at last they turned away, Joe Runciman junior and Alec Ohls junior leading the way and the others following behind through the treads worn deep by the Chinese caravan.

"People are strange," said Roy junior, the monster.

"Yeah," nodded Joe Runciman III, "People are strange."

This work is © 2015 by Christopher Blake

Christopher Blake is a reader, writer, and medical resident

Christopher Blake

from Ontario, Canada. He first discovered Lafferty in the form of a weathered copy of Nine Hundred Grandmothers in an Oxfam Bookshop and wrote "People are Strange" as a distraction from his Masters thesis on laughter and health. He therefore humbly hopes that this story gives you a chuckle, for your health's sake.

Justice
by Dan Knight

"Mr. Hieronious Smith?"

"Yes."

"Mr. Smith, my name is Holster. I'm with the Bureau of Enforced Restitution and Payments."

"Berp? You're the man from Berp?"

"I fail to see any humor in that, Mr. Smith."

"Somehow that doesn't surprise me. What does my government want now?"

"Mr. Smith, it appears you've made a number of serious misrepresentations, VERY serious misrepresentations, on the return you filed with us."

"Meaning?"

"Meaning that the company you retained to complete your return has classified you as a Four Triple B with two public service exemptions. In point of fact you are a Twelve F with no exemptions at all."

"Uh huh. Meaning?"

"Meaning, Mr. Smith, you owe us a considerable amount of money."

"Of course."

"Now, in view of the fact it's such a large sum, the Bureau will not be insisting on immediate payment. The district manager has very graciously extended you sixty days to pay the arrears. However, I must remind you, a failure to pay in full by the due date will have some very unpleasant consequences. In your case I would not rule out final closure and liquidation."

"And just *what* is that supposed to mean?"

"Salvage, Mr. Smith."

"SALVAGE!"

"Well of course salvage. Do you have a hearing impairment?"

"Just get on with it."

"Mr. Smith, you know the penalties for not meeting your payments. I think sixty days is a very generous offer and I suggest you make the best of them. Here's a breakdown on your revised of your revised assessment. It's itemized and quite clear but if you have any questions call us. Our number is on the back. Good-day, Mr. Smith."

"Give my regards to the boys back at the office."

Hieronious slammed the door loudly.

"Who was it dear?"

"Trouble."

"Again?" Luella Smith came out of the kitchen wiping her hands on an old dish towel. "What is it this time?"

"They've audited me."

"Oh Hiero, is it bad?"

"It doesn't look too good." Hieronious glanced over the assessment. "Seems Great Great Grand-dad wasn't Swiss at all. He was French."

"Oh no!"

"It gets worse. My exemptions, for Great Aunt Edith's suffragetting, and three times Great Grand-dad Penney's slavery abolitionist work, are both denied. It says that the forms were completed in a confusing manner and that there wasn't enough corroborating evidence to support them."

"How much do they say it's going to cost?"

"Let's see . . . restitution to former colonies, environmental damage from South Sea's nuclear testing, over-fishing, weapon sales . . . about $15,000 a year for each of the past five years plus interest."

"That's $100,000! We don't have that kind of money. What'll we do?"

Hieronious shook his head.

"I don't know. I just don't know."

"We could take a mortgage on my Grandparents."

"No! No matter how bad this gets. If anything happens to me that money will be enough to support you and the children. It's the only bright part of this whole thing. If they break me up you'll be better off than you are now." He put his arms around Luella's pleasantly large frame. "What I don't understand is why a girl with one full quarter aboriginal blood and looks to boot would marry a guy like me?"

Luella blushed.

"Because she loves you."

"I love you too, beautiful. I just wish I could have given you a better life. Look at this place. No furniture. No carpet. When was the last time we bought you a new dress?"

"I don't need a new dress."

"All because I was born Euro-white. I've got the blood of every major empire building race in my veins and there isn't a man anywhere that I don't owe."

"It's not your fault."

"No, but here I go off to the salvage tanks. What good will I be dead? I didn't enslave anyone. I didn't go to war. I never stole anything or raped anybody. So why me?" He sat down on the couch heavily. "Tomorrow I'm going straight down to that Acme Family Find place and find out what's going on. They goofed this up in the first place. Maybe they can get me out of it."

   ***

"I'm sorry but there's nothing we can do."

"But you admit it was your fault?"

"Oh yes, most definitely our fault. I'd it was almost criminal the way we messed up your declaration."

"So?"

"'So' what, Mr. Smith?"

"What are you going to do about it?"

The woman behind the desk smiled wryly.

"Nothing. That was all quite clear on the waiver you signed. That is your signature, isn't it? We are in no way responsible for the errors. It doesn't matter that we made a mistake. It's your problem."

"I'll get a lawyer! I'll sue you for every exemption you've got!"

"Good-bye Mr. Smith."

"I'll call the police! I'll call the papers! I'll call the Ace Heritage Place!"

"Who?"

"The Ace Heritage Place. They're your biggest competitor aren't they?"

"Mr. Smith surely you wouldn't go pestering them with this would you?"

"You bet your Navajo Grandmother I would. Just think of the things their ad boys could do with a story like this. How much business do you think you'd have if people knew they could end up salvaged for one of your little mistakes?"

"Perhaps I've been a bit hasty." She adjusted her dress and leaned forward exposing a surprising amount of skin. "I'll level with you Mr. Smith. I don't know if we can do anything about this Swiss-French mix-up. It's been checked and confirmed by the government computers and that, as they say, is that. The best we could do is to run a follow up on the two denied exemptions. They're not great. No murdered civil rights workers or anything but they're solid. They might get you ten or twelve thousand each if they came through."

It's a start. How long will it take?"

"A hundred years on one and about one hundred and fifty on the other would take . . . say two months."

"That's over sixty days!"

"Is that significant Mr. Smith?"

"Yes. I've only got fifty-nine."

"That's too bad. I don't suppose there's any point in wasting the energy then, is there?"

"You just hold your horses. You're not out of this thing yet. Do the search. I need every advantage I can get. And remember, Ace is right across the street."

"I suppose we *could* put a rush on it. But there are no promises Mr. Smith. These things take time."

"Time, lady, is about all I have left."

***

"I want to talk to Fred Greasyfingers."

"What about?"

"Business. I need some work done and I heard he could help me."

"What makes you think Greasyfingers could help you?"

"My wife's cousin, Don Littlewheels, says he does very good work. He says I should let the presidents speak for me."

The big man took the bill and held it to his ear.

"Hmmm. Nixon says you're alright. I don't know though.

You got anyone else who can speak for you?"

Hieronious grudgingly handed over another note.

"Ah, J.F.K. Much better. *Much* better." The big man smiled. "It is always good to have friends who will stand for you. Come."

Motioning for Hieronious to follow he disappeared into a narrow laneway. A twist and two turns later they were back on the street. The only person in sight was a small, dark, man dozing on a corner bench. Hieronious turned to his guide but the big man had vanished.

"Mr. Greasyfingers?"

The man on the bench looked up slowly.

"Mr. Greasyfingers, I believe the government has made a grave mistake. I was told that you could, ah, speak to them for me."

The man blinked lazily and nodded.

"They are demanding a large sum of money from me. Money I don't have. They say they will take their portion in flesh if I do not pay."

"Yes. Yes." The little man's voice was deep and resonant. "A not uncommon occurrence, Mister . . . ?"

"Smith. Hieronious Smith."

"Mr. Smith. Yes. You believe they have made an error do you? Perhaps you are not such a bad fellow as they say? I am almost convinced of it. I will need to take council of course."

He held out his hand meaningfully. Hieronious place a number of bills in it.

"It is necessary that there be ten for a council. I believe we are one short. Ah, yes. That's better. Now we begin."

Taking a small black box from his pocket he entered a nearby phone booth. After affixing it to the receiver he began a quick series of entries on a flexible plastic keyboard, occasionally stopping to glance at his wrist watch. Hieronious shuffled nervously.

"Here."

Greasyfingers shoved money at Hieronious.

"What's wrong? What happened?"

"You should feel honored citizen Smith. Not many do they spend such effort to secure. You have a Guardian Angel."

"A what?"

"A Guardian Angel. A very special . . . freind." Greasyfingers smiled. "One slip and the entire police force would be here before we had time to sneeze. I can't help you."

"You've got to!"

Greasyfingers eyed Hieronious warily.

"I've only got two days left!"

"Then you are a dead man. You have my condolences. Our business is completed."

"Thirty thousand. Two days and still thirty thousand short. Oh God, what am I going to . . . HEY! There's only nine bills here. I gave you ten!"

Like a ghost the big man had materialized next to Hieronious. Huge hands took him firmly by the shoulders.

"Thirty-*one* thousand short," he mumbled.

The walk back was much longer than he remembered.

***

"There is no point in violence Mr. Smith. You are considerably short on your assessment and the time is up!"

"GET OUT OF HERE OR I SMEAR YOU ACROSS THE DRIVEWAY!"

"A rocket launcher is no way of dealing with your social obligations Mr. Smith."

"VAMPIRES!"

A brace of tracers came from the second story window ricocheting harmlessly off the waiting armored car.

"Mr. Smith, please. We are busy people and in the interest of . . . I beg your pardon Madame? Yes, of course I'll tell him. Mr. Smith, your neighbor Mrs. LaCready says if you damage her roses it will go hard on your children. Mr. Smith? Can you hear me?"

There was a scream of frustration from somewhere in the house and then for a few minutes; silence. Some of the neighbors to cover.

"ALRIGHT! ALRIGHT! YOU WIN! You win you miserable sonafabitches. I'm COMING OUT!"

An armful of weapons tumbled out of the front door followed by Hieronious; hands on his head.

"I couldn't have gone on much longer anyways."

"Ah, I understand. We have awakened your morality."
Hieronious stopped and looked Holster in the eye.
"Lack of bullets, Holster. Lack of bullets."
They bundled him into the waiting van.

"Why are you guys so gung-ho to get me anyway?"
The armored vehicle sped through the city toward the Wrecking Yards. Hieronious appeared to be their only customer this morning.

"It's not like I've broken any laws. I've lived a quiet life. I never even cheated on my taxes. Why me?"

"Oh but you have Mr. Smith. You *have* broken the law. You have broken the first law of modern living. You have allowed yourself to be noticed by your government. As you can now see it was a very foolish thing to do."

"This is hardly my doing Holster."

"Oh, and was it not you who entrusted the filing of an extremely important document to some cheap fly-by-night company? A firm which boggled the thing amazingly I might add. We have your submission tacked up on the bulletin board back at the Bureau. It gets quite a few chuckles."

"But what have I *really* done?"

Holster looked at Hieronious with pity.

"Nothing Mr. Smith. Absolutely nothing. Just as the millions your ancestors enslaved or abused were doing.

You are not what's important here. You are worthless. It is what you represent that is of significance. Think of yourself as a sin offering. The mighty fallen hard and broken. It doesn't matter that you are a meek man. We don't want specifics clouding the beauty of the system. What pleasure could we possibly take in destroying an innocent man?

You are a monster Mr. Smith. And if you're not then we shall make you one. A rebellious unrepentant sinner to whom society extends the only kindness it can. The opportunity to make some small repayment of that vast debt you owe us and so die at least partially redeemed.

We will break you up and take from your body what we can use. The rest will be ground up to fertilize our hungry fields. There is also of course the small pleasure which some of the less refined of our citizens take in watching the proceedings: on their televisions. Justice must be seen Mr. Smith. It must be tasted and savored by all.

So, you see. You have managed to do quite a bit. It's a pity you couldn't have done more. If we had had more time perhaps you would have."

The van stopped. Hieronious was man-handled in a professional manner up a set of stairs and into the Wrecker's crushing embrace. His hands were tied and someone from the television crew came and put make-up on his face.

"It's only the local cable," she said around a mouthful of gum. "But you can never tell when someone important might tune in. Finished!"

"Okay fella, what'll it be?'

"Huh?"

"What'll it be? Condemned's choice. Where would you like me to start? Arms? Nose? Legs? How about the knee-caps? I haven't done knee-caps in ages."

"Any rules about how small it can be?"

"Nope. If you want to drag it out that's your problem."

"Okay then. Pull out my hair one strand at a time."

"How about I just rip your head off and get this show on the road?"

"Just a minute buddy. I still have some rights you know."

"STOP! STOP there's been a mistake!"

"Who's the broad?"

"Mr. Smith! Mr. Smith! Great news!"

"She's not one of them bleeding heart do-gooder types is she? They make me nauseous."

"Her? She's got about as much personal warmth as a reptile. She's my Geneo-Agent. She gets a percentage of anything she can dig up on me. While I'm still breathing that is."

"Oh, that's okay then. Greed I can understand."

"Mr. Smith, your exemptions came through!"

She raced up the platform stairs and handed an official looking document to Holster. The crowd ooooed appreciatively at her.

"It'll take a lot more than twenty thousand to get me out of this." Hieronious winced as the Wrecker changed his grip.

"It's your twice great grandfather; Joseph Penny!"

"The slave abolitionist?"

"I suppose he was an abolitionist. He was a slave."

"A SLAVE!"

Holster was checking the documents. He looked irritated. The Wrecker began to fidget.

"Is this going to take long? My coffee break starts in five minutes."

"Yes Mr. Smith, a slave. He was captured by Arab slave traders in North Africa about 1852."

"Arabs!"

"He was released on the death of his master, headed north, and started a prosperous business."

Hieronious's grin began to fade.

"But his shop was smashed by a mob and his home burned to the ground."

Holster grumbled loudly and his left eye began to twitch.

"He returned to the south and was eventually adopted by a native band. When the band was forcefully relocated by the government he died on the journey from a combination of malnutrition and disease."

"What a horrible life."

"Yes, isn't it wonderful Mr. Smith?"

"That's it. I'm off to break."

"AIEEEEE! MY FINGER! YOU TORE OFF MY FINGER!"

"Sorry buddy. Union rules. Something's got to come off or I don't get paid. Why should a working man like me suffer because of you?"

"You're free to go Smith. The papers are all in order. It looks like you might even be getting something back on top of it all."

"I'm bleeding to death!"

"Then quick, sign this so I get my commission. We working girls have to watch out for what's ours."

Hieronious rolled about the stage wildly. Holster sniffed in disgust.

"Such a fuss over a little blood. Madame, would you care to join me for lunch?"

"Delighted. Let me get my purse."

"SOMEONE UNTIE ME!"

"Congratulations Mr. Smith. You're a very lucky man. Be sure to have someone look at that wound. You can't be too careful."

This work is © 2015 by Dan Knight.

An Afterword to "Justice"
by Gregorio Montejo

In addition to founding United Mythologies Press in Weston, Ontario in order to publish the work of R.A. Lafferty, and editing a short-lived but highly important journal of lafferty studies called *The Boomer Flats Gazette*, Dan Knight was also a writer of fiction, publishing stories in such magazines as *Parsec*, and the Canadian journal of speculative fiction, *On Spec*. Knight carried on a significant correspondence with Lafferty beginning in the mid-1980's, and continuing throughout much of the 90s. The Lafferty archives at the University of Tulsa contain many of these letters, as well as a variety of short stories, both published and unpublished, which Knight sent Lafferty during these years, A copy of the original manuscript of "Justice," a previously unpublished short story, is located in the Lafferty papers in a box indicating that the tales dates from the period 1994-1996.

"Justice" is self-evidently a satire, a literary genre which Lafferty himself oftentimes practiced. Satire in the western tradition traces its origins back to the bawdy burlesques of the ancient Greek satyr plays performed during the Athenian Dionysia. In its later Horatian manifestation, developed during the Roman period, satire was used to playfully mock social vices through mild, light-hearted humor; while in its concurrent Juvenalian form, satire was employed to address perceived social evil by means of ridicule, scorn, irony, or exaggeration, in order to expose and criticize what the author took to be irredeemably foolish or vicious, particularly in the areas concerning political and social issues. This form of satire typically attempts to reduce an opposing idea or position to a caricature, all the better to heap derision upon it. Satires written in the tradition of Juvenal are often much darker than their Horatian counterparts, and are frequently characterized by outrage, invective, sarcasm, and moral indignation.[1] In many of his stories Lafferty will utilize Horatian humor to gently poke fun at genre conventions or social mores, but he is also quite adept at invoking the mocking invectives of a Juvenal, especially when denouncing the increasing routinization, bureaucratization, and resulting dehumanization of modern western societies, or when heaping literary scorn upon the course of *soi-disant* reform in post-Vatican II Catholicism.[2]

It is precisely this combination of social critique and satirical adeptness that endears Lafferty to the contemporary *enfant terrible* of French letters, Michel Houellebecq, who values Lafferty precisely because—among both contemporary genre and non-genre writers—he estimates that Lafferty is almost alone in his ability to audaciously think outside of conventionally acceptable societal parameters, along with his willingness to fearlessly mock not only reflexively received socio-political norms, but even the unthinkingly embraced ontological categories of contemporary western civilization, thus allowing us the possibility to reconceive what reality can be.[3] Houellebecq has invoked this exemplary rebellious spirit

---

[1] Cf. Dustin Griffin, *Satire: A Critical Reintroduction* (Lexington: University Press of Kentucky, 1994).

[2] See, for example, "Ishmael into the Barrens," "And Walk Now Gently Through the Fire," "The World as Will and Wallpaper." Perhaps the most ferocious instance of Lafferty's witheringly satirical moral indignation is to be found in *How Many Miles to Babylon*, published by Knight's United Mythologies Press in 1989.

[3] "Arrivée à maturité dès la fin des années 1950, elle ne donne que depuis peu de réels signes d'épuisement – un peu comme la littérature fantastique pouvait le faire, immédiatement avant l'apparition de Lovecraft. C'est sans doute pour cette raison qu'aucun écrivain, jusqu'à présent, n'a réellement éprouvé le besoin de repousser les limites – de toute façon assez flexibles – du genre. La seule exception serait peut-être cet auteur étrange, très étrange, qu'est R.A. Lafferty. Plus que de la science-fiction, Lafferty donne parfois l'impression de créer une sorte de philosophie-fiction, unique en ce que la spéculation ontologique y tient une place plus importante que les interrogations sociologiques, psychologiques ou morales. Dans Le Monde comme volonté et papier peint (le titre anglais, The World as Will and Wallpaper, donne de plus un effet

which he finds in Lafferty to push the envelope of what can be said and thought, often challenging the most cherished nostrums embraced by contemporary pluralistic societies, especially those regarding the perennially neuralgic issues of race and sex. One critic has briefly yet quite aptly described Houellebecq's Juvenalian novels as mocking condemnations of the "absurdities and hypocrisies of modern life, using a lethal mix of satire, realism and cynicism spiced with elements of science fiction and pornography, pathos and bathos."[4] As already indicated, at its most biting this sort of satire is often ominous, unfailingly contentious, and at times even scurrilous. In other words, if Juvenalian satire is to be effective, it must undoubtedly make some people angry or at least uneasy. I would venture to say that satire written in the tradition of Juvenal that is perfectly safe, which does not make anyone upset, which rocks no boats, and which incites no debates, is satire that ultimately fails precisely on Juvenalian terms.

I would contend that Knight's tale falls squarely within the parameters of this Juvenalian canon: It is a satire on race, politics, and society, influenced in part by Lafferty's mocking denunciations of the corrupting effects of modern social polity, and which on some points even seems to anticipate Houellebecq, especially its focus on the controversial issues of racial "justice" and "injustice." The thematic background of the story may have been suggested, at least in part, by the

---

d'allitéraion), le narrateur, voulant explorer l'univers jusqu'à ses limites, perçoit au bout d'un temps des répétitions, se retrouve dans des situations similaires, et finit par prendre conscience que le monde est composé d'entités de petite taille, nées chacune d'un acte de volonté identique, et indéfiniment répétées. Le monde est ainsi à la fois illimité et sans espoir ; je connais peu de textes aussi poignants. Dans Autobiographie d'un machine ktistèque, Lafferty va encore plus loin dans la modification des catégories de la représentation ordinaire; mais le texte en devient malheureusement presque illisible." Michel Houellebecq, "Sortir du XXe siècle," *Nouvelle Revue Française* 560-561 (April, 2002), pp. 117-120, at 119.

[4] Martin Pengelly, "Who is Michel Houellebecq, the French Novelist on the Charlie Hebdo Cover?" *The Guardian*, online edition, Saturday January 10, 2015:
http://www.theguardian.com/books/2015/jan/10/michel-houellebecq-french-novelist-charlie-hebdo-cover.

Canadian government's 1991 establishment of the Royal Commission on Aboriginal Peoples, which investigated Canada's removal of indigenous Canadian children from their families and their placement in church-run Indian Residential Schools as part of a greater effort to homogenize Canadian society. As a result of the commission's final recommendations, Canadian authorities issued an apologetic official "Statement of Reconciliation," which stated that the government-supported religious schools were indeed established according to a racist model of assimilation, and also set aside a $350 million reparation fund in order to recompense all those who had been affected by the Indian Residential Schools.[5] It is important to note here that the only indigenous character in Knight's satire—Luella Smith, the protagonist's wife—is also the only wholly admirable character in the story.

The tale's immediate purpose is to produce a scarifying denunciation of the excesses of identity politics, particularly a warped conception of reparations that would countenance present-day injustice in order to redress the injustices of the past. Needless to say, Knight's story is, to use current parlance, exceedingly and unapologetically politically incorrect. Indeed, it is difficult to imagine that any contemporary SF journal would publishing this story in today's highly polarized atmosphere, dominated as it is by culture wars involving so-called Social Justice Warriors in pitched battle against self-styled Puppies of both the Sad and Rabid varieties, and a proliferation of gatekeepers from across the political spectrum with ever more stringent ideological litmus tests. Frankly, this story sets out to slaughter too many sacred cows, and is designed to make too many right-thinking people uncomfortable with its uncompromisingly confrontational style, to be judged by modern standards of polite society as anything other than highly insensitive, not to mention in very bad taste. Precisely because of its blatant disregard of

---

[5] Cf. Kiera L. Ladner, "Negotiated Inferiority: The Royal Commission on Aboriginal People's Vision of a Renewed Relationship," *American Review of Canadian Studies* 31:1-2 (2001), pp. 241-264.

prevailing socio-political niceties, and even more so because of its firm historical ties to Lafferty, and that Juvenalian strain of satire within Lafferty's oeuvre which continues to inspire important new work by controversial writers like Houellebecq, the editorial staff of *FoL* unanimously agreed to publish "Justice."

This work © 2015 by Gregorio Montejo.

Bone Girl

by J Simon

Wyoming wasn't dead back then. The earth hadn't been stitched down with cold iron, the river spirits hadn't been yoked to dams. Any coyote might be Coyote, any raven might be Raven. The white man had his machines, the red his shamen: Both fought, and suffered, and uneasily agreed to share. Settlers came, though not many, and to them children were born.

When Lisha came, all the women gathered to see. The babe was pale, very pale, and a coolness seemed to radiate from her skin no matter how they swaddled her. She made no noise, offered no complaint, and they prodded at the newborn to make her strengthen her lungs with crying.

Lisha opened eyes pale as cornflower. Seeing eyes. Knowing eyes. The women crossed themselves and backed away, murmuring—praise be to the ineffable goodness of the Lord, who would allow to be born a child without a soul.

Lisha grew, though the sun never tanned her skin. She lived, though the townsfolk never dared whisper her name. Soon after her two younger sisters were married, she disappeared. Some said she'd gone to become a conjure woman up in the mountains. Others said she'd given herself as a bride to Raven, since she was too cold to warm any mortal man's bed. No one knew. Few enough cared. There it might have stood until the earth accepted her back and her name was lost to all but the wind. But the land wasn't dead—not then—and it had its own ways. Perhaps it was chance. Perhaps it was ordained. Whatever. He found her, and all else followed from that.

One day, a tall skinny tramp of a man came walking up from the arroyo, all alone, through a landscape so gorgeously desolate that not a soul dared live for miles around...

* * *

271

Mountains rose in the hazy distance, keeping watch over crumpled foothills clad in pine. Canyons stretched their narrow fingers here and there, far lesser than the child they'd eventually join to create, but no less glorious in their innumerable layers of purple and orange and—most of all—red.

There was red dust on the boots that tromped over the bedded pine needles. Dust and mud, not just from here but from a thousand places. The rest of his clothes were equally battered, equally worn, as was his slender face—but when he smiled, as he often did, the years dropped away and he became young. Water bottles clinked at his side, a heavy pack flopped on his back. He paused, wiping his brow, eyes shining with pleasure as he regarded the land. Hawks swooped and circled. Just so. He saw nothing else. Yet he, himself, was seen.

Tiny bodies scurried through channels in the pine needles. Little faces peeked up, noses twitched, eyes solemnly watched. The man sat on a stone to rest, and they were gone with hardly a rustle. The breeze picked up, high streaks of clouds gradually unfurling across the sky. Minute passed into minute.

There was no sound to announce her coming, yet he looked up. Pale skin and coal dust hair, pretty in the way a colorful spider is pretty—and just as approachable, the dour twist to her mouth speaking of barriers piled mountain-high. The breeze was cool—but the air that flowed around her seemed somehow colder. She stopped, face impassive:

"You aren't wanted here."

He looked right into her cornflower eyes, as none had dared for over twenty years, and laughed.

"Why hello," he said. "I'm Brown. From out east, actually." He offered one of his water bottles. "Care for a sip?"

"I need nothing of yours." The words were silent as stone and twice as hard. Brown shrugged equivocally. He resumed watching the hawks above.

"I'm not one to stay where he isn't wanted," he said, "but could you tell me, before I go, if you've seen any bones in these parts? Weathering out from the rocks, I mean? Big ones?"

The slightest frown creased Lisha's face. "You also... I mean, what do *you* want with bones?"

He grinned, a gesture that came easy to him. "I'll make you a deal," he winked. "You tell me *your* uses for bones, and I'll tell you mine. Here, let me guess. I'll bet you make soup."

"Enough of this. I have made of my life a cool, smooth pond, and I will brook no disturbance in it. People are... unpleasant."

Brown's grin widened. "I've made of my life a crazy, simmering stew, and I invite just about everyone I meet to jump in. Everyone has their own flavor, and few are rotten all the way through."

"You're normal," she said, each word chopped off clean as with an axe. "I have accepted the only life possible for me, and I will not have it disturbed."

"Pity. And here I felt like telling someone about the aeons-old bones of the three-horned brute I found the other day. But I guess the bizarre secrets of a mysterious vanished world wouldn't interest you, hm?"

Unfolding his lanky form, Brown began walking away, furtively glancing over his shoulder to see if she was going to call him back. Lisha folded her arms over her chest. So. He was leaving. It was what she wanted. It was what she needed. Only—

"Wait."

Brown stopped. For a time there was only the rustle of small things darting through the pine needles, the sway and surf of branches in the breeze.

A small figure, pale and translucent, faded into sight just over Brown's shoulder. The body might have been stuffed with corn husks. The face was a mask, wholly ringed by feathers. It rattled quietly and disappeared.

"Interesting company you keep," Lisha noted.

"What?"

"You didn't see that?"

"See what?" Brown asked, mystified.

Lisha gave her head a little shake. "Some people don't deserve the luck they receive. Very well. Tell me what you do with bones—but make it quick, for you're leaving right afterward."

Brown nodded, a boyish enthusiasm lighting his face as he crouched to sketch pictures in the dirt. "See," he prattled, "long ago, great monstrous thunder-lizard creature beasts roamed the earth. All that's left are their bones, which are the only keys we have to understanding the world that was. The beasts bear some resemblances to gigantic lizards... but also, in certain ways, to mammals and birds. Which were they? Or were they something else entirely? In the South Dakota badlands I found a complete set of jawbones which seem to imply..."

He all but danced across the pine needles in his desperate need to show and explain his finds to her. It was like watching the joyful paroxysms of a love-starved puppy finding its master at last. So long as he could explain his life's passion, Brown didn't much seem to care who—or *what*—was listening. Being treated like a human being, even by a raving madman, was a novel experience.

"—and getting museum sponsorship isn't a problem," he concluded, "seeing as I'm fairly lucky at finding bones. I usually go off scouting while the main crew stays back and digs. Of course, sometimes the best eyes are local eyes—ones that know the land, and know its ways." He glanced sidelong at her. "If only some kind, knowledgeable person would consent to guide me. Mm-hm. If only some improbably lovely stranger would agree to show me the way..."

A faint smile had been building on Lisha's lips. Now it vanished.

"Your success is your undoing," she told him. "It almost seems you could... like... me. The pleasure of that illusion, that dream, is far more valuable that the pain reality would bring. Leave."

Brown looked away. For a moment, just a moment, his eyes showed real hurt—and then it was gone, hidden under his usual bluff confidence. "People generally find what they look for. I look for bones." He hefted his pack, offering one last wink. "Best of fortune to you—and may you find what you're looking for. Whether you like it or not."

He headed back into the arroyo at a steady, ground-eating stride, water bottles clinking. Without really knowing why, Lisha followed, swift and silent as shadow. He couldn't have seen her, couldn't have heard her, yet Brown looked back. She glared—daring him to question her, defying him to comment—and fell in step at his side.

He almost succeeded in suppressing his smirk.

She wondered, as they walked—why am I doing this?—but the trees did not answer, and after a time she forgot to ask.

* * *

Blue sky, red earth. A river sprawled across the narrow canyon's floor in a crazy-lace intricacy of bends and bows, islets and side channels. Along the canyon walls, scrubland plants clung precariously, sere and brown, to any flat surface. Above, a lone tree—blackened and leafless, twisted by the stunting forces of long opposition—squatted over the rim.

A raven glided down, feathers gleaming like wet ink, to land in the tree, its eyes roving quick and bright over the chasm below. More birds glided across the sky, each a sleek absence of blue, to join it. One by one and two by two the ravens came, until that lone twisted tree had disappeared under as many wings as the sky has stars.

Lisha watched Brown slide down the slope, red mud crumbling under his boots. He turned to offer his hand, which she disdained. She stepped lightly down, and they headed upriver.

"Huh. How about that?" Brown shaded his eyes. "That tree up there... it's got as many ravens as you could want!"

"Yes," Lisha smiled obliquely. "As many as I want."

On they went, meandering up and down the steeply sloped sides of the canyon. Brown had an irritating habit of wandering almost at random, regardless of the obstacles nature placed in his way. He had no regard for what path was simplest or most direct—only for what happened to fascinate him at the moment. If he hadn't been so lucky at finding bones, she would have said something about it.

Brown started up a sheer slope about fifty feet high, clinging so tightly his shirt and pants quickly became caked with red-orange clay. Lisha silently shook her head, walked five paces to the right, and switchbacked her way up the far easier slope there.

"Ah!" Dangling precariously forty feet up, Brown reached out to rub fitfully at the ground. He soon uncovered the rounded end of an ancient bone, a great burl of rock larger than his own head. "Upper leg," he hazarded. "The whole bone would be about nine feet long. The creature itself might have stretched sixty to eighty feet. Too well buried to dig out." Sighing regretfully, he patiently re-covered the bone before resuming his crawl up the slope. Lisha waited for him at the top, arms folded across her chest.

"All this way to look at oddly shaped lumps of rock. I'd be hard pressed to get home before dark: Give me one reason I should stay."

"But we've only found fragments, individual bones!" Brown pleaded. "Give me a chance! Wait until we find a more complete skeleton, until we've riddled out the stories it tells, and see if you don't want to go on! Please!"

"Why do you even care? It's not as though I've done anything to help you."

"Because you like bones... for whatever reason. Because you challenge me. And because you're beautiful."

Lisha turned sharply away. Brown clambered to his feet, brushed himself off, and ambled upriver. After a moment's hesitation, she followed.

By the time they reached the next split in the canyon, the sun was already beginning to disappear behind the bluffs high above. Brown glanced along the left and right forks, shrugged, and wandered left. For once they took the easy path, directly along the banks of the muddy river. Great cliff walls rose to either side like the hands of God, their layered colors fading to a thousand ruddy browns in the diminishing light. Whirling, ever-shifting columns of bats rose off in the distance, and the great towering spires of the canyon's formations became all the more stark, all the more beautiful, in the elongating shadows of a dying light. This place had power. This place was alive.

A small figure faded into being over Brown's head, the same feather-garbed spirit as before. A short distance upriver, three more appeared—clad in earthy reds and browns, their wildly exaggerated masks suggesting raven/thief, squirrel/clown, bison/warrior. Clicking and rattling, a minor conference occurred. The three disappeared, and Brown's companion winked out and reappeared in another location, some distance back from the river. Lisha could see shrubs and wildflowers through his body as he shuffled and stomped through a slow, powerful dance, an unfettered expression of wildness and triumph—and then vanished. Brown meandered on, utterly oblivious to the invisible things of the world, his winding path drawing him gradually closer to the very location on which his guiding spirit had so recently danced.

"Look!" Brown whooped, falling to his knees. "A creature, by jove! A creature!"

He flopped down on all fours, lost to the world as he lovingly extended his arms to cradle a section of riverbank. Lisha sighed, readying herself for another ragged "bone" or minuscule fragment of jaw. She glanced down—and stared, unable to look away. The skeleton was wholly articulated and perhaps two-thirds complete. In some ways it resembled a lizard and in some ways a great land-walking bird—if either came the size of a deer.

Shaking off his reverie, Brown yanked out a notebook and began writing—landmarks and locations first, then sketching the specimen itself in meticulous detail. Seeing the monster, Lisha began to understand Brown's passion. So powerful, so graceful, so perfectly designed—and yet it had no place in the world, no relation to any living thing. Lisha smiled faintly. Why, it was practically her sister.

"A predator, by the teeth," Brown mumbled. "Or scavenger. Being a reptile, lethargic and slow, it would have stood upright to survey potential prey..."

On his pad, a lizard-like creature was taking shape: Standing awkwardly upright, tiny arms dangling useless, tail dragging on the ground behind it. Lisha looked at the sketch—and shocked herself by bursting out laughing.

"*That's* what you think she looked like?"

"Do you have any other suggestions?" Brown asked, taken aback.

"I wouldn't break her back in two places to make her conform to that ridiculous upright stance."

"Well, how else could it be?"

Lisha knelt beside him, gently splaying her fingers over

the entombed beast. She tested, probed, let her consciousness seep into the bones. Breathing deeply, she cleared her mind and let the bones' shape and nature reveal their function.

There was no miraculous revelation, no sudden and complete knowledge of the ancient creature's workings—only a series of hunches, feelings, small knowledges. Opening her eyes, Lisha took Brown's pencil and began a sketch of her own. He watched her a while, rolling his eyes in bemused tolerance, before finally grabbing the pencil back so he could start reworking her admittedly inferior artwork. Lisha grumbled, letting him draw in the proper proportions and musculature—but snatched the pencil back when he threatened to alter something she knew was so. Back and forth they went—arguing, explaining, drawing, agreeing—both so enmeshed in their respective passions they didn't even notice the sky steadily growing darker. When they were done, a new sketch had emerged from Brown's peerless anatomical knowledge and Lisha's intimate rapport with the bones. It showed a fleet, forward-facing lizard-bird, parallel to the ground and capable of devastating attacks.

"You... are... amazing!" Brown cried. Lisha had time only to look up, eyes widening—and then he kissed her. For a moment, just one lingering moment, she forgot that such things were not for her. Then Brown pulled back, flushing and flustered. "I'm sorry. That wasn't very gentlemanly. And I'm not really sorry, which I guess is what I'm sorry for. If you gather."

"I have to leave."

"You... what?" Brown gaped at her. His hair was wild, his clothes one big lump of mud, his expression bewildered. Lisha looked away, if only for a moment. Lord, he was beautiful.

"I have to leave." Her voice was steady. Good. She would have expected it to be shaking.

"But why?"

She pursed her lips and blew a cold white plume of mist over Brown's face: He shivered as a thin rime of frost formed on his stubble. "You may love what part of me is human. But that is, after all, only part. You don't want to see the rest."

"Don't be so sure," he said gamely. "You're not the only

person with problems. You're not the only person to ever hurt."

Lisha closed her eyes. It ached, knowing what was to come. Why not just walk away, leave him here? But no. If she didn't show him, prove to him what she was, she would always have to wonder what might have been. She had to do it. No matter how much it would hurt to see his fear—or taste his contempt.

Lisha seated herself on a big pile of leaves, twigs, and other detritus that had accumulated at the bottom of a nearby cliff. Her fingers swept slowly back and forth over the mound. Her breathing calmed. Her awareness sank down, down, into the earth below—seeking out the small perfect treasures of the little things that had died.

"Is it so profane, to bring them back?" she said softly, not looking up. "In creatures so tiny, the spark of animus—of life?—is small to begin with. I need only sacrifice a small bit of myself to summon them back. It never stops hurting—but they come back. And they serve me. And they love me." Her cool fingers pressed into the ground. "That... is what I do with bones."

A slight rustle stirred the ground, almost too quiet to be heard. A rapid series of small sharp pains jolted Lisha, a series of almost imperceptible spasms shaking her body. Slowly, in bits and pieces, the earth began to move.

Spiders crawled stiffly from the heaped debris. Some were missing legs. Some were missing heads. Others were just disembodied parts, spasming and kicking and struggling to move. Half-eaten mice burrowed out of the pile, accompanied by faceless voles. Fragments of centipede scurried and clicked. A small bird, neck twisted and eyes absent, pushed up from the heap. Bit by bit, a carpet of death emerged to cover the mouldy earth.

"Now do you see?"

Brown sat down. His hands trembled, and he had to swallow several times before he could speak.

"Well. That's interesting," he said, managing to keep most of the shake from his voice. "Are they truly alive, or just... puppets?"

Lisha stared at him. He was trying. God above, he was

trying. "These, at least, are puppets," she said. "Had I more time, and a more complete body, and no cold iron within a hundred yards—I could bring something truly back."

"Interesting. Interesting." He forced a laugh. "See? That wasn't so hard. I like you just the same."

"Then you lie," Lisha said coldly. "Kiss me. Kiss me now."

He started to lean toward her. At the same time, the carpet of death contracted upon her—climbing up and over her, covering her as thickly as they'd covered the earth itself. Tiny legs tickled her hands, her arms, her neck. Faithfully, silently, lovingly they covered her face until there was nothing left but her eyes. Struggling to control himself, Brown leaned closer. Closer. All was still, all silent save for the click of chitin and the rustle of moving limbs. Spiders and centipedes crawled lightly over her lips. Brown stopped, his body tense as a guy wire, eyes staring wide and white at the film of decay that danced upon her skin.

All at once Brown crumpled to the earth, his face twisted with grief and regret. Lisha gazed impassively at him. So. The truth was known. It was liberating, in a way, to know that things never changed. Once again her life could be a cool, smooth pond. Feeling nothing. Disturbed by nothing. She bowed her head, and the little creatures—dead once more— fell from her body like a drift of ashes. It was done.

"I will leave in the morning," she said, her every breath a cold white vapor on the air. "Do not look for me tonight. You will not find me."

Brown lay on the ground, fingers clenching awkwardly at the dirt. Lisha stood, and left without a backward glance.

* * *

Forested hills stretched lazily to the horizon. Here, there, a plume of steam marked the vented breath of the living earth. Somewhere out there lay wild-colored pools, hot as fire and vivid like no hue on earth: Great vats of bubbling, steaming, gasping mud: The gaping pits of geysers: The stinking waters that never froze. Lisha stood atop a hill and waited for the sun to rise. Perhaps it was time to return there a while. A year. Forever.

A clinking and clattering came up behind her. She told herself not to look back, not to subject herself to reality. She failed.

"And a fine morning to you!" Brown said, tipping her a wink. "Ready for the hike back to town? If we start now, we could even get back before nightfall."

Lisha stared at him, flabbergasted. "What about last night?"

There was a catch in his smile, a tension to his laugh—but still he met her eye, direct and unafraid.

"You're still a challenge. You still like bones. Your ideas may be wholly and individually wrong, but the ardent debate they inspire is the lifestuff of science itself. I will not leave you. You must, if such is your wish, leave me. Shall we be off?"

Lisha growled under her breath. "You maddening... insane... *wretched* creature. What does it take to discourage you? Do I have tie you down with cords woven from the sinews of the gods?"

"Yes, that would probably do it," Brown agreed, cheerfully digging through a pack of trail rations. "By the way, do you like jerked beef? Not that you have a choice."

She wanted to wring his skinny neck. At the same time, something deep inside her wanted to laugh with relief. She was all emptied out. She'd shown him everything, and still he insisted on deluding himself. This wasn't how it was supposed to be. For so long she'd clutched to herself a single comforting truth: Her "life," such as it was, had been forced upon her by an uncaring world. If *she* was the one to leave *him*, wouldn't it put the lie to everything?

Brown ambled easily southward. Lisha glared at his retreating back for long moments before slowly, reluctantly moving to follow.

Hour by hour, they worked their way down from the hills and canyonlands. The sun was bright, wildflowers abloom, and the awkward silence between them gradually faded into a peaceful quiet, a shared appreciation of the world around them. Brown occasionally commented on this bone or that creature, telling the stories of his recent finds. Now and then he'd suffer a sudden inspiration—"My Lord! The pre-ocular skull gap! Of course!"—and he'd be off on one of his hairy tours of speculation. Lisha had communed with too many animals, had co-inhabited their bodies and minds too thoroughly to stand by and merely tolerate his wild inaccuracies: She challenged, Brown questioned, and in the ardor of their subsequent debates the miles flew by. By mid-afternoon, as they crossed a silken, wind-rippled plain of sunflower and high grass, Lisha found she didn't really *want* to leave. Her mind knew better, and she still held Brown at greater-than-arm's-length by simple instinct: But it was a comfortable sort of discomfort, being with him.

The closest human beings lived no closer to Lisha than a full four day hike... or so she'd thought. To her surprise, they came upon a haphazard little town—obviously of recent construction—on the afternoon of that very day. Not far up the river stood a small grouping of tents and excavations where dozens of persons eased bones from the earth with meticulous care.

"My expedition," Brown sheepishly explained. "We were going to hike out to the canyonlands before we even started looking, but... well, about five minutes out, I stubbed my toe on a bone-bed of ancient herbivores. Most of the group hasn't even bothered to move out of the hotel. Come on—I've got to tell them about my finds!"

"I think I'd rather wait here," Lisha muttered. The town was ugly to her, sitting amidst a great stain of earth broken and tamed to the plow. The taint of cold iron was everywhere, a diffuse aura of nearly imperceptible deadening. Beyond that—there were people. Many people. It was not without misgivings that she followed Brown into the village. Her skin was still pale. Her flesh was still cold. She was still *different*.

Indeed, folks turned and stared as the two of them walked past. Brown waved, smiled, called greetings to those he seemed to know slightly. None responded. None smiled. Lisha locked eyes with one woman, who promptly looked away and made the sign of the cross.

"Conjure woman..."

Brown continued to greet the townsfolk, confused and increasingly hurt by their closed, angry manner. He tried harder, grinning as he teased a young farmsteader, but the man just spat at his feet. Lisha bit her lip until there was blood, locked eyes with the man. Smiled. *Now* he looked away.

"What's wrong with them?" Brown murmured, obviously pained.

Lisha slowly shook her head. She could care less about the townsfolk. Twenty years' exposure had created numbness enough for that. But here was a man who still, after all this time, honestly didn't understand what was wrong with her. It was beyond belief.

"You do, don't you?"

Brown glanced back, startled. "Huh?"

"You do. See me as human."

"What? Were you thinking you were a badger?" he asked solicitously.

Lisha gazed at him. It was a strange feeling. Unique. Almost, she might understand what it felt like to have the sun warm one's skin. "You're an idiot. But then, if I like you—and I admit nothing—I suppose that makes me an idiot, too."

Brown grinned, reaching out as if to take her hand. Lisha flinched back. Ruefully shaking his head, he led her on toward the hotel.

"Hoy!" cried a thick, somewhat slurred voice. "Brown!"

Back along a side street, a pretty little veranda jutted from a tavern, wreathed in potted prairie flowers. Several men sat around its lone table—foremost among them the steel-haired, florid man who had called Brown's name. The broken veins of a career drinker wandered across his face and nose— indeed, he clutched a slopping-full mug in each fist right now—but his body was compact, his expression canny, the pistol on his belt meticulously clean. When sober, this must be a formidable and intelligent man indeed.

"Edwards," Brown said amiably. "I read your monograph on *plateodontus*. Fascinating specimen. What's that, the ninetieth species you've described?"

"Eighty-two," Edwards said, glowering from behind his mug. "Two more than you, Brown. Two more!" His gaze— cold, calculating, probing—passed over Lisha's face. "So." His voice cracked with a drunk's sudden anger. "My doctorate against your ignorance, Brown, my learning against your *nothing*. My hundreds of hirelings and thousands of scouts against your ragged mob of students. My meticulously planned expeditions against your lazy walking tours. Still I can hardly stay a species ahead of you. And why?" His finger rose to point at Lisha, trembling slightly. "Conjure women! Bone-wishing! Fornicating with the devil's wife!"

"Oh, *really*," Brown said. Edwards rose to his feet, white-faced and trembling, ignoring the efforts of his companions to hush him. One attempted to take the man's pistol away, but succeeded only in unending his ammunition pouch. Iron-clad "fairystoppers" spilled to the porch in a rattling mutter, but Edwards could hardly be bothered to notice.

"MISCREANT!" he roared. "I'm better than you, Brown! I'm smarter than you, more meticulous than you, harder working than you! You steal my fame! You steal my finds! You steal my career! *THIEF*! Face me like a man!"

"Let's get out of here," Brown sighed, guiding Lisha away down the street. "In the morning he'll be properly mortified, find it somewhere within his vast ego to say something that could almost be interpreted as an apology, and we'll talk bones a while. Just so long as your room in the hotel isn't too near his..."

"No." Lisha gave her head a little shake. "I've been reminded too forcefully and in too many ways why I gave up on humanity. I'm not staying. Not here, anyway. I'll meet you at the hotel tomorrow morning. And then..." She gazed speculatively at him. "...we'll see."

"At least let me walk you back," Brown pleaded. "The smaller the town, they say, they more dangerous it as at night."

"Who says?"

"Oh, you know." Brown smiled disingenuously. "People."

Lisha said nothing. But she walked, and he walked with her. Almost, their hands touched. At the edge of town they parted. Lisha walked out into the high prairie grass, her mind whirling in many directions. Some of them good. Some of them pleasant.

So it was when she heard the shot.

Even as she ran—she knew. A small crowd of townsfolk gathered around the crumpled figure. Too late. An infinity too late. The hole was small, but it had been made by lead—lead alloyed with cold iron. The life within had been extinguished far beyond her power to rekindle. Lisha shoved past men and women, threw herself down at the body's side, pulled it over onto its back.

Still Brown wore his gentle smile—as he would forever more.

* * *

Tall grasses dipped in the morning breeze, bowing their respect to the passed. Morning's dew shone bright in the coming light, a thousand thousand seas of shining tears. Dozen by dozen, the ravens glided near, dipped their wings in final salute, and passed.

It had been a long night, a dark vigil. Brown was dead. Nothing could change that. Yet—even as she'd failed to welcome him in life—she couldn't bring herself to abandon him in death. It had been a night for many things. Dragging his corpse away from town, away from cold iron. Supervising the small burrowing animals that had removed the pistol-ball and done such repairs as could be managed. Sealing her lips over his until an icy, preserving coldness had suffused his entire body. All of it useless—demented rituals performed for the sake of one who could never appreciate them. And yet she could not bring herself to let go. Lisha had not wept. There was a great space inside her where the tears should be, and every time she looked at him it just got emptier and emptier...

A lone figure, clad wholly in funereal black, worked its way toward her position on the hill. Edwards drew within hailing distance, hat held respectively in hands. He glanced at the stiff body, white and frost-rimed, that lay near Lisha. Twisting his hat in his hands, face downcast with contrition, he called to her.

"Have they, ah, discovered who shot him yet?"

Lisha said nothing: Edwards nodded gravely. "Some things remain forever beyond our ken. Still. A darker day I've never seen. A brilliant man. The only one who could stand his own in an argument with me." He sighed regretfully. "I've decided to fund his expedition through to completion—without taking a single bone, you understand, or taking credit for a single species. It's what's right, that's all. Also, I'm going to fund an illustrated book of his finds. It should stand second in the classroom only to my own."

The man was annoying. Lisha stared at the ground, waiting for him to go away. If every townsperson trod up here, hauling cold iron precariously close to Brown's...

Lisha stopped. Cold iron. Edwards' holster was there. So why didn't she feel the deadening taint of his pistol? She turned on him, her smile slow and sinuous.

"You regret Brown's passing?" she asked mildly.

"Immensely," Edwards said, clearly troubled. "A terrible accident, terrible. Could I bring him back, I would."

"You seemed less kindly disposed toward him last night."

"Drunken ranting, devoid of intellect. I was a shame to myself and my profession, and regret it wholly. I was not myself."

Lisha nodded. Thinking. Considering. "What's gone can't be saved," she quietly said. "Brown's memory would best be served by discovering the biggest, most spectacular bones of all time—and I'm sure he'd be honored to have you, his greatest colleague, be the one to find them. Let me join you."

"Well... it *would* be as he wanted," Edwards mused, "and I can't well leave a helpless woman to fend for herself on the frontier. Yes, I believe it would be a kindness to let you join my company."

Turning her back on him, Lisha leaned down, once more placing her lips over Brown's. New frost formed, growing deeper, thicker, slowly fusing into big, blocky crystals of ice.

"He comes with us," she said, a certain imperturbable coolness coming over her face.

"Ah..." Edwards glanced distastefully at the frozen body, but the avaricious dream of spectacular new finds had already been awakened in his eyes. "Naturally, my lady. Of course he must be present."

Edwards offered his arm. Suppressing the slightest of shudders, Lisha took it.

* * *

A procession of more than three hundred tromped

through the pine forest, from diggers and cooks to mule-tenders and scientists. Lisha led, Edwards just behind, and pretended she knew the way to the spectacular bones she'd promised. Mice criss-crossed the ground, scouting as best they could with tiny eyes and limited intellect. Ravens flew to either side, their keen vision spotting shiny things and unusual shapes. Finding bones wasn't as easy as she'd rashly assumed: Through all of yesterday and most of today, she hadn't found a thing.

Reigning in her frustration, Lisha headed instinctively for the deepest, greenest, most vital heart of the ancient forest—yet the comfort she'd come to expect was not there. The expected vitality and life was somehow deadened.

Lisha stopped, hand raised. Edwards called the entire convoy to a halt, looking expectantly at her.

"All iron must be discarded," she announced, "or wrapped very, very thickly under multiple blankets. We're getting close," she added, more to forestall groans and questions than out of any actual hope of success. Edwards hesitated, but finally nodded his agreement. Grumbling, directing many a hard glance at Lisha, the men began the laborious process of complying.

While they worked, Lisha hiked a ways ahead—well out of sight, well out of hearing. Already the life's breath, the sense of presence was returning to the forest. It was a wholeness, a natural purity that even Brown, in time, might have understood.

Brown. She'd thought herself dead to emotion, yet in that one thought was such need, such pain, such longing...

A quiet rattle caught her attention. Looking up, she found a small, translucent figure hovering over her, its mask-face ringed all the way around with feathers.

"So." She smiled crookedly. "Am I your friend, now? What luck can you bring me?"

The spirit rattled again. Deeper in the forest, a grinding click answered—then another, and another, until all the forest echoed with an impossible cacophony of rattles and clicks, scrapes and whistles. Lisha gaped at a forest suddenly bristling with scores, hundreds, thousands of ghostly little figures, seemingly one for every branch and puddle and stone. She blinked—and they were gone. All save for Brown's cornhusk spirit, who gazed impassively down at her a moment longer before winking out.

A coyote slipped from the trees, tongue lolling out of a sly grin. He trotted away, paused, looked back over his shoulder to see if she were following. Somewhere in the forest, a faint rattle sounded.

That very afternoon, the expedition discovered an enormous skull weathering from a hillside, its terrible jaws bristling with teeth the size of bananas. Lisha bowed her head in silent thanks. In the distance, a coyote yipped and sprinted away.

* * *

The sheer organized furor of an Edwards-managed excavation was something to behold. Each group unearthed its allotment of bones with a controlled urgency, as if racing to finish before some unseen competitor could beat them to it. Edwards strode from group to group—railing, shouting, encouraging, instructing. He loved the work, he loved the bones. If he listened to no opinion but his own, if he brooked no deviation from his orders, if he gleefully anticipated the acclaim *edwardodontus* would bring—would anyone have done differently in his position? Lisha stood off to the side, ignored and forgotten, silently communing with the earth. Little shudders continuously passed through her, and an invisible ripple radiated from herself, crawling slowly across the countryside...

Darkness came. As per Lisha's instructions, all cold iron was again hidden and cached away. Men ate, drank, talked. Fires died. Men retired to their tents. Midnight came and passed.

Under the near-total dark of an ashen moon, Lisha approached the half-exhumed monster. Truly immense. Truly fearsome. A dramatically enlarged version of the lethal hunter she and Brown had found in the canyon. Somewhere in the distance—late though it was—she could hear Edwards still talking, still drunkenly carrying on in his pride and accomplishment. Bowing her head, she began.

All across the countryside, a million little dead things began to stir. A million fiery stings lanced into Lisha's heart, ripping out bits of her own life to feed the rising swarm. For a mile around, the earth crawled. Tiny things, dead things emerged from the ground, closing with inexorable patience on their mistress. Pain like molten metal screamed through Lisha's nerves. Her back arched. Her muscles clenched. Her teeth bared in a feral grimace, eyes rolling back until there were only whites. A trickle of blood, black in the darkness, tracked down from the corner of her mouth. Still the dead things came. Slow. Inexorable. Obedient.

Dead things poured into the excavation in a trembling, writhing tide. Lisha swayed as the sea of tiny bodies combined, joined, weaved into a single flesh. Binding themselves to bone. Uniting into tendon and skin, muscle and horn. There was no light under that extinguished moon—yet a distant lantern provided just enough illumination to show an impossibly vast figure laying where once had been bones.

"Rise," Lisha said. The beast—immense, powerful— ripped itself from the earth in a rain of dirt and stones. Slowly, purposefully it stood: Flesh crawling and changing by the moment; Huge calcareous teeth meshing together in an abattoir large enough to take a buffalo whole; Composite eyes each glistening like a cluster of a million tiny orbs.

"Scream," Lisha said. The beast raised its head and issued a strangled, sodden cry. The camp stirred, mens' worried voices calling back and forth. Someone opened their tent. Someone unveiled a lantern.

Then there were screams.

"Walk," Lisha said. The beast stomped toward camp, one splayed foot pounding before the next. Men screamed. Men ran. Running, fleeing, scattering in all directions. In moments all was quiet—or nearly all. Just one man remained, too drunk, too proud, too sure of himself to ever run away. Standing before his tent, red-faced and defiant, standing his ground until the last.

Lisha walked toward him. She felt empty, scraped clean as a drinking-gourd, as if the slightest breeze could knock her over. The great terror-beast stood over her, blotting out the sky with its enormity, beetles and bits of spider sifting down from its corrupt mass. Edwards waited, finding it somewhere within himself to glare imperiously at her. Defiant. Unafraid, or pretending to be so. There was something admirable in that.

Lisha met his eyes. Edwards did not look away.

"It was you that shot him."

"It was," he admittedly gravely, "and it will torture me. Always. I envied Brown—but I respected him. What I did in that drunken haze will be a cross upon my neck for all my remaining days."

"I know." Lisha looked away. "You could at least have had the grace to be a monster. Something wicked. Something deserving of retribution. But you're not. Your ethics are your law—at least when you're sober. You'd never kill for the sake of revenge, never claim a life for a life. You aren't evil."

Edwards sighed, relaxing visibly.

"No," Lisha said quietly. "*You* aren't evil."

The faintest of smiles touched her lips. Edwards' eyes went wide.

"Kill," she said.

It was over before she even finished saying the word.

* * *

Later, but not too much later, Lisha stood alone under an ashen moon, face upraised. Forty feet long and twenty feet tall, the mighty terror beast leaned over her. For just a moment, bloodied jaws and pale lips touched. And then the beast collapsed, becoming earth once more as it gave back all the life she'd sacrificed to animate it. Yet there was something more. She felt over-full, stretched taut with energy. Then it occurred to her—Edwards, or what remained of him. She had more life than she needed.

Hour after long hour she hunched over Brown's cold, unmoving form. With dawn's first light he began to breath. With the warm morning breeze, his heart began to beat. Yet his eyes were empty, his mind an unchanging smoothness as vast as the great plains. It was too late. Brown was dead—for only his body lived. Lisha curled into a ball, shivering. After so many years. After so much pain. It wasn't until now she finally learned to weep.

A little cornhusk figure appeared, cradling an incredibly delicate web of color and thought between its hands. It drifted down, touched Brown, and was gone.

Brown coughed. His eyes found Lisha. Then he smiled, and all the years and worry dropped away from his face and left him young.

"You're still wrong... about everything," he breathed. "But ah, I like you anyway."

She knelt by his side, not quite able to meet his eyes. "Not many people get a second chance to live."

"I know. And I'm grateful."

"I wasn't talking about you."

She still didn't look at him. But slowly, timidly, Lisha reached out and took Brown's hand in her own.

J Simon is an author and programmer based in Wisconsin. His most recently published novel, Fossilized Gods, is available at majra.org. Some years ago, he read Lafferty's "Eurema's Dam" in the Robert Silverberg edited anthology The Best of New Dimensions, and has never been quite the same since (or before really).

Barstone

by Stephen R. Case

Barstone hadn't always been a hill in the park. He hadn't always waited under his cloak of dirt. Once he stood like a man, walked about even, probably ran and talked. Not that he didn't talk now.

"Tone," I would ask him. I would stand at his shoulder where the grass always grew a bit longer because the mower could never quite get that dip between his shoulder and neck. You wouldn't know it was a shoulder and neck though. You had to look at it right. "Tone," I would ask, "why don't you get up? How long are you going to let these plants and this dirt work its way up over you?"

He would rumble real deep like he did the first time I heard him and realized it wasn't just a hill sitting here in the park. "They cover me up," he would say, "and grow on the outside 'cause there's nothing on the inside."

"And that's shit, Tone," I would say, and the pools that were his two eyes would stare out mournfully. "You know it is. Just flex those knees and stand. Walk on out of here."

But Barstone would tell me that the roots had wrapped him too deeply, that the soil was too heavy, and that his seat of stone had formed to his skin.

"What was it made you sit in the first place?" I would ask him. I had asked him many times before, but I never got a real answer.

I used to walk the three-legged mutt I had through the park, and just like you I saw the rise of Barstone's shoulders and the low dome of his brow and called it a hill. One day though my dog decided to do her business on its slope, and I heard him speak.

"Obliged," he said, and it was clear immediately that nothing was speaking other than the hill itself, and that if you looked at it quite correctly there in the sloping light you'd realize it was indeed old Barstone, nearly reclined, chin on chest, trees sprouting up along the slope of his arms.

"Obliged if you'd have your dog to that elsewhere," he said.

"What are you?" I'd asked, and he rumbled back his name like a boulder sliding down a skree.

After that I took the time to stop and speak with him when I was able. He never stirred, and people walking the path below might have been quite sure I was crazy as I stood alone and seemed to speak to nothing and no one on that particular hill. I'm not sure if they would have heard his answers or if they would have simply believed it to be the thunder of an approaching storm.

The mutt got antsy before storms, racing back and forth in the tiny apartment, and the only thing that seemed to sooth her was—ridiculously—taking a walk in the park with the thunderheads piling up on the horizon. That seemed to be when Barstone was the most inclined to talk. Something about the shifting air masses seemed to stir him. In the winter he'd be muffled under snow, and in the summer the sun made him sleepy. Before a storm you could catch him almost chatty.

"Didn't always sit on stone," he mumbled once on a particularly heavy afternoon. The mutt was chewing some grass contentedly. She'd throw it back up on the carpet as soon as we were inside, but I was more interested in hearing what Barstone had to say than stopping her.

"Didn't?" I asked.

"Didn't. Before these knees bent for the last time, they were flesh like those." I supposed he was talking about mine. "Could bend them back and forth. Could use 'em to walk out in the sun or the rain."

I nodded. "Bigger than most though, I'd assume."

"Bigger knees," he agreed. "Bigger feet. Bigger arms."

"How tall are you, Tone," I asked, "if you were to stand up?"

The soil shifted very slightly under my feet. It was a shrug, the closest thing Barstone would ever come to movement.

"Taller than a house, taller than a tree maybe," he mumbled.

"Like old Paul Bunyan?"

"Like old Barstone," he said.

"Well then," I said. It would rain soon, and when it rained Barstone's eyes overflowed and he cried. "Well."

"It was a woman, you know, as to make Barstone come to rest on the stones and in the dirt," he said.

"Really?" That was the first I'd heard him speak of anything from before, of where or when or why he had been a man and come to rest like a mountain in the park of his name.

"Aye."

I'd go back soaked, I was sure, and it looked to be a bad one too. But how often is it you hear a hill tell you about the loves it had when it was a man?

That was it though. He just said "Aye" and waited until the rain started and his eyes ran down across his chin.

Another day I watched the sun set, and it came down like fire on Barstone's shoulders. The trees that grew there were ablaze, and in the breeze every leaf caught the light and held it like it was saying good-bye for the last time. I walked the park without the mutt, listening to the voices in the grass, and when I reached the slope of his broad shoulders, he spoke as well.

"She was quicksilver," he said. When he spoke each syllable was a drawn out sigh. "There was never a moment of stillness within her."

"Who, Tone?" I asked him, though I thought I surely knew.

"Came here when there wasn't much else but a pathway through the forest," he said. "Walked out of the hills to the east, where they said his momma had been a mountain and his father a thunderhead. It didn't matter."

"What did you do?"

"Whatever anyone did in those days," he sighed. The sun was dropping fast. "We tore out the forests and dredged the river and laid out the streets that you pass without seeing. When there were enough fields cleared from the forest and boats in the river, they built a school for the families that had come. Passed it one day and saw the red planks like blood and saw her standing at the doorway."

"I thought she didn't stand, Tone," I said. "I thought she was never still."

"Not standing like a mountain stands," Barstone said. "Not standing still—never still. Stood like a willow in a windstorm, with students streaming out around her. They were quiet—they were motionless beside her."

I crouched in the hollow where Barstone's hand was only a mound of earth and five low boulders that splayed out on the grass.

"Walked together after that," he said, his voice as low as the dying light, "down paths that had become streets lined with husks of houses instead of trees. Walked beyond those out into fields that were still new, and she was never still. Watched her like the play of light on water."

The first stars had come out, and in the growing chill I heard Barstone's joints crack and pop beneath me.

"Will you go walking tonight, Tone?" I asked him. I had never heard him speak so much.

"Not tonight," he said. His wet eyes reflected the starlight clearly. "Roads aren't wide enough to let old Barstone pass, and no one will carve new ones."

When Barstone sang, everything in the town cried, and people would wake up with their eyes wet and not know why. I begged him not to that night, and he promised he wouldn't. When I walked out of the park though, the trees were moaning. I dreamed that night of silver rivers, and the dogs outside were howling.

I guess I had always just assumed that I was the only person who knew that Barstone lived in the park, but one day the girl in the coffee shop stopped me and said that she knew why Barstone would never move.

"You know him?" I asked dumbly. She had stopped out of the blue beside my table, and when I gawked upward at her she dropped into the chair opposite me.

"I run in the park in the mornings. Usually he's not awake when I pass, unless he's been up all night anyway."

"Singing," I said with my head in my hands.

She nodded. "I dreamed last night I lived in a house of porcelain dolls, and every one was broken."

"I begged him not to."

I wasn't sure whether she worked there or not. People would come and go behind the bar, and it was the sort of place if you were a local you could come in and brew your own pot. I had seen her there often but never spoken to her.

"It was my grandmother," she said, leaning over the table.

"Barstone is your grandpa?"

She wrinkled her nose, which set freckles dancing on her cheeks and chin.

"No. But my grandmother is in all his stories. She was a teacher here a hundred years ago."

"Your grandma couldn't be that old."

Someone came and set a cup of coffee in front of her. She stared into it like it was one of Barstone's eyes.

"Could have and was."

I shrugged.

"They courted. It was conservation of momentum."

"What?"

Her coffee was half-gone, and her slender hand beat the air like a butterfly as she spoke. "She was slight and quick, and he was large and slow. She would have burned herself out in a year or two. When I was a kid, she could sit in the sunlight all afternoon and not stir beyond the needles in her lap. But by then Tone himself was too slow—he had absorbed all her momentum."

I blinked. "I don't think that's how it works. To conserve momentum—"

She cut me off with a flutter of the hand. "For billiard balls, maybe. Not people. Not stories."

I watched her drink the rest of her coffee. Between us my laptop waited with its steady blinking cursor.

"So that's it?"

Again the freckles shifted, and it took me a moment watching them scatter up her cheek to realize it was smile.

"Not it. Barstone's still there, right? Still sitting like a stone."

"No." I shook my head. "I mean, that's the whole story about him and your grandma? He was big and slow and she was fast and slight, and so now he's big and unmoving and she's slight and still?"

"Was. She passed a few years back."

"I'm sorry."

She set her coffee cup down. "She said it happened the first time they kissed. He won't tell you this, but my grandma used to sit and look out over the hills and talk about him like he was going to walk up the path any time."

"But he wasn't your grandpa?"

"Hush. No. My grandma married a trainman—my grandpa, but that was later. She said that the first time she kissed Barstone he sat on the hillside all night, and she finally had to leave him at sunrise."

"That's . . . bizarre."

"Stranger than a talking hill?"

I shrugged.

"She thought maybe he was just flustered, as he had always been slow with words and was pretty much in love with her. The next time it happened though, he didn't stir for a week. She'd go out to find him after school, and she'd put her head up against his chest and lay awhile and hear his heart thudding slowly and steadily. They would sit together in the park because there wasn't any bench in town large enough for him."

I nodded absently. My coffee had arrived, and she reached around my computer and took a sip.

"The third time was after he asked her to marry him. He was moving so slowly that it had taken the better part of an evening, and by then she sort of had an idea of what was going on, but she was so surprised and pleased she kissed him again. He never stood up after that. He was on one knee, but by winter he had levered himself around so that he was sitting like he is now. That was the last my grandmother saw him move, though she waited three years."

"Conservation of momentum, huh?"

It was her turn to nod.

"How come it didn't work the other way? Why didn't she speed him up?"

"He was bigger."

I realized that was the best explanation I'd get, so the nod was echoed a third time. I reached for my coffee and found the rim still warm from her lips.

"So," I said, tasting her breath with the coffee, "how did you know that I talked to your grandmother's old, broken, hillside beau?"

"He spoke of you," she said. "He told me to look for a scarecrow with a three-legged dog." Again the freckles shifted.

We walked in the park together after that, often with the mutt but often without. If we paused beside Barstone's hill, he would rumble in his throat in greeting. By the next summer we were preparing a wedding, and I came to find Barstone alone.

"You going to build Barstone a road?" he asked, and the ripples of his eye-pools danced.

"How wide would it need to be to get you to walk it?"

The slight shifting of the ground told me he shrugged. "Don't suppose that road will be torn for quite some time. In the meantime, you'll marry her granddaughter."

"You think so?"

"I see plenty on these paths."

"I suppose so."

The leaves on the tree that sprouted at Barstone's elbow were quivering, and it took me a full minute to realize he was laughing, a sound too low to hear. "Suppose you came to ask this old hill to roll down and sit outside the church."

"We'd be honored. But you won't, and I understand. Do you think she'll slow me down? Or speed me up?"

"Hard to tell." His voice was slowing, fading off with the clouds moving down toward the horizon.

In the morning the boulder that was Barstone's first finger had shifted or settled or pulled itself slowly up, and there in the black soil beneath was a golden ring with a single small diamond. I took it and thanked him, but he said nothing.

\#

Afterward we went to the park often, and when there were children we took them as well. Each year the trees were taller on Barstone's shoulders and the moss had grown up farther along his arms. The pools of his eyes became lidded with overhanging limbs, and he would only speak when his low voice was echoed by thunderheads. We moved when my job took me east, and I can now only imagine that he is still there waiting, a silent hill in a parkland, waiting for the roads to widen for his passing.

This work is © 2015 Stephen R. Case.

Letter from Alan Dean Foster to R. A. Lafferty

THRANX INC.
19 Sept. 91

Dear Rafael;

As Virginia has no doubt informed you, I'm delighted to take your story RAINY DAY IN HALICARNASSUS for the anthology of original humorous fantasy that I'm editing with Marty Greenberg. I have no problem with its previous appearance in the limited-edition booklet and am glad it will now receive a much larger audience.

Virginia informs me that you have chosen to stop writing. So be it. She explains that it's because you feel unappreciated. Well, *of course* you're underappreciated, Rafael! You're a *writer*, for God's sake. You have a unique style, distinctive wit, and a deliciously skewed view of the cosmos. You don't chum out endless volumes of homogenized pap for the general public. If you're going to act like that how else can you expect to be except underappreciated?

Remember what a colossal flop MOBY DICK was here in the U.S. when it first appeared? Folks wanted more of Melville's south seas travelogues like TYPEE and OMOO. I mean, what the hell was all this brooding and mooding about the nature of man doing in an otherwise neat book about whaling? Talk about slowing up the action!

My own personal theory is that any artist, in any field, has to be dead for at least a hundred years before an objective evaluation of his work can be rendered anyway. So why are you worrying about it now? Would you rather be like, say, poor Henryk Sienkiewicz? Remember him? Nobel prize for literature, 1905. Wrote QUO VADIS and the PAN MICHAEL trilogy (the greatest work of Polish fiction and some damn fine stories). Who reads him, who "appreciates" him today? If you're writing for appreciation, you're *always* gonna be disappointed. Write for yourself. Write for your cat (if you don't have a cat, get one). Write for the ages. Write slow and for your own amusement and we'll publish the stuff after you're dead.

But to give up something you can do that nobody else can because you feel underappreciated ... nawww.

I held off getting a computer until three years ago because I was afraid I wouldn't be able to do what the fourteen year old kid down the block could do, and that someone would find out, spread it around, and make me a laughing stock. But the damn things work, and make writing a lot easier. Takes the work out, puts the fun back in. You can even get 'em with a 19-inch screen, if your eyes are giving you trouble (I use a 14-inch).

Virginia says you made a vow to quit. Last writer I know who made that vow was Robert Silverberg, about ten years ago. He lasted about eighteen months. Know what I think? I think you're writing right now, in your head. I don't think you can escape it. Putting it down on paper, that you can escape. Conjuring, concocting, observing, commenting ... that I don't think you can get away from.

Or maybe you can. Rossini quit. That's about 46 grand operas we haven't got, because he got lazy, or selfish, or tired, or felt underappreciated. What a waste.

Oh well. Whatever you end up doing, or not doing, rest assured there's more than one other *writer* out here who appreciates the hell out of you.

Sincerely yours

Alan Dean Foster

R. A. Lafferty's Reply to Alan Dean Foster

Tulsa, Okla
Sept 22, 1991

Alan Dean Foster

Dear Thranx Inc:

I think I'll get me an alternate name for one of my alternate personalities. Of course I could never come up with anything as slick as 'Thranx Inc', but maybe I could devise a pretty good one.

Virginia Kidd has a talent for reading the minds of all her clients and friends and unraveling their innermost thoughts and feelings. Unfortunately it is a flawed talent, and I doubt whether she has ever been right yet.

I certainly did not stop writing because I felt unappreciated; I've never said so or indicated so in any way; and I've never felt unappreciated. I am not a self-centered person, and only such can ever feel unappreciated. Only half of the persons in the world are self-centered, and the other half are world-centered. To quote myself, as I often do, "I have a certain affection for myself, as I would for any other ungifted and clumsy and funny-looking person of long, if casual acquaintance. I run into myself constantly, and so I am one of the most familiar persons around. But I wouldn't list myself among the fifty most interesting persons I know, and certainly not among the fifty persons I care for most deeply. An exasperated lady once said "I don't know how you can be so dumb and create such smart characters." And I answered honestly "Because I take all my characters, or almost all of them, from life, and I am fortunate in knowing some very smart people."

But the fact is that I quit writing when I noticed that I had started to write drivel. I hadn't a bad case of the drivels, but I saw that it might become so. I had also begun to yearn for many of the things I had to shove aside to make room for my writing. And after twenty-five years of writing I decided to take up all my old hobbies again. I didn't 'make a vow to quit', but I may have told Virginia so when she wanted me to write a story for a certain book and I didn't want to do it.

Since then, when the other old timers ask me why I've quit writing, I tell them honestly "I quit because I'd started to write drivel. Have you noticed the kind of drivel that the over-seventy writers are writing nowadays?" This makes the over-seventy writers kind of mad, and justly so.

And the second reason I quit was that the arthritis and cramping in my hands became so bad that I could not write on anything for more than about three minutes at a time. So I quit on my 70th birthday, which will be seven years on November 7th. Now I have time to read Plutarch in Greek and St. Augustine in Latin (and Padraic Pearse in Irish). I was at the ChiCon WorldCon a couple of weeks ago, and I haven't given up my love of Science Fiction. In fact I have time to read a little more of it than I did when I was writing it. I am moderately wealthy and I seem to be happier than most of the people I survey. Dammit, I'm out to pasture, and the pasture's green. And the work-place is full of thistles.

Good luck to you in everything, Alan

R. A. Lafferty 1715 . S. Trenton, Tulsa

Rossini did things backwards. He started out writing drivel, and it was very popular. He wrote better and better stuff, and it was less and less popular. His last and best opera, William Tell, was the only one both good and popular. but in his long retirement he was the happiest and probably busiest man in Europe. He had it all right and in order.

Letter from Alan Dean Foster Nominating Lafferty for the Arrell Gibson Life Achievement Award

THRANX INC.
21 Mar 94

Dear Ms. Hamilton;

When I first encountered the work of Raphael Aloysius Lafferty I was convinced I had stumbled across the chromatic, scintillating prose of some whacked-out twenty-five year old with an IQ of 210 and perpetually dilated pupils who dwelt in the bowels of Haight-Ashbury in San Francisco, emerging only to occasionally deliver himself of wry comments on the state of the cosmos at assorted memorable university lectures and poorly-lit coffeehouses.

Imagine my surprise on first meeting R.A.L. when he turned out to be a gold-toothed, pot-bellied, balding ex-electrical engineer from Tulsa, who favored not exotic coffees but traditional spirits and was more at home with the history of science than radical polemics.

I once tried to write a story in the Laffertian style, only to end up snarling my syntax so badly it threatened to strangle me. Only Lafferty can do Lafferty. In my opinion he is the most distinctive stylist the field of modern science-fiction/fantasy has yet produced. Plunging into a Lafferty story is akin to being attacked by a radiation-mutated game of scrabble, being assailed by all the words in the English language that *aren't* in the Oxford dictionary but somehow should be, buying a ticket on a subway named Moebius.

You don't <u>read</u> a Lafferty story. You grab hold of the tail and hang on for the ride, usually getting doused but not battered along the way. He's a Leprechaun, Lafferty is. Words are his rainbow and revelation and delight the gold in the pot at the end. He's the only scribe I've ever met whose smile matches exactly the way he writes. He's an honest candidate for the Nobel, but since the dynamite man's heirs haven't asked me about him, I'll recommend him instead for the Arrell Gibson Life Achievement Award. R.A.'s Achieved, he's Lived, he's even Gibed (I don't know how you Arrell). There are a number of American writers who deserve more recognition than they've received, and Lafferty belongs right up there on top of the pile.

With greatest of pleasure I remain, yours sincerely,

Alan Dean Foster

Born in New York City in 1946, Alan Dean Foster was raised in Los Angeles. After receiving a Bachelor's Degree in Political Science and a Master of Fine Arts in Cinema from UCLA (1968, 1969) he spent two years as a copywriter for a small Studio City, Calif. advertising and public relations firm. His writing career began when August Derleth bought a long Lovecraftian letter of Foster's in 1968 and much to Foster's surprise, published it as a short story in Derleth's bi-annual magazine The Arkham Collector. *Sales of short fiction to other magazines followed. Since then, Foster's short fiction has appeared in all the major SF magazines as well as in original anthologies and several "Best of the Year" compendiums. His published works includes more than 100 books. Foster's work to date includes excursions into hard science-fiction, fantasy, horror, detective, western, historical, and contemporary fiction.*

His website is www.alandeanfoster.com

An Interview with Harlan Ellison

by Andrew Mass

I've been working on a documentary film about R. A. Lafferty. I've likely contacted some of you about doing an interview and if I haven't, I may still. So far everyone has been overwhelmingly generous with their time and ideas. Having worked as a journalist in the past I can assure you that this is not always the case, or even typical. Lafferty, it seems, inspires an openness and willingness to share among his fans, friends and colleagues. But why?

I suppose it's for the same reasons I would read passages, or entire stories, out loud to whomever happened to be in my field of vision—ending with a resounding, "have you ever heard anything like that?" It's why this journal was created and (perhaps I shouldn't admit this) I was genuinely surprised and delighted with the high level of writing and analysis here, or why the Facebook group is so active, why we post Shelfies (TM) online and discuss ways to publish and popularize Lafferty to a wider audience. None of this was happening when I first had the notion to make a documentary; it was just my way of sharing, of reading out loud.

Harlan Ellison clearly feels the same way. He was kind enough to sit down and talk about "Ray" in his home earlier this Summer, and on short notice. In point of fact, I'd say he was entirely eager. While portions of this interview will eventually make it into the documentary, I thought some of you might enjoy having a more complete transcript, edited only for redundancy and for when we strayed too far off-topic. I'd like to thank the editors of *Feast of Laughter* for creating this marvelous journal and, of course, everyone who has been willing to share their time and love of Lafferty.

One final note I should make about Harlan Ellison is that he is quite the performer: often conveying as much information with wildly gesticulating hands and extreme facial muggings as with his words. There's no real way to illustrate that emotion here, so I thought I'd just say that Harlan clearly had strong feelings for his buddy Ray. When he said, "God, I loved him," he was bent over with his head in his hands, having a moment.

When did you first hear about R. A. Lafferty?

Raymond (Raphael) Aloysius Lafferty was the white man equivalent of the Invisible Man. He had been working at jobs that were middle American, fairly un-auspicious, and had burning in him ideas that were untold and unthought of. The first time I got wind of him was a little story that was published by, I believe, Terry Carr—he was the editor of the Ace Specials.

Lafferty submitted the story cold and it was called "Narrow Valley." The instant I read it, it was as if there had been a cosmic explosion. You could tell that this was an intellect that had been waiting to pop, that he had all these stories in him and nowhere to go with them and didn't know he was a writer. He may have been working as a freight man, or shoveling coal, one never knows, but once he started writing it was the explosion of a nova.

Terry started buying him immediately. I started reading him and talking him up to all my friends. And this was the period that was called the New Wave—Samuel R. Delaney, Joanna Russ, Kate Wilhelm, Damon Knight...and Ray Lafferty, who was not like any of us because he was much older than us, but fit right in. We knew nothing about him and saw nothing of him because he was the invisible ghost. When he showed up at a convention, imagine our amazement when he would suddenly POP into a room full of people partying and go "Bang Bang!" and vanish.

I followed him like a mongoose because I thought he was the *ne plus ultra* of brilliance. He was quiet. He was pleasant, he was incredibly religious, he was a devout Catholic. I am a devout atheist and I got him to write stories for me, and he wrote one for *Dangerous Visions*—which he wrote, I didn't prod him with a scimitar—he wrote it, and it was brilliant. And afterward he wrote me a letter and said "you are the Imp of Satan." Every time we got together he would sit beside me drinking, just throwing them back, and I don't drink, so I'm always cold stone sober, and the two of us would sit there like the Imp of Satan and the Hand of God and he would tell me what an Imp of Satan I was.

Why did he think you were the Imp of Satan?

Because I had gotten him to write stories that he probably felt were not holy enough or were in defiance of God's will. (Pause) I don't ask people what their beliefs are, I don't care if they're Scientologists. I don't care if they eat cats.

Did Lafferty proselytize or did he keep it to himself in person?

Ray was deeply religious. Everything had God in it one way or another. And I wouldn't get into it with him. I wouldn't say, "God is a creation of man. There is no God. There is no one with a big beard up there." That's illogical. That's the mind of man working.

It does seem like religion is a pretty fertile place for a writer. I think I read a quote from you that said the Bible was one of your main sources of inspiration.

Well, the Bible is a myth and all myths are ripe ground for hoeing and every myth should be retold as many times as you can, in as many settings as you can, using whatever mythology or technology or futurism you can think of. The more you retell it, the more you re-stage it, the better it is because it's the basic myths. Whether it's man against man, man against nature or man against himself—those are the only three basic tales, whether you tell Cain and Abel or Adam and Eve or you tell Noah and his sons—it's all the same myths, just retell it more cleverly and restate it so someone will say, "that's fresh". That's what a writer does.

I occasionally use religion. Not as much, because I don't believe in it. I believe in it as much as fairies, elves and gnomes, and I use them sparingly as well.

It seems like Lafferty is drawing from some different places than most...

Yeah. Lafferty was deeply wise, deeply philosophical, well read, brainy and yet not stuffy. And he could take a simple idea and say, "now wait a minute, look at it this way," and he would turn the mirror and you were looking at it from that side and say, "oh my God, I didn't think of that," and then he would tell a story. And the people in his stories were interesting and they were human.

He had lived with people so he was able to relate to the average working man and woman, the average thinking man or woman, and average idiots who fall over their own shoelaces. All of whom make up the great panoply of the walking dead who appear in stories and are only made interesting because of the brains of their writer.

What about structure? Is structure something you think about a lot as a writer, because Lafferty seems to have created some new ones?

Structure is one of those things that when they ask you about, it's like love. What is love? What is structure? Structure is what works. You build a house, it gets no cracks, doesn't fall down—structure's ok. Ray wrote sparingly, wrote like... probably the closest thing to what Ray wrote is the way the modern, noir detective novelists write. He wrote a simple, direct story. When he wanted to get complex he would write a novel like *Okla Hannali*. He would write an involved novel in which there was a complex philosophy that had to be expressed, but it was always expressed in structure and you could follow it—and you never got lost with Ray, you could go back and look it up and say, "oh, that's where I misread," and you'll see that he had it all there. Ray built a good foundation, good characters and his dialog was always succinct and precise and payed off. And he also knew how to form a phrase.

How do you start a story?

When you start a story there are several ways of doing it. When I start a story I like to not know where I'm going. I'll come up with a title. I'm doing a story now called "The Last Survivor of the Bataan Death March." It has nothing to do with the Bataan Death March. It opens with a guy sitting on a curb watching dirty water run down a curb, and a human face with no skull and no bones behind it, just the mask of a face, washing down the curb and catching on weeds and pieces of paper, and then him getting it up and looking at it—and I have no idea where it goes from there, but I think what it has to do with is the concept of the guilt of the survivor. That one child who survives of twelve who went to Dachau has to live with the fact that they lived—there's no guilt there, but there is a thing called the guilt of the survivor, "why did I survive and no one else?" And I think this guy sitting there watching is going to be a manifestation of the guilt of the survivor. And his whole family and everything that's happened to him, everybody else has gone, and Ray perceived the pain that lies at the sole of the human spirit.

This is my wool gathering and it may not be his philosophy at all but I see in Ray a brightness of intellect that says everybody lies to you. When you meet someone and say "how are you?" and they say "oh, I'm fine," their son just came out of rehab, their daughter is hooking for five dollars with a pimp, their mother has got brain cancer and their husband is cheating with the intern, and she has three spinal taps in her. And yet, "oh, I'm fine." It's a lie. It's just a lie. But people find it more convenient not to have to suffer somebody saying, "Oh I'm sorry you're in pain," and so they lie. And so everybody lies 24/7. I'm incapable of lying, which makes me a cranky, mean-spirited, hard to deal with, disrespectful person. I will not lie. You ask me a question I will tell you the absolute truth. You won't like it, necessarily. But you will get the truth from me. And then they say, "he was rude," and I have to live with that. And I've been living with that forever.

You came to the right town then.

What, Hollywood? As opposed to Detroit? As opposed to New York?

There's a famous book about Hollywood called, *Hello, He Lied*.

There's an old New York joke, where an Iranian walks up to someone and says, "Where is the Chrysler building, or should I go fuck myself?" Hollywood is no better and no worse than any other city in the world. I'm telling you, you're going to lie to me, if I say "how are you," what are you going to say to me?

I'm pretty good.
No you're not. You've got the same shit that I got. You're getting on. You're above the water, floating. La Di Da...moving right along to Ray Lafferty. Ray Lafferty always spoke his mind, there was very little chit-chat with Ray. Ray and I would sit at a bar, because that's where Ray was comfortable. Ray was a drinker. And I was the Imp of Satan, cold stone sober. All I cared about was that Ray Lafferty was a giant in my mind, and a great writer, a great, great writer. One of the unsung great writers of American fiction.

You said he was one of the first people you thought of when you conceived of putting together *Dangerous Visions*.
Yeah.

You also said he was part of the New Wave, but I wonder if he fit in, or really thought of himself as part of that group?
Ray fit in because the group absorbed him. He may not have thought he was part of the New Wave, but the New Wave took one look at Ray Lafferty and said, "Oh my God, he knows what we're doing and he's been doing it." He was already there, with no name for it. He was the artist before there was a name for the art.

Earlier you made it sound like you had given him some ideas on what to write about for *Visions*. Is that true or did you just ask him to write whatever he wants?
Well, originally I had said to him, tell the story you have never been able to tell. Everybody resisted that because, it's that humble brag, "I already told the stories I wanted to tell." No, don't give me that shit. What story have you never been able to tell about labor relations, about religion, about sex, about sadness, about the emptiness, the hollow at the center of the human heart, about man's brutality to men, men's brutality to women, women's brutality to men and women?

It's interesting because Lafferty is often so funny on the surface but halfway in you realize how violent...

Violent! And truthful. He would not back away from pointing out, yes, this is the way they smile at each other, and here's where the knife went in. There was a staunchness, there was a steel rod at the core of every Lafferty story. His stories mattered, that's the important thing. Lafferty's stories mattered. When you read them and were done with them they left a mark upon you. Even something that seems as slight as "Narrow Valley," which I think is one of the ten greatest stories I have ever read, is an idea so overwhelmingly original that it's up there with "The Purloined Letter," with *The Haunting* [*of Hill House*] by Shirley Jackson...*Moby Dick*. I mean, it's really literature because, short as it is, it is succinct and powerful. And that is another key word with Lafferty: powerful. He would hit you under the heart and you would feel it.

You were instrumental in bringing about the transformation of Science Fiction into literature in people's minds and making sure the best of it was getting out there...

Well, the best were always writing a kind of literature... *milieu fantastique, noir*, phantasmagoria, that which had not been thought. They used the tools of science fiction: space travel, robots, aliens, other worlds, but they were impertinences—they were like Wells using a time machine. They were devices to tell stories about human behavior.

When I and others felt restricted by what had been Science Fiction for thirty or forty years we said we're going to go on our own way, we're going to use these impertinences to our best end, whenever they're available, but here's what the story is really about: It's always being late, "Repent Harlequin!," said the ticktockman, the guilt of the survivor, why I didn't cry when my father died, why it took twenty years for me to finally burst into tears in a totally different venue, why I had four marriages and was off women forever until I found the light of my life. These are the things that matter, the things that really carry us from day to day.

Ray was carried from day to day. The fact that he had a

drinking habit, I don't know whether it spurred him or impaired him. I don't know whether having such a profound religion, and I mean he was nutsy fagan about Catholicism, whether he believed it and it was his center-post or it was a delusion that kept him from seeing his own destiny, is beyond me. One cannot know. All one knows at the end of the game is what is left behind in the stories. "Oh what fools these mortals be," as Shakespeare said. At the end of the day what's left is the work, the structures, the houses. It can be Levittown with all the houses looking alike or it can be the Taj Mahal.

Why did Lafferty become difficult to publish at some point, or perhaps publishers didn't want to publish him?
Who said that?

I have a collection put out in Chapbooks, presumably because he couldn't get them published elsewhere.
He wrote so much. And after a while, they... well, I don't know... Publishers are essentially, and I say this as politely as I can, they are not just blind men and women staggering around in a stalagmite cavern, bumping their heads, falling over and bleeding to death—they are just dick-wads. They are assholes with bow ties and jumpers, all of whom think they know everything and know nothing... So at some point it was obvious that the Science Fiction people would have loved to continue publishing Lafferty novels, but his fans were so rabid that they grabbed all they could get, short works, and did them as Chapbooks.

One day somebody will assemble the complete works of R. A. Lafferty and it will be a nice big book. It will have all the short stories and the novels and everything. And he will be treated the way Robert Silverberg and I and A. E. van Vogt and James Blish have been, because these were the important writers. R. A. Lafferty is top of the heap—no one better.

You've worked a lot in television and movies and Lafferty never did, as far as I know he had no interest in it, except I'm sure he would have liked the money...
I don't think Ray gave a shit about money. I mean he may have, but in all the time I knew him he never mentioned

money—how much he got paid for a story or a book. Very seldom will you hear me mention money, unless I've gotten some money out of someone and then I just give it to Susan, because I don't really care about the money. But if you get the money you know you're being paid for doing good work. And everybody wants to interview me the way they want to interview you; they want to do films, they want to do Lafferty films, everybody wants something from you. Every gift has a fish hook in it. I've got here seventeen requests for interviews, some of them I'll give...

Why did you give it to me?
Because you sent me a nice letter, because of Lafferty, not necessarily in that order. Anytime I can ever praise Ray Lafferty...

To get back to TV, Lafferty seemed, especially in something like *Not to Mention Camels*, with Media Lords and the un-electronic people, to have something against modern media—did you ever talk about that subject?
We talked about television. He liked my phrase, that it was a "glass tit," and he said it was, like me, the Imp of Satan. What he said to me, not often, was that television, while offering linkage to the world was in fact drawing you away from everything.

Picasso said that "art is either a revolutionist or a plagiarist" and you were quoted as saying that *Dangerous Visions* was "constructed along the lines of revolution." Do you think revolution is important and necessary, and do you think Lafferty thought so too?
Yeah. Absolutely.... One of my favorite quotes is, I think, Walt Whitman, that those who forget the past are doomed to relive it. All debt to the future is in the present but if you forget where you've been you're a blind man walking. You're a stalagmite, in a cave.

What do you think about the state of speculative fiction today, it seems to have gone mainstream?
Long since. Long since. Almost everybody working in

"mainstream" today—and it had been done before we started doing it, Mark Twain, going back to Lucian of Samosata— almost everyone has taken a crack at it at one time or another. I don't like the names, but if I have to call it something I'll stick with speculative fiction. Everyone gets pigeonholed— if they're in Science Fiction, then you're a *Transformers* movie.

I don't think people thought of Lafferty as a writer who engaged in predicting the future, with spaceships and such, but in retrospect he did seem to predict things like social media...

Ray and Phil Farmer were two of the really great prognosticators. They had an eye on it. I think Ray was not an optimist, there was a lot of optimist in him, but I think Ray and I alike, you know the glass half-full... we both think the glass is half-full and all of it will poison you.

I tend to be fairly cynical. I don't mean to be, but inevitably my thoughts come back to that. It may be that I picked up too much Ray Lafferty—God I loved him. If Ray was anywhere within fifty miles of where I was, I'd go. I think Ray liked me. There are some people in this life, who if they like you, it's as big an honor as if the King of England had come to visit at your home.

Do you have a favorite story, you mentioned "Narrow Valley" before?

Well, "Narrow Valley" and all the ones in *Nine Hundred Grandmothers*. This is like... Talking to your audience, looking right into the camera (turns to camera): Telling you to dip into R. A. Lafferty is like saying to you that you're walking through a large desert and suddenly you see a hillside and you go to the hillside and you begin brushing away the sand and suddenly you discover a golden door with a lock on it, and you begin fiddling with the lock and miraculously it opens for you. You open it and you look in and suddenly you're looking into Aladdin's Cave and you have discovered the miraculousness of the universe. You go in and you say, well maybe I'll only pick up this lamp, maybe a Genie will come out of it, or I'll only pick up this group of doubloons and maybe it will last me all my life... Oh, look at this carafe, I'll pick up this—and next thing you know it's a million years later and you've spent a million years looking at Ray Lafferty's stories.

Ray Lafferty is like that. Asking me what my favorite story is is like saying "what's you're favorite song, who's the most beautiful woman you've ever slept with?" My wife, of course. I've had five wives, I've slept with movie stars. If you ask me, I've got no contest, it's my wife. What's the most interesting Ray Lafferty interview I've ever given? This one is. So what's my favorite Ray Lafferty story? The one you find.

This work © 2015 by Andrew Mass

Andrew Mass is a New York based writer who has worked as a copywriter and creative director in digital advertising for most of the last 15 years. He also had an enjoyable stint at NY Public Radio, and as a financial journalist. Andrew studied China at university and spent 1987 at a college in Nanjing. Sometime in the late '90s he stumbled upon a Lafferty book and has been pleasantly bewildered ever since.

"Lafferty Bang Bang" © 2015 Anthony Ryan Rhodes

Don't Just Read Lafferty, Be Lafferty!

RA LAFFERTY MASK

I recommend taping a stick or tightly rolled piece of paper to the mask.

Mask by **Anthony R. Rhodes,** Oct 2015

http://arr-illustrator.blogspot.com

"Portrait of the artist as a cranky old man from Tulsa"

Download an 8 ½" x 11" template at
mask.feastoflaughter.org.

This work © 2015 Anthony Ryan Rhodes

Anthony R. Rhodes is not a shy man. He does not have test anxiety. He has never experienced stage fright. He has paralyzing fear that a box of sewing pins will fall, crash, and spill across the floor. Anthony is a quiet man. For the last 25 years he has worked with persons with disabilities or studied to do so and made no art whatsoever. For the illustrations in this volume he blew out more than a few cobwebs, cracked a few knuckles and toes, and learned the software Inkscape. Anthony does not have a website to display his work, but if he did you might find it at http://arr-illustrator.blogspot.com. He is from Tulsa, Oklahoma.

Tell It Funny, Og

by R. A. Lafferty

In the beginning the world was good-humored, good-natured, genial, and funny. And the True Tales from the Beginning will always remember this.

My own researches on how it was in the "dawn days" reveal that the first tales ever told were not only pleasant and funny but they also had elements of the "shaggy dog stories," "shaggy bear stories," and "shaggy people stories" in them. But what those earliest tales really were might be called "shaggy ogre stories". The shaggy or hairy ogres were the first story-tellers, and they will probably be the last. Og the Ogre, the seventh son of the seventh son of Adam himself, was not the first of these story-tellers, but he is the first we know by name.

Most story-tellers and story-writers are funny-looking, as I wrote in my previous epistle; they *do* have bug-eyes. They *are* "bug-eyed monsters". They must have panoramic vision; they must see everything; they could not be good story-tellers without this wide vision. But only the bug-eyes have this panoramic vision.

And they do have outsized ogre ears, knobby and bumpy and sometimes hairy. They would not be superb eavesdroppers or conversation-listeners without them; and they would not have their story materials if they did not eavesdrop massively on unsuspected and often quite distant talkers.

The convoluted hairs of their hairy ears may be antennae that pick up waves on other than audio frequency. Og the Ogre, in all his descendants, does have this strong sensing, equal to that of the animals. He can see well, he can hear well, and he can smell superbly.

Story-tellers are intended to be funny-looking, and stories are intended to be funny. The first unfunny stories were literary disasters, but they did not appear early.

People and situations were pleasant and funny from the

beginning. Strange lands were pleasant and funny. I remember the persons swallowed by a very large whale and their nine day journey through the fantastic lands and towns in his belly: strange and funny lands, those! Animals were funny and friendly, and so were the aliens. The pleasant and humorous aliens were of ancient establishment. The idea that there might be something unpleasant or unfriendly about aliens came much later.

Alien monsters were pleasant and funny. One early and almost forgotten piece of history tells that Adam, in addition to naming all the sub-lunar creatures, also named the nine hundred and ninety-nine species of creatures who had their homes and nests above the moon, on other moons or trabants or asteroids or planets. And after they were named, the super-lunary creatures went back to their own places, with friendly memories of Earth, the 'naming place'. So we do have nine hundred and ninety-nine alien species, monstrous but friendly, waiting to meet us again.

About the story-tellers and the story-writers — well, the writers were almost as early as the tellers. Someday I will recount the invention of moveable type by Og the Ogre. It was living moveable type, very small flat-fish or alphabet fish who hopped into the hopper on voice command and printed their individual letters on pulp made of larch-wood. The alphabet fish could spell better than Og could, and their printing was very neat. But from the very first there were difficulties with the printed stories, difficulties of distribution and of profit margin mostly, so printing wasn't a great thing in the early days.

The good-humor and funniness of the early stories (all of them were Science-Fiction or Knowledge-Fiction Stories) was not all expressed in extreme hilarity and horse-laughter. (In the beginning, horses laughed like horses, and men laughed like men.) The expression was urbane, civilized, deep and rich humor; it was universal, and often it was outrageous.

In their deep and pleasant and often outrageous humor, Homer and Rabelais were full blood-brothers, and the time discrepancy between them may be disregarded. Ogres are not subject to time to the same degree that other folks are. Paleogrammarians have written thousands of foot-notes to explain the verbal anomalies of Homer when the real explanation was that he was writing comic verse and that he created wry and goofy verbalisms for the fun of it. Neither Homer nor Rabelais was often guilty of the sin of pomposity.

There is rollicking good-humor all through every Scripture. Samson, the riddle-telling judge and strong man, is full of high spirits even when going down to Gaza and to his death. David is full of fun when he invents the story of his victory over Goliath and sings it to his own harp music. Goliath was not that big, nor David that small; and moreover Goliath was killed by another warrior, Elhanan. But a story-teller can always fictionize accounts. There is a lot of fun in Balaam and his talking donkey, and in Ezekiel's account of those primitive flying machines. Who were those early barnstorming aviators anyhow?

All the old Asian tales were comic, the Ramayana, the Panchantra Fables, the Epic of Gilgamesh, the Shiva stories, the Mahabharata, the Druga stories, the Incarnation of Vishnu (there was a vaudeville act a few thousand years later that used many of his quick-change tricks). There was a giantism running through many of these old tales, and their being sacred tales was no inhibition to their being funny. There is nothing funnier than a Skyful of Giants.

The Greek and Roman myths are full of fun, though there is often stark pain mixed in with it. The Cúchulain stories of Ireland are funny, and the Peredur story of Wales. All the Medieval stories are funny, some of them intentionally so, some of them unintentionally. There's a lot of good humor to be found in American Indian stories and in African stories. And the Arabian Nights stories are almost total fun.

But something, almost from the beginning, has been seeping in to diminish the good-humor of the stories of our Earth. I do not know whether the tales of the friendly nine hundred and ninety-nine monstrous and alien species are subject to the same spoiling as are the tales of our own world. Everything in the world, in every world, is either good-humored or bad-humored. So all the bad-humored things were once locked up in an iron cavern and the iron doors made firm with bolts and locks. But some of the bad-humored things seep out and ooze out under the iron doors, and they do their damage to us.

What if we are the only species whose good-humor is being rusted and rotted away? What if, on the Day of Reunion, the other nine hundred and ninety-nine species will reject us because of our insufficient or tainted humor?

The seven bad-humored and unfunny devils who eat ourselves and our narratives alive are Pretentiousness, Pomposity, Presumption, Pontificality, Pavoninity or Peacockery, Pornography, and Pride, these seven offenses to all life. They have oozed out from under the iron doors and then they have inflated themselves immeasurably.

Of the writers of more-or-less modern Science Fiction, Verne had the endless depth of good-humor, Mark Twain had it, Poe had a lot of it (his queer effect is due to his going from pleasant humor to horror in an instant); Wells had it in his Science Fiction but not always in his Political Fiction. But A--- and a second A--- and B--- and C-- have not had it. Van Vogt and black-hearted Bester and Sturgeon and Sheckley have the good humor, but D--- and another D--- and still a third D--- have it not. Old Burroughs (what a hairy-ogre brain he did have!) was full of the juice, and Arthur C. Clarke has at least enough to save his soul. Even Heinlein (this is hard to believe, and yet you'll stumble over instances of it) has patches of good humor and near funniness that croak out in another voice than his regular one. But E--- and F--- and G--- lack the bright thing completely. There are a hundred who have it and ninety-nine who fail it. And the failures may destroy the rest, as they have done in so many other fields. There is now only one art on our earth that has not gone rigid and dead-ended, and that is Science Fiction. It is worth saving; and if it is saved, it may rekindle some of the other arts.

There is one way to do it. Take all the code-named, insufficient, bad-humored, spawn of the seven devils, grind them up small, hammer them down, pulp them back under that iron door again. Pay no attention to their wails. They came from that fetid place, and they must go back there. And seal the iron door at its bottom with blow torches and welding torches this time. It was neglected to do this before.

I offer this solution as illuminated and unsullied literary criticism and necessary and preventive mayhem. And the enforcing of this decision will give some liveliness and some noisy scenes. It will also give a whole new cycle of tales worth telling.

Tell them funny, Og.

June 19, 1980

Configuration Of The North Shore
by R. A. Lafferty

The patient was named John Miller.

The analyst was named Robert Rousse.

Two men.

The room was cluttered with lighting, testing, and recording equipment. It had several sets of furniture that conferred together in small groups, sodas, easy chairs, business chairs, desks, couches, coffee tables, and two small bars. There were books, and there was a shadow booth. The pictures on the walls were of widely different sorts.

One setting. Keep it simple, and be not distracted by indifferent details.

"I have let my business go down," Miller said. "My wife says that I have let her down. My sons say that I have turned into a sleepy stranger. Everybody agrees that I've lost all ambition and judgment. And yet I do have a stirring ambition. I am not able, however, to put it into words."

"We'll put it into words, Miller, either yours or mine," Rousse said. "Slip up on it right now! Quickly, what is the stirring ambition?"

"To visit the Northern Shore, and to make the visit stick."

"How does one get to this Northern Shore, Miller?"

"That's the problem. I can locate it only very broadly on the globe. Sometimes it seems that it should be on the eastern tip of New Guinea, going north from the D'Entrecasteaux Islands and bypassing Trobriand; again I feel that it is off in the Molucca Passage toward Talaud; and again it should be a little further south, coming north out of the Banda Sea by one of the straats. But I have been in all those waters without finding any clue to it. And the maps show unacceptable land or open sea wherever I try to set it."

"How long?"

"About twenty-five years."

"All in what we might call the Other East Indies and dating from your own time in that part of the world, in World War II. When did it become critical?"

"It was always critical, but I worked around it. I built up my business and my family and led a pleasant and interesting life. I was able to relegate the Thing to my normal sleeping hours. Now I slow down a little and have less energy. I have trouble keeping both sets of things going."

"Can you trace the impression of the North Shore to anything? Transfigured early memory of some striking sea view? Artform-triggered intuitions? Can you trace any roots to the evocative dream?"

"I had an inland childhood, not even a striking lakeview in it. And yet the approach to the North Shore is always by a way recognized from early childhood. I don't believe I have any intuition at all, nor any sense of art forms. It is simply a continuing dream that brings me almost to it. I am rounding a point, and the North Shore will be just beyond that point. Or I have left ship and wade through the shallows; and then I have only a narrow (but eerie) neck of land to traverse to reach the North Shore. Or I am, perhaps, on the North Shore itself and going through fog to the place of importance, and I will have the whole adventure as soon as the fog clears a little; but it doesn't. I've been on the verge of discovering it all a thousand times."

"All right. Lie down and go to dreaming, Miller. We will try to get you past that verge. Dream, and we record it."

"It isn't that easy, Rousse. There's always preliminaries to be gone through. First there is a setting and sound and smell of place near the surf and a tide booming. This watery background then grows fainter; but it remains behind it all. And then there is a little anteroom dream, a watery dream that is not the main one. The precursor dream comes and goes, sharp and clear, and it has its own slanted pleasure. And only then am I able to take up the journey to the North Shore."

"All right, Miller, we will observe the amenities. Dream your dreams in the proper order. Lie easy there. Now the shot. The records and the shadow booth are waiting."

Shadow booths reproduced dreams in all dimensions and

senses, so much so that often a patient on seeing a playback of his own dream was startled to find that an impression, which he would have said could in no way be expressed, was quite well expressed in shadow or color or movement or sound or odor. The shadow booth of the analyst Rousse was more than a basic booth, as he had incorporated nearly all of his own notions into it. It reproduced the dreams of his patients very well, though to some extent through his own eyes and presuppositions.

First was given the basic, and Rousse realized that for his patient Miller this was New Guinea, and more particularly Black Papua, the stark mountain land full of somber spooky people. It was night; the area seemed to be about fifty yards from the surf, but every boom and sigh was audible. And there was something else: the tide was booming underground; the ocean permeated the land. Guinea, the mountain that is an island, was a mountain full of water. The roots of the mountain move and sigh; the great boulders squeak when the hammer of the tide hits them; and on the inside of the cliffs the water level rises. There is a feeling of being on a very large ship, a ship a thousand miles long.

"He has captured the Earth-Basic well," the analyst Rousse said. Then the basic faded back a bit, and the precursor dream began.

It was a flat-bottomed rowboat from some old camping trip. He was lying on his back in the bottom of the boat, and it was roped to a stump or tree and was rocking just a little in the current. And here was another mountain full of water, but an island one of much less bulk, and the ice-cold springs ran out of its sides and down its piney shoulders to the shingle of the creek bank. Fish jumped in the dark, and blacksnakes slid down the hill to drink. Bullfrogs echoed, and hoot owls made themselves known; and far away dogs and men were out possuming, with the baying carrying over the miles. Then the boy remembered what he must do, and in his dream he unroped the boat and shoved into the stream and ran his trout line. From every hook he took a fish as long as his arm till the boat was full and nearly swamped.

And from the last hook of all, he took a turtle as big as a wagon wheel. He would not have been able to get it into the boat had not the turtle helped by throwing a booted leg over the side and heaving himself in. For by this time it was not so much like a turtle but more like someone the boy knew. Then he talked for a while with the turtle that was not exactly a turtle anymore. The turtle had a sack of Bull Durham and the boy had papers, so they rolled and smoked and watched the night clouds slide overhead. One of them was named Thinesta and one was named Shonge, which chased the first and would soon have him treed or caught, if they did not run into the mountain or the moon first.

"Boy, this is the life!" said the turtle. "Boy this is the life!" said the boy.

"He's a poet," said Rousse, and this puzzled him. He knew himself to be a cultured man, and he knew that Miller wasn't.

Then the little precursor dream slid away, and there began the torturous and exhilarating journey to the North Shore. It was coming around a point in an old windjammer on which all the men were dead except the dreamer. The dead men were grinning and were happy enough in their own way. They had lashed themselves to rails and davits and such before they had died. "They didn't want it bad enough," the dreamer said, "but they won't mind me going ahead with it." But the point was devilish hard to turn. There came on wind and driving spray so that the ship suffered. There was only ashen light as of false dawn. There was great strain. The dreamer struggled, and Rousse (caught up in the emotion of it) became quite involved and would have been in despair if it were not for the ultimate hope that took hold of him.

A porpoise whistled loudly, and at that moment they rounded the point. But it was a false point, and the true point was still up ahead. Yet the goal was now more exciting than ever. Yet both the current and the wind were against them. Rousse was a practical man. "We will not make it tonight," he said. "We had better heave to in this little cove and hold onto what advantage we have gained. We can make it the next time from here."

"Aye, we'll tie up in the little cove," one of the dead men said, "we'll make it on the next sortie."

"We will make it now," the dreamer swore. He jammed the windjammer and refused to give up.

It was very long and painful, and they did not make it that night, or that afternoon in the analyst's office. When the dream finally broke, both Miller and Rousse were trembling with the effort and the high hope was set again into the future.

"That's it," Miller said. "Sometimes I come closer. There is something in it that makes it worthwhile. I have to get there."

"We should have tied up in the cove," Rousse said. "We'll have blown backwards some ways, but it can't be helped. I seem to be a little too much in empathy with this thing, Miller, I can see how it is quite real to you. Analysis, as you may not know, has analogs in many of the sciences. In Moral Theology, which I count a science, the analog is Ultimate Compensation. I am sure that I can help you. I have already helped you, Miller. Tomorrow we will go much further with it."

The tomorrow session began very much the same. It was Guinea again, the Earth Basic, the Mountain Spook Land, the Fundament permeated with Chaos which is the Sea. It boomed and sighed and trembled to indicate that there are black and sea-green spirits in the basic itself. Then the basic adjusted itself into the background, and the precursor dream slid in.

The boy, the dreamer was in a canoe. It was night, but the park lights were on, and the lights of the restaurants and little beer gardens along the way. The girl was with him in a cave; she had green eyes and a pleasantly crooked mouth. Well, it was San Antonio on the little river that runs through the parkways and under the bridges. Then they were beyond the parkway and out of town. There were live-oak trees overhanging the water, and beards of Spanish moss dragged the surface as though they were drifting through a cloud made up of gossamer and strands of old burlap.

"We've come a thousand miles," the girl said, "and it costs a dollar a mile for the canoe. If you don't have that much money we'll have to keep the canoe; the man won't take it back unless we pay him."

"I have the money, but we might want to save it to buy breakfast when we cross the Mississippi," the boy said. The girl's name was Ginger, and she strummed on a stringed instrument that was spheroid; it revolved as she played and changed colors like a jukebox. The end of the canoe paddle shone like a star and left streaks of cosmic dust on the night water as the boy dipped it.

They crossed the Mississippi, and were in a world that smelled of wet sweet clover and very young catfish. The boy threw away the paddle and kissed Ginger. It felt as though she were turning him inside out, drawing him into her completely. And suddenly she bit him hard and deep with terrible teeth, and he could smell the blood running down his face when he pushed her away. He pushed her out of the canoe and she sank down and down. The underwater was filled with green light and he watched her as she sank. She waved to him and called up in a burst of bubbles. "That's all right. I was tired of the canoe anyhow. I'll walk back."

"Damn you, Ginger, why didn't you tell me you weren't people?" the dreamer asked.

"It is ritual, it is ordering, the little precursor dreams that he makes," Rousse said.

Then the precursor dream glided away like the canoe itself, and the main thing gathered once more to mount the big effort. It was toward the North Shore once more, but not in a windjammer. It was in a high hooting steamship that rode with nine other ships in splendid array through one of the straats out of what, in concession to the world, they had let be called the Banda Sea.

"We come to the edge of the world now," the dreamer said, "and only I will know the way here."

"It is *not* the edge of the world," one of the seamen said. "See, here is the map, and here we are on it. As you can see, it is a long way to the edge of the world."

"The map is wrong," the dreamer said, "let me fix it." He tore the map in two. "Look now," the dreamer pointed, "are we not now at the edge of the world?" All saw that they were;

whereupon all the seamen began to jump off the ship, and tried to swim back to safety. And the other ships of the array, one by one, upended themselves and plunged into the abyss at the edge of the water. This really was the edge of the world, and the waters rushed over it.

But the dreamer knew the secret of this place, and he had faith. Just in time he saw it, right where he knew it must be, a narrow wedge of high water extending beyond the edge of the world. The ship sailed out on this narrow wedge, very precariously. "For the love of God be careful!" Rousse gasped. "Oh hell. I'm becoming too involved in a patient's dream." Well, it *was* a pretty nervous go there. So narrow was the wedge that the ship seemed to be riding on nothing; and on both sides was bottomless space and the sound of water rushing into it and falling forever. The sky had also ended — it does not extend beyond the world. There was no light, but only ashen darkness. And the heavy wind came up from below on both sides.

Nevertheless, the dreamer continued on and on until the wedge became too narrow to balance the ship. "I will get out and walk," the dreamer said, and he did. The ship upended itself and plunged down into bottomless space; and the dreamer was walking, as it were, on a rope of water, narrower than his boots, narrow as a rope indeed. It was, moreover, very slippery, and the sense of depth below was sickening. Even Rousse trembled and broke into cold sweat from the surrogate danger of it.

But the dreamer still knew the secret. He saw, far ahead, where the sky began again, and there is no sky over a void. And after continuing some further distance over the dangerous way, he saw where the land began again, a true land mass looming up ahead.

What was dimly seen, of course, was the back side of the land mass, and a stranger coming onto it would not guess its importance. But the dreamer knew that one had only to reach it and turn the point to be on the North Shore itself.

The excitement of the thing to come communicated itself, and at that very moment the watery rope widened to a path. It was still slippery and dangerous, it still had on each side of it depths so deep that a thousand miles would be only an inch. And then for the first time the dreamer realized the fearsomeness of the thing he was doing. "But I always knew I could walk on water if the thing got bad enough," he said. It was a tricky path, but it was a path that a man could walk on.

"Keep on! Keep on!" Rousse shouted. "We're almost there!"

"There's a break in the path," said Miller the dreamer, and there was. It wasn't a hundred feet from the land mass, it wasn't a thousand feet to the turning of the point and the arrival at the North Shore itself. But there was a total break. Opposite them, on the dim land mass, was an emperor penguin.

"You will have to wait till we get it fixed," the penguin said. "My brothers have gone to get more water to fix it with. It will be tomorrow before we get it fixed."

"I'll wait," the dreamer shouted. But Rousse saw something that the dreamer did not see, that nobody else had ever seen before. He looked at the shape of the new sky that is always above the world and is not above the abyss. From the configuration of the sky he read the Configuration of the Northern Shore. He gasped with unbelief. Then the dream broke.

"It may be only the quest-in-itself motif," Rousse lied, trying to control himself and bring his breathing back to normal. "And then, there might, indeed, be something at the end of it. I told you, Miller, that analysis has its parallels in other sciences. Well it can borrow devices from them also. We will borrow the second-stage-platform from the science of rocketry."

"You've turned into a sly man, Rousse," Miller said. "What's taken hold of you suddenly? What is it that you are not saying?"

"What I am saying, Miller, is that we will use it tomorrow. When the dream has reached its crest and just before it breaks up, we'll cut in a second stage booster. I've done it before with lesser dreams. We are going to see this thing to the end tomorrow."

"All right."

"It will take some special rigging," Rousse told himself when Miller was gone. "And I'll have to gather a fair amount of information and shape it up. But it will be worth it. I am thinking of the second stage shot in another sense, and I might be able to pull it off. This isn't the quest-in-itself at all. I've seen plenty of them. I've seen the false a thousand times. Let me not fumble the real! This is the Ultimate Arrival Nexus that takes a man clean out of himself. It is the Compensation. If it were not achieved in one life in a million, then none of the other lives would have been worthwhile. Somebody has to win to keep the gamble going. There has to be a grand prize behind it all. I've seen the shape of it in that second sky. I'm the one to win it."

Then Rousse busied himself against the following day. He managed some special rigging. He gathered a mass of information and shaped it up. He incorporated these things into a shadow booth. He canceled a number of appointments. He was arranging that he could take some time off, a day, a month, a year, a lifetime if necessary.

The tomorrow session began very much the same, except for some doubts on the part of the patient Miller. "I said it yesterday, and I say it again," Miller grumbled. "You've turned sly on me, man. What is it?"

"All analysts are sly, Miller, it's the name of our trade. Get with it now. I promise that we will get you past the verge today. We are going to see this dream through to its end."

There was the Earth Basic again. There was the Mountain booming full of water, the groaning of the rocks, and the constant adjusting and readjusting of the world on its uneasy foundation. There was the salt spray, the salt of the earth that leavens the lump. There were the crabs hanging onto the wet edge of the world.

Then the Basic muted itself, and the precursor dream slid in, the ritual fish.

It was a rendezvous of ships and boats in an immensity of green islands scattered in a purple-blue sea. It was a staging area for both ships and islands; thence they would travel in convoys to their proper positions, but here they were all in a jumble. There were LST's and Jay Boats, cargo ships and little packets. There were old sailing clippers with topgallants and moonscrapers full of wind, though they were at anchor. There was much moving around, and it was easy to step from the ships to the little green islands (if they were islands, some of them no more than rugs of floating moss, but they did not sink) and back onto the ships. There were sailors and seamen and pirates shooting craps together on the little islands. Bluejackets and bandits would keep jumping from the ships down to join the games, and then others would leave them and hop onto other islands.

Piles of money of rainbow colors and of all sizes were everywhere. There were pesos and pesetas and pesarones. There were crowns and coronets and rixdollars. There were gold certificates that read "Redeemable only at Joe's Marine Bar Panama City." There were guilders with the Queen's picture on them, and half-guilders with the Jack's picture on them. There were round coins with square holes in them, and square coins with round holes. There was stage money and invasion money, and comic money from the Empires of Texas and Louisiana. And there were bales of real frogskins, green and sticky, which were also current.

"Commodore," one of the pirates said, "get that boat out of the way or I'll ram it down your throat."

"I don't have any boat," said the dreamer. "I'm not a commodore; I'm an army sergeant; I'm supposed to guard this box for the lieutenant." Oh hell, he didn't even have a box. What had happened to the box? "Commodore," said the pirate, "get that boat out of the way or I'll cut off your feet."

He did cut off his feet. And this worried the boy, the dreamer, since he did not know whether it was in the line of duty or if he would be paid for his feet. "I don't know which boat you mean," he told the pirate. "Tell me which boat you mean and I'll try to move it."

"Commodore," the pirate said, "move this boat or I'll cut your hands off."

"This isn't getting us anywhere," the dreamer said, "tell me which boat you want moved."

"If you don't know your own boat by now, I ought to slit your gullet," the pirate said. It was harder to breathe after that, and the boy worried more. "Sir, you're not even a pirate in my own outfit. You ought to get one of the sailors to move the boat for you. I'm an army sergeant and I don't even know how to move a boat."

The pirate pushed him down in a grave on one of the green islands and covered him up. He was dead now and it scared him. This was not at all like he thought it would be. But the green dirt was transparent and he could still see the salty dogs playing cards and shooting craps all around him.

"If that boat isn't moved," the pirate said, "you're going to be in real trouble."

"Oh, let him alone," one of the dice players said. So he let him alone.

"It's ritual sacrifice he offers," Rousse said, "He brings the finest gifts he can make every time. I will have to select a top one from the files for my own Precursor."

Then it was toward the North Shore again as the Precursor dream faded.

It was with a big motor launch now, as big as a yacht, half as big as a ship. The craft was very fast when called on to be, for it was going through passes that weren't there all the time. Here was a seacliff, solid and without a break. But to one who knows the secret there *is* a way through. Taken at morning half-light and from a certain angle there was a passage through. The launch made it, but barely. It was a very close thing, and the cliffs grouped together again behind it. And there behind was the other face of the seacliff, solid and sheer. But the ocean ahead was different, for they had broken with the map and with convention in finding a passage where there was none. There were now great groupings of islands and almost-islands. But some of them were merely sargasso-type weed islands, floating clumps; and some of them were only floating heaps of pumice and ash from a volcano that was now erupting.

How to tell the true island from the false? The dreamer threw rocks at all the islands. If the islands were of weed or pumice or ash they would give but a dull sound. But if they were real land they would give a solid ringing sound to the thrown rock. Most of them were false islands, but now one rang like iron.

"It is a true island," said the dreamer, "it is named Pulo Bakal." And after the launch had gone a great way through the conglomerate, one of the islands rang like solid wood to the thrown rock. "It is a true island," said the dreamer, "it is named Pulo Kaparangan."

And finally there was a land that rang like gold, or almost like it (like cracked gold really) to the thrown rock. "It is true land, I think it is," said the dreamer. "It is named Pulo Ginto. I think it is. It is the land itself, and its North Shore should be the Shore Itself. But it is spoiled this day. The sound was cracked. I don't want it as much as I thought I did. It's been tampered with."

"This is it," Rousse urged the dreamer. "Quickly now, right around the point and you are there. We can make it this time."

"No, there's something wrong with it. I don't want it the way it is. I'll just wake up and try it some other time."

"Second stage called for," Rousse cried. He did certain things with electrodes and with a needle into Miller's left rump, and sent him reeling back into the dream. "We'll make it," Rousse encouraged. "We're there. It's everything you've sought."

"No, no, the light's all wrong. The sound was cracked. What are we coming to — oh no no, it's ruined, it's ruined forever. You robbed me of it."

What they came to was that little canal off the River and into the Sixth Street Slip to the little wharf where barges used to tie up by the Consolidated Warehouse. And it was there that Miller stormed angrily onto the rotten wooden wharf, past the old warehouse, up the hill three blocks and past his own apartment house, to the left three blocks and up into the analyst's office, and there the dream and reality came together.

"You've robbed me, you filthy fool," Miller sputtered, waking up in a blathering anger. "You've spoiled it forever. I'll not go back to it. It isn't there anymore. What a crass thing to do."

"Easy, easy, Miller. You're cured now, you know. You can enter into your own full life again. Have you never heard the most beautiful parable ever, about the boy who went around the world in search of the strangest thing of all, and came to his own home in the end, and it so transfigured that he hardly knew it?"

"It's a lie, is what it is. Oh, you've cured me, and you get your fee. And slyness is the name of your game. May somebody someday rob you of the ultimate thing!"

"I hope not, Miller."

Rousse had been making his preparations for a full twenty-four hours. He had cancelled appointments and phased out and transferred patients. He would not be available to anyone for some time, he did not know for how long a time.

He had a hideout, an isolated point on a wind-ruffled lake. He needed no instrumentation, he believed he knew the direct way into it.

"It's the real thing," he told himself. "I've seen the shape of it, accidentally in the dream sky that hung over it. Billions of people have been on the earth, and not a dozen have been to it; and not one would bother to put it into words. 'I have seen such things—' said Aquinas. 'I have seen such things—' said John of the Cross. 'I have seen such things—' said Plato. And they all lived out the rest of their lives in a glorious daze.

"It is too good for a peasant like Miller. I'll grab it for myself."

It came easy. An old leather couch is as good a craft as any to go there. First the Earth Basic and the Permeating Ocean, that came natural on the wind-ruffled point of the lake. Then the ritual offering, the Precursor Dream. Rousse had thrown a number of things into this: a tonal piece by Gideon Styles, an old seascape by Grobin that had a conic and dreamlike quality, Lyall's curious sculpture "Moon Crabs," a funny sea tale by McVey and a poignant one by Gironella. It was pretty good. Rousse understood this dream business.

Then the Precursor Dream was allowed to fade back. And it was off toward the North Shore by a man in the first craft ever dreamed up, by a man who knew just what he wanted, "The Thing Itself," by a man who would give all the days of his life to arrive at it.

Rousse understood the approaches and the shoals now;

he had studied them thoroughly. He knew that, however different they had seemed each time in the dreams of Miller, they were always essentially the same. He took the land right at the first rounding of the point, leaping clear and letting his launch smash on the rocks.

"There will be no going back now," he said, "it was the going back that always worried Miller, that caused him to fail." The cliffs here appeared forbidding, but Rousse had seen again and again the little notch in the high purple of them, the path over. He followed the path with high excitement and cleared the crest.

"Here Basho walked, here Aquin, here John de Yepes," he proclaimed, and he came down toward the North Shore itself, with the fog over it beginning to lift.

"You be false captain with a stolen launch," said a small leviathan offshore.

"No, no, I dreamed the launch myself," Rousse maintained. "I'll not be stopped."

"I will not stop you," said the small leviathan. "The launch is smashed, and none but I know that you are false captain."

Why, it was clearing now! The land began to leap out in its richness, and somewhere ahead was a glorious throng. In the throat of a pass was a monokeros, sleek and brindled.

"None passes here and lives," said the monokeros.

"I pass," said Rousse.

He passed through, and there was a small moan behind him.

"What was that?" he asked.

"You died," said the monokeros.

"Oh, so I'm dead on my couch, am I? It won't matter. I hadn't wanted to go back."

He went forward over the ensorcelled and pinnacled land, hearing the rakish and happy throng somewhere ahead.

"I must not lose my way now," said Rousse. And there was a stele, standing up and telling him the way with happy carved words.

Rousse read it, and he entered the shore itself.

And all may read and enter.

The stele, the final marker, was headed:

Which None May Read and Return

And the words on it—
And the words—
And the words—

Let go! You're holding on! You're afraid! Read it and take it. It is *not* blank!
It's carved clear and bright.
Read it and enter.

You're afraid.

LAFF LIBS

And Methulselah Marvels a Maker

There was a yowl "Voices across the far side of existence!

_____."

<small>HUMOROUS CURSE IN BAGARTHACH STYLE RHYMING VERSE</small>

Most declared defections against _____

<small>ONTOLOGICALLY RELEVANT NOUN</small>

are really defections against _____. Every old book with

<small>DOGMATIC SYMBOL</small>

_____ in its binding knows we can defect against one

<small>SURREAL ASPECT</small>

without revolting against the other.

"For a restructured reality," called the eccentric billionaire with the

_____ beard. "_____,

<small>ANTHROPOMORPHIZING QUALITY</small>   <small>GLEEFULLY ZANY INTERJECTION</small>

leave no man stolid in all those _____

<small>ORDINARY BUT SYMBOLIC SETTING, PLURAL</small>

least we paint me dead."

By Anthony R. Rhodes in proudly pitiful imitation

List of Contributors

The Ktistec Press Editorial Board:
    Kevin Cheek
    Gregorio Montejo
    John Owen
    Rich Persaud
    Daniel Otto Jack Petersen
    Anthony Ryan Rhodes

Contributors:
    Niyaz N. Abdullin
    Robert Bee
    Christopher Blake
    Stephen R. Case
    Kevin Cheek
    Harlan Ellison
    John Ellison
    Andrew Ferguson
    Alan Dean Foster
    Martin Heavisides
    Paul Kincaid
    Dan Knight
    R. A. Lafferty
    Lissanne Lake
    Andrew Mass
    Gene McHugh
    Gregorio Montejo
    MPorcius
    Rick Norwood
    Roman Orszanski
    Rich Persaud
    Daniel Otto Jack Petersen
    Charles Platt
    Anthony Ryan Rhodes
    Bill Rogers
    Darrell Schweitzer
    J Simon
    Dena C. Bain Taylor
    Don Webb

The Northeast Lafferty League and The Mercer County Library Present

Writer Guest of Honor:
Michael Swanwick

Artist Guest of Honor:
Lissanne Lake

Lafferty Ghost of Honor:
Mary Mondo

LAFFCON1

The world's first and only R.A. Lafferty Conference

Join us for Ghostly Argonautics, Astrobean Politics, Camiroi Scholarship, Bagarthatch Verse, Guesting Time Bench Seating, Snuffles-Style Worldbuilding, and more! Panels will include: "These Misshapen Waves: Lafferty And The New Wave," "Of The Bums And Impoverished Scholars: The State of Lafferty Studies," "Biographical Notes: Documenting Lafferty," "Whatever Happened To Painting? Lafferty And The Visual Arts," and "Several Steps Removed From Original: Reading Lafferty." Refreshments provided by the Friends of The Library- Lawrence Branch.

Registration is preferred and begins May 2, 2016. **Participants must register online.** Go to www.mcl.org, click on the "Program" tab at the top of the page. Click "Adult Programs" and register for Laffcon1.

Mercer County Library
2751 Brunswick Pike
Lawrenceville, NJ 08648

www.laffcon.org

Saturday
June 4, 2016